International Studies on Military Ethics

THE SERIES IS EDITED UNDER THE AUSPICES OF THE INTERNATIONAL SOCIETY FOR MILITARY ETHICS IN EUROPE (EURO-ISME)

VOLUME 1

The titles published in this series are listed at *brill.com/isme*

Responsibilities to Protect

Responsibilities to Protect

Perspectives in Theory and Practice

Edited by

David Whetham
Bradley J. Strawser

TUTA SUB AEGIDE PALLAS · 1683

BRILL
NIJHOFF

LEIDEN | BOSTON

Cover illustration: United Nations peacekeepers drive past local residents as they custody an United Nations convoy, heading to Rutshuru to relaunch UN operations in the area, north of the provincial capital of Goma, Congo, November 3, 2008. UN peacekeepers will "do the maximum" to protect civilians in rebel-threatened Goma, UN peacekeeping chief French Alain Le Roy warned during a visit to the eastern Democratic Republic of Congo city Monday. AFP PHOTO/Yasuyoshi CHIBA.

Library of Congress Cataloging-in-Publication Data

Responsibilities to protect : perspectives in theory and practice / edited by David Whetham, Bradley J. Strawser.

pages cm. -- (International studies on military ethics ; volume 1)

Includes papers presented at the second annual conference of the European Chapter of the International Society for Military Ethics held at the UK Defence Academy in Shrivenham in 2012.--Preface.

Includes bibliographical references and index.

ISBN 978-90-04-28037-3 (hardback : alk. paper) -- ISBN 978-90-04-28038-0 (e-book : alk. paper)

1. Responsibility to protect (International law) I. Whetham, David, editor. II. Strawser, Bradley Jay, editor.

KZ4082.R467 2015
172'.42--dc23

2015005584

This publication has been typeset in the multilingual "Brill" typeface. With over 5,100 characters covering Latin, IPA, Greek, and Cyrillic, this typeface is especially suitable for use in the humanities.
For more information, please see www.brill.com/brill-typeface.

ISSN 2214-7926
ISBN 978-90-04-28037-3 (hardback)
ISBN 978-90-04-28038-0 (e-book)

This book is printed on acid-free paper.

MIX
Paper from responsible sources
FSC® C109576

Printed by Printforce, the Netherlands

This volume is dedicated to the memory of Dr David Fisher who sadly died in February 2014. His experience at the heart of UK government policy-making informed his insights into the practicalities of military ethics, and he was never shy in pointing out the limitations of more abstract moral reasoning in the real world when he moved from his distinguished civil service career into academia.

• • •

As a mature research student, he completed an impressive PhD thesis on *Morality and War*, subsequently published by Oxford University Press in 2011. The book was awarded the highly prestigious WJM MacKenzie Book prize by the Political Studies Association in 2013 and represents an important contribution to Just War scholarship.

• • •

David was a lively and popular participant in the military ethics community, and was a strong supporter of the International Society for Military Ethics, its aims and goals. His distinctive laugh, incisiveness and razor sharp wit will be sorely missed and our community is the poorer for his passing.

Contents

Preface

Created in 2011, Euro ISME is the European Chapter of the International Society for Military Ethics (ISME) set up in 2005 in the United States with which it maintains tight bonds.[1] Following the example of the objectives of the latter, the European association is aimed at developing research, education, and training in the field of professional military ethics. Euro ISME, which gathers university professors, researchers, as well as civilian and military executives based in and beyond Europe, focuses its work on a specific European approach in order to identify, develop, and promote the best practices within the Armed Forces of the member countries of the European Defence Community. At the same time, it emphasises fruitful exchanges with other continents such as Africa and South America in order to encourage similar initiatives there.

This book is the first official product of the association and reflects the main thoughts which resulted from its second annual conference held at the UK Defence Academy in Shrivenham in 2012. The developed subject matter – 'The Responsibility to Protect' – is a recent concept which seemed to us both interesting and important to study. Indeed, inherited from the "humanitarian right of interference" promoted by Bernard Kouchner, the responsibility to protect has emerged in the international debate in the 90s, in a context marked by the inability of the international community to react to the mass atrocities committed against the civilian populations of Rwanda and Bosnia-Herzegovina.[2] The United Nations only acknowledged this concept in the final document of their World Summit in September 2005. The heads of States gathered in New York solemnly asserted that it was incumbent to the international community, within the framework of the United Nations, to implement the diplomatic, humanitarian, and other appropriate peaceful assets, complying with Chapters VI and VII of the United Nations Charter, in order to help protect the populations from genocide, war crimes, ethnic cleansing and crimes against humanity. The endorsement of this concept by the Heads of States and Governments of the entire world is a major political innovation: for the first time, there was a broad consensus on the idea that there is, not a right, but a duty of interference from the part of the international community against massive violations of human rights committed in a State.

---

1 The original ISME itself evolved out of an organization known as JSCOPE; that is, the Joint Services Conference on Professional Ethics.

2 Note that in this volume, one of the contributing authors disputes both that the present notion of R2P evolved out of the "right of interference" model promoted by Kouchner and that it is a recent concept.

As one would expect from an organisation interested in the practical application of morality and ethics, this volume looks at more than simply the Responsibility to Protect in terms of humanitarian intervention. It also looks at what this means for the people actually doing the interventions and those directly affected by them. For example, the soldiers charged with acting on behalf of the international community, the medics sent with them, or the people that are being protected. What responsibilities do states have towards their own soldiers when sending them to protect 'other' people?

I am, therefore, particularly glad that the Euro ISME association can bring some of its expertise to reflect on this area in this volume in order to make it better known, to make some of its aspects more precise, and possibly open new avenues for future development.

Brigadier General Benoit Royal
President of Euro ISME

List of Contributors

Don Carrick
is an ethicist specialising in military and medical ethics. He earned his BA in philosophy and his MA in applied ethics from the University of Hull. Following a long career as a lawyer in private practice, he returned to academic life in 2003. Don has taught philosophy and law at Hull, and now teaches medical ethics at the University of Leeds, where he is an Honorary Research Fellow in applied ethics. He is co-director of the Military Ethics Education Network, based at the University of Hull and has published on the Just War Tradition, military ethics education, and military-medical ethics, He is senior editor of Ashgate Publishing Ltd's Military and Defence Ethics series. His latest book, edited with Michael Gross, is *Military Medical Ethics for the 21st Century*.

Dr Mark Clegg
has spent his professional career engaged in the pursuit of protecting people. During a successful 23-year career as a senior officer in the Royal Air Force his primary focus was force protection. This involved him planning and directing activities with the primary aim of protecting personnel in hazardous environments in the UK and overseas. On leaving the military, he was appointed as the UK lead for a pan-European Union civil protection initiative drawing together the differing standpoints of European states in pursuit of enhancing a collective approach to emergencies. Mark was also appointed as a fellow of the Post-war Reconstruction and Development Unit of the University of York where he conducted work focusing on building resilience in the face of natural and man-made disasters. He continues to manage complex resilience projects in challenging environments. Mark has a PhD in International Relations and a Masters in Strategic Studies from the University of Aberdeen as well as a BA in International Studies from the Open University. He is an Associate Consultant of the UK Emergency Planning College.

Dr Anthony Dew
is a Royal Navy Doctor. He joined the RN in 2000 and has worked in most military environments including ships, submarines and a tour as a Senior Medical Officer in Afghanistan. He does not claim to be an expert in land conflicts but has researched the employment of medical personnel in the military as part of his staff training and MA in Defence Studies. He has an interest in medical ethics particularly in the military environment.

Dr David Fisher
taught ethics and war in the Department of War Studies at King's College, London, where he was awarded a PhD in 2010. He was a senior official in the UK Ministry of Defence, Foreign Office and Cabinet Office, serving as defence adviser to the Prime Minister and UK Defence Counsellor to NATO. He was the Co-chairman of the Council on Christian Approaches to Defence and Disarmament and a regular contributor to books and journals on defence an ethical issues. *Morality and War – Can War be Just in the Twentieth-first Century?* won the 2012 W.J. Mackenzie prize as best book of the year in political science. He co-edited *Just War On Terror?- A Christian and Muslim Response?* and he was the author of *Morality and the Bomb,* written when he was a research fellow of Nuffield College, Oxford.

Dr Shannon E. French
is the Inamori Professor in Ethics, Director of the Inamori International Center for Ethics and Excellence, and a tenured member of the Philosophy Department with a secondary appointment in the law school at Case Western Reserve University in Cleveland, Ohio, USA. She is also a Senior Associate at the Center for Strategic and International Studies (CSIS) in Washington, DC. Dr. French received her Ph.D. in philosophy from Brown University in 1997. Prior to starting at CWRU in 2008, she taught for eleven years as an Associate Professor of Philosophy at the United States Naval Academy and served as Associate Chair of the Department of Leadership, Ethics, and Law. She is the author of many scholarly publications, including *The Code of the Warrior: Exploring Warrior Values, Past and Present,* editor-in-chief for the *International Journal of Ethical Leadership,* and an associate editor for the *Journal of Military Ethics.*

Dr Anthony I. Jack
directs the Brain, Mind and Consciousness lab at Case Western Reserve University, and holds appointments in the departments of Cognitive Science (primary), Philosophy, Psychology, Neurology and Neuroscience. After high school, he worked briefly at the Harwell Nuclear Physics Laboratory before starting undergraduate studies in physics and philosophy of science at Oxford University (Balliol College). After the first year, he switched topics and took his BSc in psychology and philosophy. He then studied for his PhD in the Department of Psychology at University College London, working on visual awareness – his thesis explored the intersection between experimental psychology and philosophy. Subsequently he trained and worked at two major centers for cognitive neuroscience: the Institute of Cognitive Neuroscience in Queen Square London, and the department of Neurology, Washington

University in St. Louis. Prof. Jack's work has been published in leading neuroscience, psychology and philosophy journals, and focuses on human reasoning, morality and consciousness.

Dr Peter Lee
is a Portsmouth University Principal Lecturer in Military and Leadership Ethics based at Royal Air Force College Cranwell, where he specialises in the politics and ethics of war and military intervention, the ethics and ethos of remotely piloted aircraft operations, and the politics and ethics of identity. In November 2012 Dr Lee transferred from King's College London after four years in the Air Power Studies Division and continues to lecture across a range of diverse subjects, from international relations to terrorism and insurgency. In 2012 he published his first book entitled *Blair's Just War: Iraq and the Illusion of Morality*. In addition, he has recently published on the ethics of UAV operations and is regularly invited to lecture on this and other subjects to military, academic, political, religious and wider audiences. From 2001 to 2008 Dr Lee served as a Royal Air Force chaplain.

Sophie Paul
joined the Royal Air Force in 1995 after having studied History at Cambridge University and has enjoyed a 20-year career in military intelligence. Starting as an intelligence watch officer in 1996, Wg Cdr Paul has served in posts from the tactical to strategic levels, whilst also spanning intelligence disciplines, undertaking roles specialising in human intelligence, operational intelligence and imagery intelligence. During this time she has deployed on operations in support of the Iraq No Fly Zones working from Kuwait for Southern Watch and then numerous times to Turkey for Northern Watch. She also deployed in support of the Tornado GR4 during the conflict with Serbia as well as a subsequent tour in a different role in Kosovo. Her last operational deployment was Afghanistan for Op HERRICK. A keen sportswoman, Sophie has captained the RAF Ladies Ski Team to several successes. Married with two sons, Sophie is currently in a Cyber-related post as defence gears itself to harness and defend against threats in this rapidly expanding and swiftly developing area.

Brigadier General Benoit Royal
is research fellow closely associated with professional ethics at the Research Centre, Saint-Cyr Coëtquidan School, General Royal has accumulated significant command experience during his career. He has spent more than ten years of his career working outside of France: Germany, Polynesia, Reunion as well as the Ivory Coast, and he has completed several overseas courses

(United Kingdom, Nepal, USA). General Royal is a graduate of the War College and attended both the Centre for Higher Military Studies (CHEM) as well as the Institute for Higher Studies in National Defence (IHEDN). He spent three years as the Head of Army Corporate Communications and this was followed by three years as the Deputy Director Army Recruiting. He has been the Commandant of the School of Artillery since 1st August 2013. Additionally, since June 2012, General Royal has been the President of the International Military Ethics Society in Europe. He is the author of numerous articles published in civilian and military periodicals, as well as several books, like the most famous translated into English, *"The Ethical Challenges of the Soldier – The French Experience."*

Dr Bradley Jay Strawser
is an Assistant Professor of Philosophy in the Defense Analysis Department at the US Naval Postgraduate School in Monterey, California and a Research Associate with Oxford University's Institute for Ethics, Law, and Armed Conflict. Prior to his current appointments, Dr. Strawser was a Resident Research Fellow at the Vice Admiral James B. Stockdale Center for Ethical Leadership in Annapolis, Maryland. Previously he taught philosophy and ethics at the US. Air Force Academy in Colorado and the University of Connecticut. Before his academic career, Strawser served as an active duty officer in the US Air Force for nearly 8 years. His research focus is primarily ethics and political philosophy, though he has also written on metaphysics, ancient philosophy, and human rights. His work has appeared in such journals as *Analysis, Philosophia, Journal of Military Ethics, Journal of Human Rights,* and *Epoché.* He recently published *Killing By Remote Control: The Ethics of an Unmanned Military* (New York: Oxford University Press, 2013), an edited volume on the many moral issues raised by drone warfare.

Group Captain Colin Sullivan
has completed over twenty seven years military service in the Royal Air Force. As an aviator on Chinook helicopters and more recently as a Flight Operations Officer, he has been involved in multiple operational deployments around the globe including the Balkans, Africa, the Middle East and Afghanistan. During these operations he has witnessed the best and worst that humanity can offer. As a graduate of the UK's prestigious Advanced Command and Staff Course he has studied the application of military capability from the strategic to the tactical level. In addition to his military studies, he also completed a Masters Degree in International Studies at Kings College London.

Dr Jean-Baptiste Jeangène Vilmer
holds degrees in philosophy (BA, MA, PhD), law (LLB, LLM), and political science (PhD). A former postgraduate fellow of the MacMillan Center for International and Area Studies, Yale University, postdoctoral fellow at the Ecole Normale Supérieure (ENS Ulm) and at McGill University's Faculty of Law, and Lecturer in international relations at the Department of War Studies of King's College London, he is now a policy advisor on security issues at the French Ministry of Foreign Affairs, teaching the laws and ethics of war at Sciences Po Paris and the Ecole Spéciale Militaire de Saint-Cyr (French military academy). Please note that this article does not represent the views of the French ministry of Foreign Affairs. The author of 15 books including Pas de paix sans justice ? (Presses de Sciences Po, 2011) and Ethique des relations internationales (PUF, 2013), he won an Académie Française prize for La Guerre au nom de l'humanité. Tuer ou laisser mourir (PUF, 2012, preface by Hubert Védrine).

Dr David Whetham
is a Senior Lecturer in the Defence Studies Department of King's College London, based at the Joint Services Command and Staff College at the UK Defence Academy where he coordinates or delivers the military ethics component of courses for between two and three thousand British and international officers a year. In Spring 2011, David was a Visiting Fellow at the Stockdale Center for Ethical Leadership, Annapolis, and in 2009, David was a Visiting Fellow with the Centre for Defence Leadership and Ethics at the Australian Defence College in Canberra. He is also a regular visiting lecturer in military ethics at the Baltic Defence College, and the Royal Brunei Armed Forces Command and Staff Course. Publications include Ethics, Law and Military Operations (Palgrave, 2010) and Just Wars and Moral Victories: surprise, deception and the normative framework of European war in the later Middle Ages (Brill, 2009). David is the Vice President of the European Chapter of the International Society for Military Ethics (Euro ISME) which holds an annual conference for military practitioners, academics and defence policy-makers. He is married with two children, and in his spare time, David is a Magistrate on the Wiltshire bench, fences with the medieval longsword and epée and plays the trombone.

Robert Wilton
is an international relations and security sector professional, an advisor, and a writer. After studying at Oxford (and subsequently London), he spent ten years

working for the UK Government in the Ministry of Defence, Cabinet Office and Foreign Office. He increasingly specialised in the Balkans, covering amongst other things events in Kosovo (1999), Serbia (2000) and Macedonia (2001), as well as writing daily briefings for the Prime Minister during the 2003 Iraq campaign. In 2006 the UK Government asked him to become independent security advisor to the new Prime Minister of Kosovo, at the latter's request. His work has included reviewing the capacity of the Prime Minister's Office, helping design the future defence and security sector, and advising the Kosovo team during their current negotiations for the recognition of independence. He has published articles and reviews on Balkan history, culture and politics, and is the author of the Comprollerate-General series of historical dramas, as well as several prize-winning short-stories.

CHAPTER 1

The Moral Responsibility to Aid Others

David Whetham and Bradley J. Strawser

Imagine you are walking along a quiet beach and you see a young child struggling in the waves, clearly drowning and in need of aid. You glance around and find yourself alone. You see that rescuing the child will incur some cost to you: your brand new linen suit will get ruined by the ocean water. Still, nearly everyone agrees that you are morally bound to enter into the water and save the young child. One might say you have a responsibility to do so; to come to the aid of this child and protect it from harm.

This basic moral concept, that we are at times obligated to help others, is at the heart of this book and behind the doctrine known as the 'Responsibility to Protect'. That phrase, often referred to simply as 'R2P', has become a stand-in for the view that we, not as mere individuals but as whole societies, nations, states, and even the entirety of the 'international community', can at times take on a moral responsibility to aid others, perhaps with military force if necessary, in other societies and states that are not our own. Of course, we are now a long way from talking about saving a young child from drowning on the beach, but are invoking the far more contentious concepts of military intervention, collective responsibility, the justified use of force, and much more. Can intervention of this type be justified along the same lines as the duty to save the young child? Can it be permissible, much less morally required, to intervene in the affairs of others in this way, or is such meddling forbidden?

Historically, we can pick out several instances of interventions that could plausibly claim to have an R2P basis of the type we are alluding to here, though each is contentious in its own right. The multi-state military coalition that engaged in military intervention in Libya in 2011 is one recent example that many R2P advocates cite. The NATO intervention in the former Yugoslavia in 1999, or the US 'Operation Uphold Democracy' in Haiti in 1994 are others. Looking further back, many will reference the 'United Nations Operation in the Congo' peacekeeping force in 1960, or, far more contentiously, perhaps even a subset of the Spanish-American War, particularly the Cuban War for Independence in 1898. Each of these military interventions could be claimed – and were so claimed – to be good faith efforts at coming to the aid of others in grave peril; of fulfilling one's moral obligation to one's fellow humanity.

 | DOI 10.1163/9789004280380_002

But the belief that it can be ethically required, or even permissible, to intervene in the affairs of another state has not always enjoyed the popularity R2P currently commands in international affairs. Indeed, across the modern era there has been a complete reversal of received wisdom on the permissibility to intervene. There is a clear progression of thought from the view that any kind of intrusion by one group into the affairs of an independent state is wrong, no matter the motivation, slowly evolving to a view that such interference could at times be permissible, all the way to the conclusion that interceding by military force can even be obligated. To trace out the story of evolving views on intervention, we have to go back several hundred years to the formation of the modern nation-state, through the bloody wars of the 20th Century, and into the conscience challenging conflicts and genocides of the very recent past.

We start at what most consider the birth of the modern international order: the Peace of Westphalia and the emergence of the so-called Westphalian Model for nation-states. The Peace of Westphalia was a set of treaties that effectively ended the awful and destructive wars that had ravaged Europe for the past several decades, the Thirty Years' War and the Eighty Years' War. Both of these wars were waged in large part over religious disagreements and the desires of powerful ruling families to exert what they held to be right belief or conduct on others, including other states. The Peace of Westphalia ended these wars by forcing the recognition of the mutual sovereignty of rival states. The model for a modern state was born with the simple idea that each state is sovereign over its own people and within it's own borders; it is not for another state to dictate their religion or how they are to live or meddle in their affairs. Each state is its own, self-enclosed 'black box' of independent rule and authority.

This strong view of state sovereignty that became orthodox following the Peace of Westphalia was wed to a robust principle of non-intervention. The political order and international stability – so desperately needed after the destruction and chaos brought about by endless war of the previous century – was built upon respect for a given state's sovereignty within their own borders, and the view that one ought to keep one's nose out of other's business, to put a colloquial phrase on it. A related concept is the critical normative value of autonomy. Etymologically, autonomy derives from the Greek *autos* and *nomos*, meaning, literally 'self-law' or 'self-rule'. The Westphalian model demands that each state has unbridled autonomy and that it is wrong for one state to attempt to intervene into another state's affairs and thereby violate its autonomy.

Importantly, modern just war theory is built upon this notion of respecting state sovereignty and autonomy. On Michael Walzer's conventional reading of the just war tradition, often framed through his so-called 'legalist paradigm', we are to view competing states in the international order as members of a joint community where the only crime one can commit against the other is 'aggression'.[1] Aggression is defined explicitly in terms of violating another state's sovereignty. This can be done by directly infringing upon its territorial integrity or in some other way abridging its autonomy. Just war theory traditionally holds that it is only this act of aggression – violating another states sovereignty – that can serve has a legitimate just cause for war.

The philosopher John Stuart Mill famously argued for a strict principle of non-intervention. Speaking of his own home state, Great Britain, at the time unrivalled in might throughout the world, he declared that "if other nations do not meddle with it, it will not meddle with them."[2] We find in Mill the articulation of respecting autonomy as an argument against intercession, and not merely for the state's autonomy itself, but for the people's autonomy within it. He viewed external intervention as a violation of autonomy because, even if it were designed to aid those on whose behalf it is fought, he argued, it still was forcing one's will upon another. As he put it, "To go to war for an idea, if the war is aggressive, not defensive, is as criminal as to go to war for territory or revenue; for it is as little justifiable to force our ideas on other people, as to compel them to submit to our will in any other respect."[3]

Surprisingly, however, as Mill continues his argument, his reasons appear to become more paternalistic, rather than based in solely respecting autonomy. Mill suggests that a primary reason for non-intervention is because "there can seldom be anything approaching to assurance that intervention, even if successful, would be for the good of the people themselves."[4] And his reasons for thinking it would not be good for such people is not merely because it would violate their autonomy but because, apparently, those being aided must not properly value their autonomy in the first place, or, in any case, they *wouldn't* properly value it after it was "bestowed" upon them from external interveners. As Mill put it, "If they have not sufficient love of liberty to be able to wrest it from merely domestic oppressors, the liberty which is bestowed on them by other hands than their own, will have nothing real, nothing permanent."[5]

If Mill sounds overly harsh here against those who might be rescued by external interveners against an oppressor, it's important to understand the

1 Michael Walzer, *Just and Unjust Wars* (Basic Books, 1977).

2 John Stuart Mill, "A Few Words on Non-Intervention," 1859.

3 *Ibid.*

4 *Ibid.*

5 *Ibid.*

context in which he was writing. Mill was far more concerned that an imperialistic state would abuse the notion of a goodwill intervention as a cover for their own expansionary policy, and thereby infringe upon the autonomy of people in other states, than he was concerned with helping, say, a dissatisfied minority faction in rebelling against their ruling state. Moreover, remember the desire to maintain stability in the international political order was derived centrally from a desire for peace. The thought is that avoiding war, even if that war is waged for the best of motives, is better than the costs of war. Maintaining stability by not intervening in the affairs of others, and respecting their autonomous rule, seems the better of two evils.

But after Mill's time the world trudged through the first half of the 20th Century and the utter devastation caused by two World Wars. After the horrors of such wars, and in particular the heinous crimes states committed against their own people and people brought under their rule, the world was forced to question the wisdom of 'letting each to their own'. The very idea of genocide, brought appallingly to fore most prominently by the holocaust, cast the idea that one is absolutely forbidden from intervening in others affairs as morally quaint. Such horrors shouted to the world that there must be *some* limits to a state's sovereignty; that a state cannot be a true 'black box' within which it can do as it pleases, even against the very humanity of the people living within it.

Once some limits to sovereignty are recognized we see the start of a transition from viewing intervention as something that is morally forbidden, to something that can be morally permissible, in at least some cases. The post-WWII world agreed that there were, indeed, limits on sovereignty, and that sovereignty can thus be over-ridden in some cases. Sovereignty is still a good to be protected; but it is not an inviolable good that can never be outweighed by even greater moral demands. The formation of the United Nations was itself a nod towards this new consensus. It made clear that other states within the international community could cast judgment upon one another state's actions and, in some extreme cases, permissibly do something about it. Walzer himself offered three explicit cases where state sovereignty could be overridden: to intervene in successions, to intervene in civil wars to restore balance, and to intervene when gross violations of human rights "insult morality" and render sovereignty arguments cynical and irrelevant. On just war theory grounds, the idea of intervention here is consistent: if a given state has committed such crimes against its own people, it is considered to have given up its own sovereignty. The very basis for respecting its autonomy is negated, and, as such, intervening militarily against it is not an act of aggression. Such a shift results in a permission, under the right circumstances, to intervene.

Given the horrors which shocked the world into being more open to intervention into a state's affairs, we might here return to Mill and see that perhaps he was more open to the idea than a quick read of his work assumed. We see in Mill's argument against intervention an admittance that if the wrongful harms against the individuals under the rule of a given state are severe enough, then even he thinks intervention can be warranted. Mill says as much when he writes that it would, indeed, be permissible to intervene in order "to procure the abandonment of some national crime and scandal to humanity, such as the slave-trade."[6] Although it was not the slave-trade, perhaps the holocaust would have been just such a 'scandal to humanity' as Mill had in mind. In any case, we see that post-WWII the idea that it was permissible to intervene become standard.

Yet in the decades since WWII, tragic events have pushed the world to move even beyond mere moral permission for intervention. Consider what unfolded in Rwanda in 1994. Violence erupted between two long-conflicted ethnic groups, the Hutus and the Tutsis. The violence quickly turned into undeniable genocide. While as many as 2 million innocent civilians were slaughtered, the world's militaries stood by watching, doing nothing. Indeed, the small UN-led peace-keeping military presence that was in Rwanda at the start of the conflict fled after facing domestic political pressures. Reeling from such events, the international community began to ask not only if it was permissible for other states to intervene in such a case, but perhaps ethically mandatory – not far from the obligation faced upon discovering the drowning child at the start of this introduction. The genocide in Rwanda shocked the conscientious of the world into questioning whether not only might it be permissible, but perhaps it is morally required to intervene to prevent grave evil.

This shift in thinking was made manifest in a United Nations' inquiry in 2001 by the International Commission of Intervention and State Sovereignty (ICISS). UN Secretary Kofi Annan queried the international community whether there were cases where they *must* – not if – but must respond to protect innocent lives. The answer given was unambiguous, as it was in this report by the ICISS that the phrase "responsibility to protect" first appeared. The growing consensus was established as orthodoxy at the 2005 UN World Summit. There 191 member states agreed with the shift in the language of obligation to intervention represented by R2P. Specifically, four main points detailing what the responsibility to protect entailed were outlined at the summit:

6 *Ibid.*

1. States are responsible for protecting their populations from genocide, war crimes, crimes against humanity and ethnic cleansing.
2. The international community should encourage or assist states to exercise the responsibility.
3. The international community should use diplomatic, humanitarian, and other peaceful means to protect populations threatened by these crimes.
4. When a state "manifestly fails" in its protection responsibilities, and peaceful means are inadequate, the international community *must* take stronger measures, including collective use of force.[7]

R2P has since continued to develop as a standing doctrine of the UN and, broadly, of the international community as a whole. These basic propositions, if actually implemented, put significant moral burdens on the 191 member states who agreed to them. Today we are presently seeing this new consensus of a duty to take action play out as R2P is invoked to justify multi-lateral actions such as the 2011 intervention in Libya or, presently, those who argue for intervention into Syria's civil war.

So then, now that we have this moral trajectory laid out before us – a slow moving shift from thinking intervention is impermissible, to permissible in some cases, to even obligatory – let us return to where we started. If we grant this trend that there are situations where a moral duty arises to aid others, a plethora of other difficult questions come to the fire. Whose duty is this? Is it 'assigned', as it were, to any one particular collective or individual, or is it an impersonal, 'free-floating' duty? Just how high a cost is one required to take on in fulfilling one's duty to help others? And consider the militaries who engage in such humanitarian interventions. Should institutions designed for national self-defense even be used in such ways? These and countless other moral questions are the topic of on-going work in the R2P field, and several of them are touched upon in this volume.

To help clarify some of these ethical puzzles, consider again the thought experiment that opened this chapter, that of the drowning child on the beach. The case is a take on Peter Singer's classic thought experiment, where you stumble across a child who is drowning and whose rescue would be easy for you to accomplish, but your brand new – and rather expensive – shoes would

7 See paragraphs 138–139 of the *United Nations 2005 World Summit Outcome Document*, 15 September 2005, accessed at: http://www.un.org/en/ga/search/view_doc.asp?symbol=A/RES/60/1

get ruined.[8] Would someone be committing a wrong, if they chose to not rescue the child so as to not damage their expensive shoes? Most think yes; that we must save the child, our shoes be damned. But now imagine that you were not alone when you came across the child, that there were several other people with you, and you all had expensive shoes on. It would only take one of you to ruin your shoes to save the child. So who should it be? Who should have to bear this cost?

This is precisely the dilemma the international community finds itself in for many cases of R2P. Any number of states could intervene to stop a given genocide. On whose shoulders should the burden to do so fall? Some answer this question by suggesting that the burden to aid others falls on those who are most capable to carry out the rescue.[9] Consider a slight modification on the drowning child on the beach case. Imagine that you come across the child as before, but now your friend, who happens to be a highly trained lifeguard, is with you. Many think that the moral burden will fall on him to save the child. This is not only because he serves in this particular role as a lifeguard – many will take him to have an additional role-based duty to save the child. But it may also be simply because he is more capable of swimming out and saving the child. Since he is more capable, the cost he'd have to bear to fulfill the duty may in some ways actually be less.

To see this, imagine that far more than expensive shoes or a new linen suit is at stake for the rescuer. Imagine that the child is drowning in rather dangerous ocean waters, and that the risk that a rescuer may herself drown in the rescue efforts is very real. Once we raise the costs of aid high enough, many think the duty to intervene drops away and becomes, instead, a mere permission rather than an obligation. Again, we see that the international community may find itself in just such a case for humanitarian intervention. The costs to preventing genocide may well be significant loss of life to one's own people or astronomical, even bankrupting economic costs. Consider the incredible costs the prospect of a long drawn out intervention into Syria could pose to any state – especially given the recent history of the decade long occupation, and

---

8 See Peter Singer, *The Life You Can Save* (New York: Random House, 2010), for one of many places Singer employs this thought experiment.

9 See James Pattison, *Humanitarian Intervention and the Responsibility to Protect: Who Should Intervene?* (Oxford: Oxford University Press, 2010). Also see, Pattison, "Legitmacy and Humanitarian Intervention: Who Should Intervene?" *The International Journal of Human Rights* 12.3 (June 2008): pp. 395–413. Pattison also discusses the possibility of, and current limitations to and problems with, the idea of a cosmopolitan standing army controlled not by any state but by the UN itself. See "Humanitarian Intervention and a Cosmopolitan UN Force," *Journal of International Political Theory* 4.2 (2008): pp. 126–145.

budget destroying, occupation of Iraq by the United States. If the costs are high enough, does the responsibility to protect still have the force of moral demand?

Combining this question with the one of capability to rescue may give us a partial answer. Imagine you are on the beach and spied the drowning child, even with the dangerous waters which could cost you your own life, but you were also accompanied by a world-champion swimmer, Michael Phelps perhaps. Imagine that the waters, while potentially lethal for you, would pose no real risk of death to Phelps (even though the ocean may still ruin his suit). Would Phelps still be obligated to rescue in such cases, even while you are not? Many will think so. If this is true, then it shows that the relative capability of the rescuer, and the ways in which that capability can lower the costs of aid to the rescuer, may actually determine whether one has a duty to help, or a mere permission.

Some take this to be decisive in the question of humanitarian intervention.[10] For states with powerful militaries and robust economies, like the US, the UK, or many NATO member states, the costs of intervention may be a reasonable one they are morally required to take on, given the high stakes at play, such as stopping genocide. While for other states with less powerful militaries, or more fragile economies, the prospect of intervention might be a cost far too high to reasonably demand of them. If this is right, it raises its own series of puzzling questions. Is it fair to the Michael Phelps of the world for them to bear the burden of R2P, simply because they happen to be more capable of carrying out such moral demands? And, if so, perhaps it drives a perverse incentive to intentionally reduce one's intervention capabilities so as to not bear such demands – to intentionally be a poor swimmer so as to ensure that one is never asked to save a drowning child.

We cannot begin to adequately answer such questions here, but these and many other puzzles give rise to a host of objections against the plausibility of R2P. For example, R2P also appears to shift the burden of proof away from justifying intervention to a need to justify a failure to act. This is surprising as one could start to ask of any intervention, "Why did you intervene here to stop this genocide, but not over here, where there was an equally bad humanitarian crisis?" One may also object that the soldiers asked to undertake the life and death risks of humanitarian intervention did not 'sign up for this', as it were. Rather, presumably, most militaries are founded upon the idea of national self-defense, not the defense of others on the other side of the world. If so, is it right to ask soldiers who agree to risk their life for home and country to do so for another's home and country? Finally, if R2P requires intervention anywhere

10 Again, see Pattison, cited above.

there are significant unjust threats to innocents, consider the so-called "Global War on Terror" (GWOT). Since terrorism perpetrated by international non-state actors directly harms innocent civilians the world over, can the GWOT efforts actually be justified as a mere extension of R2P on behalf of those affected by terrorism? And if so, to what extent are the GWOT efforts required to go?

This contentious and complex web of ethical conundrums remains tangled for R2P today. And it is upon this background that the chapters of this book are situated. They each attempt to give us a fine-grained look at a particular angle or aspect of the ways in which the moral responsibility to help others has impacts in the real-world militaries and institutions upon whom this duty is thrust. This volume aims to give us a 'practitioner's perspective' on these questions and engages issues that intersect with R2P in pragmatic ways, rather than the more austere academic works that usually dominate the field. In what follows, we will offer a brief outline of the book and describe what each chapter is after.

* * * *

David Fisher's chapter charts the way humanitarian intervention moved in and out of favour over the last 30 years. Apparently, it was again out of favour following the unpopular and controversial Iraq conflict. However, much to many people's surprise, as a particularly vicious civil war unfurled in Libya in 2011, the UN Security Council passed Resolution 1973, authorising all necessary measures to protect civilians and civilian populated areas. Fisher explores whether or not this was a final outing for the liberal interventionist model, or whether it instead, represents a demonstration of why this type of humanitarian intervention may indeed have a future. Fisher employs the Just War Tradition to provide a useful framework for determining if and when such intervention might be justified or even required in the future.

Consistent with the beach rescue theme that began this chapter, what if the CPR following the rescue from the sea results in a broken rib. Does the person being saved have the right to object or even complain about the way in which they were rescued? Does it matter if they asked for help or not? The chapter by Robert Wilton explores what the Responsibility to Protect idea felt like from the perspective of someone who was intimately involved with the practical results of the policy. Wilton was well-placed to do this, specialising in Balkan affairs while working for the UK Government, before being asked by the Prime Minister of Kosovo to provide advice and support in reforming the fledgling state's institutions in the run up to the declaration of independence before finally being appointed as the *Chief of the European Mission in Kosovo*. Wilton argues that when Tony Blair and Bill Clinton led the world into Kosovo in 1999, it seemed to be the first of a new breed of interventions embodying Britain's 'ethical foreign policy' and the doctrine of just humanitarian action set out by the British Prime Minister in his famous Chicago speech, and building on American regret about non-intervention in Rwanda. However, Wilton believes that while there might be other limited interventions, the NATO engagement in Kosovo will turn out to have been the first and last of its kind, a kind made possible by the perceived failures in Bosnia and now made impossible by the perceived failures in Afghanistan and Iraq.

Wilton's chapter, written from a practitioner's perspective, reviews the Kosovo intervention as an apparently clear example of 'force for good': the threat and use of force, with limited actual commitment of material and relatively limited human cost, to remedy a clear example of human suffering and to bring stability and democracy, a mission that had some immediate success in 1999 and subsequently reached a new point of achievement with the recognition of a democratic, multi-ethnic independent state. The chapter reviews the ways in which the success was achieved. It also suggests various aspects of the intervention which were not, arguably, so successful. The exploration of the apparent successes and the consideration of the possible failures in Kosovo offer a new synthesis of argument on what makes for effective intervention, and on the limits to the good that force can do.

Peter Lee's chapter looks specifically at the Doctrine of the International Community as articulated by the British Prime Minister, Tony Blair. Setting out principles that sound very similar to those found in the Just War Tradition that Fisher's chapter discusses, Blair expounded the rare conditions under which the principle of the inviolability of state sovereignty might be set aside: specifically, in the cases of genocide, oppression leading to population displacement and regional instability, and illegitimate regimes. By taking two case studies in which Blair was heavily involved, Kosovo (1999) and Iraq (2003), and judging Blair on his own criteria, Lee concludes that the strength and moral credibility of the justifications put forward for the two military interventions can be judged very differently.

Fitting with the Euro ISME aspiration of exploring ethical concepts from multiple national perspectives, the next chapter moves from a British take on the Responsibility to Protect idea to a French one. Vilmer's chapter sets out to challenge the concept by providing a realist critique of its origins, substance and current expression. Moving through a series of 'myths', Vilmer debunks one misunderstanding after another, concluding that for the rest if the world, R2P is the equivalent to what the *droit d'ingérence* has been for the Francophone world: a highly marketable, but more or less meaningless concept, defended effectively by its supporters. However, he also argues that one can be critical of the manifestation of the current popular concept without completely abandoning the idea of intervention justified on humanitarian grounds in certain situations.

Moving from the perhaps more traditional idea of seeing protection in terms of those who cannot protect themselves, the next chapters in this volume now turn to another, less explored aspect of the subject, reflecting on the obligations and duties to look after those who are sent to protect others. Not wishing to expose the British military or its personnel to liability, the Chief of the Defence Staff, Admiral Boyce, refused to commit the British military to war in 2003 until he was satisfied that the order was legal. Constitutionally, this was a challenging time for the United Kingdom, and yet if one is to take the idea of a Responsibility to Protect seriously, how could this not also be seen to apply to those who are being sent into harm's way? While this reflects one type of obligation towards our service personnel, Mark Clegg's chapter approaches the whole notion in a slightly different way, by focusing on exposure to physical harm rather than legal liability. How do you balance force protection of one's own personnel against the lives of those you have been sent to protect? By examining the evolution of US policy in Iraq and then Afghanistan, Clegg charts the challenges of getting this balance right and the problems, practical, operational and political with both 'selling' such a policy and actually putting it into practice on the ground.

Military medical ethics provide a rich seam of moral conundrums for mining.[11] In their chapter, Dew and Carrick, one a Royal Navy doctor and the other a philosopher, explore the ways that military medicine has been transformed in recent years. The intense period of conflict since 2001 has led to remarkable advances in medical treatment for combat injuries, leading to substantial increases in survivability rates for the wounded. Part of this has been made possible by the provision of medical attention at the point of the injury being sustained meaning that medical personnel are no longer remote from the battlefield in the way that the founders of the International Committee of the Red Cross may have initially envisaged. They are now an integral part of the combat effectiveness of troops *in* combat and arguably, this has blurred the traditional boundary between combatant and non-combatant as a result.

Military medical personnel are protected in the sense that although they are with combatants, they themselves are considered non-combatants. However,

11 E.g. see Duncan Blair, 'To Whom Does a Military Medical Commander Owe a Moral Duty?' in D. Whetham (ed.), *Ethics, Law and Military Operations* (Palgrave, 2010).

in a chicken-and-egg type situation, they now find themselves being deliberately targeted by their opponents. If they wear the visible protective insignia, they find themselves being more vulnerable rather than less. But if they remove it, are they any different from the combatants they are deployed with? What does this mean for their own responsibility and duty to protect the wounded in a warzone? Drawing on personal experience and interviews with deployed medical personnel and the commanders who are charged with protecting them, Dew and Carrick explore some of the practical implications for deployed medical personnel in today's conflicts, including the dilemma about how much and what type of activity they can be justified in participating in, especially in small units where individual survival requires group protection. They argue that medical personnel are conferred their protected status by their duty to others, and this confers a responsibility on the force with which they serve to ensure that they are not employed to do things that compromise this protection, regardless of the challenges posed by the contemporary operating environment.

The military environment, and the defence and security sector as a whole, is one in which individual rights and safety are often considered to be necessarily subordinate to the needs of the 'greater good'. Command and control within such an environment requires that people accept and trust that either the organisation as a whole, or at least those in charge of policy and direction, are doing things for the right reasons. It is often considered that people who challenge or speak out in such an environment risk not only their own position, but the broader security of all – defence is simply not an area that can allow its 'dirty laundry' to be aired in public. The intent of Group Captain Colin Sullivan's contribution is to argue why encouraging whistleblowing in the military environment is, counter intuitively, something that should be encouraged rather than stifled. This is justified in terms of looking at what it is that you are actually trying to protect.

Jack and French's chapter focuses on an exciting new area of research that may have profound implications for teaching and understanding military ethics – neuroethics. The way we train our soldiers for the contemporary operating environment requires that they have a high degree of mental flexibility in the field. They should be trained in a way that optimizes their ability to fluidly switch among roles such as active combatant, peacekeeper, and military escort/trainer. These tasks require different mental processes and skills. By asking our troops to be both highly analytic and highly empathetic, we appear to be asking for the impossible, resulting in potentially destructive levels of cognitive dissonance. However, they argue that it is possible, with good training based on the right kind of warrior code emphasising honourable conduct, to be able to reconcile to protect the lines that must not be crossed under any circumstances.

They point out that military ethics is not alone in facing such challenges. For example, a surgeon is expected to have a good bedside manner one moment, but not to exhibit empathy in the operating theatre. Successful surgeons cope by ensuring they are tuned into the cues and cognitive context that make the adoption of the appropriate cognitive mode a relatively straightforward matter. In combat, where lethal force may be required, empathy may not only be counterproductive, it could be lethal. However, there is a difference between dehumanization and objectification of a foe. The former is associated with atrocities, while the latter, where one temporarily views an enemy as a part of a machine one is opposed to rather than as a beast, can provide a way of creating sufficient moral distance to do what is necessary at the time, without removing the awareness after the fact that it was a human being that was killed as a result. Such a temporary and localised moral distance can help soldiers deal with the guilt of their actions without removing guilt from the picture entirely – just as surgeons do not feel guilt for cutting into their patients, because they know it was for a good end, but if they carelessly cut too much, just as if a soldier goes beyond what is necessary, some guilt *is* appropriate.

Military training must be focused upon facilitating the mental readiness of troops to achieve a fluid and appropriate transition between different states and to ensure that cues and context are appreciated and understood. Thus, Human Terrain Systems can be seen as ways to ensure that sociocultural understanding is enhanced, minimising the dehumanisation or even objectification of a people. Doing this effectively helps to protect civilian populations, vulnerable parties and our own troops from the debilitating effects of mental trauma that can result from bad ethical decisions in life and death situations. Troops should not be asked to love their enemies while inflicting suffering and death upon them. Some objectification is necessary, but training them to hate or dehumanize their opponents is counterproductive and highly damaging to the safety of all parties to the conflict.

Consistent with the alternative approaches to the responsibility to protect explored in the chapters in the second half of this volume, Wing Commander Sophie Paul's chapter takes a whole new angle on the R2P debate. It deals with a different aspect of 'responsibility' and exploring it from an angle that few have considered before. Within the way this concept is normally considered, we (the West) are concerned with protecting those populations who are unable to protect themselves, implicitly through no fault of their own. Focusing on the individual level, this chapter begins to explore the question of whether placing oneself at risk should or could negate the state's responsibility for its own citizens when they end up in harm's way. Paul's examination concentrates in particular on the case of journalists operating in insecure environments, sometimes against the advice of those who understand the risks. Even where they are not acting against advice, many of the changes to the contemporary operating environment explored by Dew and Carrick in their chapter affect journalists in similar ways to military medics. They can find themselves deliberately targeted for doing a job that has traditionally conferred a protected status, but in today's wars, actually seems to attract even more danger. If journalists deliberately place themselves in harm's way, are they responsible for any harm caused by their rescue? How does the state balance their rights against those of the collective whole? Should culpability be a factor influencing one's response or is that irrelevant to the state's duty to protect its citizens? From the perspective of the UK, the chapter draws on social contract theory and different philosophical approaches to try and make sense of current state practice towards protecting journalists in combat zones. In the process, Paul raises a number of fascinating and pertinent points that have relevance beyond the case study itself.

On the whole, the volume offers a surprisingly wide range of chapters in terms of content and topics. Each chapter engages moral questions which are themselves either directly or obliquely related in important ways to the doctrine of R2P. Given the sad realities that our future world likely holds – more violence, turmoil, and unrest – these questions are pressing, relevant, and even urgent; and the analysis of them, as this book offers, is very much needed.

The editors would like to thank the team at Martinus Nijhoff Publishers for their patient efforts in bringing this volume to press. Particular thanks go to Lindy Melman and Bea Timmer. We also thank our contributors for their excellent work and dedication, without which there would be no book. We are indebted to these fine scholars and practitioners. Additionally, Brigadier General Benoit Royal has our sincere gratitude for his prescient foreword. Our heartfelt thanks also go to the International Society for Military Ethics – Europe (Euro-ISME) for the society's unwavering support, peer reviews, and encouragement of this book. Finally, we thank our wives, Sarah and Abbi, and our children, Alfie, Toby, Lily, and Norah, for their ceaseless love and support throughout this long project.

CHAPTER 2

Libya: A Last Hurrah or Model for the Future?

David Fisher

At the beginning of 2011, with the US committed to ending its military engagement in Iraq and a growing awareness of the difficulties of protracted operations in Afghanistan, it may have seemed not unreasonable to suppose that the era of liberal interventionism was over. But then in March 2011 came the successful NATO intervention in Libya. Was this intervention just a last hurrah of the old interventionist regime? Or does it represent a new model for interventions in the future?

Humanitarian intervention has been in and out of favour over the last three decades. For much of the time it has been out of favour. In 1994 the international community did nothing to prevent the genocide in Rwanda nor did it stop the 1995 massacre at Srebrenica. But, from the 1999 NATO intervention in Kosovo through to the UN Summit in September 2005 that endorsed an international Responsibility to Protect, humanitarian intervention was briefly in favour. But largely as a result of the unpopular intervention in Iraq and the lack of progress in Afghanistan, by the beginning of 2011 humanitarian intervention seemed once more out of favour.

But then, to the surprise of many, the Libyan intervention took place. On 17 March 2011, following an earlier plea for help from the Arab League, the UN Security Council passed resolution 1973. This authorised UN members to take all necessary measures to protect civilians and civilian-populated areas under threat of attack in Libya. NATO operations commenced on 19 March and continued until 31 October. By then the Gaddafi regime had been overthrown and a new Libyan Government was in power, committed to establishing democracy. There is a long way still to go before the democracy is secure. But the military operation was an outstanding success.

So was this intervention just a last hurrah of the moribund regime of liberal interventionism? Or does it represent a new model for interventions in the future? Does humanitarian intervention have a future? Predicting international affairs is notoriously difficult but, drawing on just war thinking, I suggest that the Libya intervention both could and, more importantly, *should* be a model for the future. It should be a model because it was a just intervention. But it should also be because the Responsibility to Protect (R2P), for the sake of which the intervention was undertaken, is so important a principle, that, having only recently rediscovered it, we should not now – only eight years after

 | DOI 10.1163/9789004280380_003

the UN Summit that endorsed it – allow it be lost. We should try to ensure that humanitarian intervention does have a future.

Libya – A Just Intervention?

The Arab Spring began in December 2010 in Tunisia with widespread popular protests following the death of a street vendor that rapidly led to the overthrow of the regime and the departure into exile on 14 January 2011 of the Tunisian President, Ben Ali. The wave of popular protests spread quickly to neighbouring countries. On 15 February 2011 the arrest of a human rights activist, Fethi Tarbal, provoked street protests in Benghazi. 14 protesters were killed by security forces on 17 February and a further 24 in clashes that attended the funeral procession of one of the protesters killed the previous day. The protests rapidly spread elsewhere. By 24 February anti-government militias had taken control of Misrata. The reaction of the Gaddafi regime in seeking to suppress these uprisings was swift and brutal. The brutality of the response prompted the UN Security Council to pass Resolution 1970 on 26 February. This resolution, recalling 'the Libyan authorities' responsibility to protect its population' (words echoing the 2005 Summit declaration), imposed sanctions on Gaddafi and his family and an embargo on the supply of arms to Libya. It also referred the actions of Gaddafi's security forces to the International Criminal Court for investigation of war crimes.[1]

Ignoring such international condemnation, Gaddafi mounted a major counter-offensive with tanks and aircraft to wrest back control from areas seized by the rebels. As his tank forces massed outside rebel-controlled Benghazi, Gaddafi threatened the civilian inhabitants of that populous city in a radio broadcast, 'We will come. House by house, room by room'.[2]

To the surprise of most commentators the UN Security Council reacted decisively to these events. On 17 March 2011, following an earlier plea for help from the Arab League, the UN Security Council passed resolution 1973. This resolution, as expected, imposed a no fly zone. But the resolution also underlined 'the responsibility of the Libyan authorities to protect the Libyan population' and the Security Council's 'determination to ensure the protection

1 UNSCR 1970, accessed on 27 February at: http://www.un.org/en/ga/search/view_doc.asp?symbol=S/RES/1970(2011)

2 Maria Golovnina and Patrick Worsnip, 'U.N. Approves Military Force; Gaddafi Threatens Rebels, Reuters, March 18, 2011, accessed on March 20, 2011 at: http://uk.reuters.com/article/2011/03/18/idINIndia-55670020110318

of civilians and civilian populated areas'. It accordingly authorised Member States:

> acting nationally or through regional organizations or arrangements, and acting in cooperation with the Secretary-General, to take all necessary measures to protect civilians and civilian populated areas under threat of attack in the Libyan Arab Jamahiriya, including Benghazi, while excluding a foreign occupation force of any form on any part of Libyan territory.[3]

The resolution was passed with 10 votes in favour, none against and 5 abstentions from Russia, China, Brazil, India and Germany. 'All necessary measures' is the accepted UN diplomatic phrase for military action. The unexpected alignment of Germany with Russia and China (habitual sceptics of UN intervention) rather than its NATO Allies – Britain, France and the US – occasioned much criticism and reflected German concern over how the operation might develop and its reluctance to see its own military forces involved, particularly with impending local elections in Germany.[4]

While the resolution does not itself explicitly refer to the 2005 Summit declaration on the Responsibility to Protect, the language used, with its emphasis on 'the responsibility to protect' civilians closely echoes the language of that declaration. The 2005 declaration is also explicitly quoted in the chain of previous UNSCR resolutions to which UNSCR 1973 refers.[5] The military action authorised by the UN Security Council in resolution 1973 can thus justifiably be regarded as the first military implementation of the Responsibility to Protect doctrine.

Military operations against Libya followed swiftly after the UN vote. On 19 March French and Italian aircraft undertook reconnaissance missions and French aircraft attacked tanks outside Benghazi. US and UK ships and submarines launched cruise missile attacks to degrade Libyan air defence capabilities

---

3 UN Security Council Resolution 1973, *The Guardian*, March 17, 2011, accessed March 18, 2011 at: http://www.guardian.co.uk/world/2011/mar/17/un-security-council-resolution

4 Richard Rousseau 'Why Germany Abstained in UN Resolution 1973' January 22, 2011, accessed on February 12, 2012 at: http://www.foreignpolicyjournal.com/2011/06/22/why-germany-abstained-on-un-resolution-1973-on-libya/

5 UNSCR 1973 invokes UNSCR 1738 which reaffirms UNSCR 1674 of 28 April 2006 which 'reaffirms the provisions of the 2005 World Summit Outcome Document regarding the responsibility to protect populations from genocide, war crimes, ethnic cleansing and crimes against humanity', viewed on 15 July 2013 at: http://www.unrol.org/doc.aspx?n=S-Res-1674%20on%20protection%20civilians%20in%20armed%20conflict%20%2828Apr06%29.pdf

in order to prevent subsequent attacks on coalition aircraft. Coalition operations rapidly expanded in scope and participation, including, importantly, Arab forces provided by Qatar and the United Arab Emirates. Command and control of all the coalition operations was taken over by NATO on 31 March. NATO planes flew over 26,500 sorties, including 9,700 strike missions.[6] In addition to air operations, small units of French, British and Qatari Special Forces operated on the ground. After NATO planes had mistakenly bombed forces of the National Transitional Council (NTC) in early April, UK Special Forces were despatched to help direct and coordinate air operations to avoid further accidents. A SAS unit was subsequently deployed in late August to train and mentor NTC units.[7]

The NATO mission was concluded on 31 October. By then the Gaddafi regime had been overthrown, with the dictator himself slain by rebel militia, and a new Libyan Government was in power, committed to set up a democracy. Progress since then has been mixed. A major security problem continues to be posed by the operation of armed militias and the continued failure of the central government to control them.[8] Apart from the lynching of Gaddafi, one of the most disturbing incidents was the murder of the US Ambassador in an attack on the US consulate in Benghazi on 12 September 2012, amid protests over an anti-Islamic film distributed on the internet. This attack provoked, however, mass protests against the Islamist group believed responsible for the murder. Moreover, contrary to the forecasts of many pessimists, the country has not split up into different tribal or ethnic areas. Democratic elections were successfully held in Libya on 7 July 2012 and were won by the moderate National Forces Alliance. After protracted negotiations Parliament approved the formation of a coalition government on 31 October 2012. This was a major step forward, although the central government remains weak and has yet to extend its control to all parts of the country.

Were the NATO operations justified? The just war principles provide helpful guidance for assessing when interventions may legitimately be undertaken and for ensuring they are conducted and concluded with due ethical restraint. The principles are relevant to any application of force. They are, however, of particular importance for an operation, such as that in Libya, undertaken for

6 Operation Unified Protector Final Mission Stats 2 November 2011, accessed on December 12, 2012 at: http://www.nato.int/nato_static/assets/pdf/pdf_2011_11/20111108_111107-factsheet_up_factsfigures_en.pdf

7 Mark Urban, 'Inside Story of the UK's Secret Mission to Beat Gaddafi', *BBC News*, January 19, 2012, accessed on January 20, 2012 at: http://www.bbc.co.uk/news/magazine-16573516

8 See, for example, Hisham Matar, 'In Libya, Fear is Back', *The Guardian*, July 30 2013: 'Under Gaddafi We were Afraid of the State. Now Its Weakness Imperils all We Have Achieved'.

humanitarian objectives, not least since the humanitarian rationale of an operation may be undermined by the unethical conduct of those involved. So how do NATO operations in Libya fare against the just war criteria?

Just war teaching prescribes a number of tests that have to be met for a war to be just. Before a decision is taken to go to war it is necessary to be satisfied that the action is undertaken with:

- Just cause
- Right Intention
- Competent Authority
- as a Last Resort
- and be Proportionate. That is, the harm likely to be caused should be judged not to outweigh the good to be achieved, taking into account the probability of success.

In the conduct of a war two further tests have to be met:

- The harm judged likely to result from a particular military action should not be disproportionate to the good to be achieved by that action (the principle of proportion)
- Non-combatants should not be deliberately attacked (the principle of non-combatant immunity).

Finally the war should end in the establishment of a just peace.[9]

So let us consider the Libyan intervention against each of these criteria. First, was there a **just cause**? The Libyan intervention – unlike that in Iraq – was an avowedly humanitarian operation authorised to 'take all necessary measures to protect civilians and civilian-populated areas under threat of attack'. It was undertaken to halt a humanitarian catastrophe – the slaughter of civilians in Libya – that was taking place. It was also, importantly, undertaken in accordance with the international Responsibility to Protect principle, which had been endorsed by the UN Summit in September 2005. This had placed on the international community a responsibility to protect citizens from genocide, war crimes, ethnic cleansing and crimes against humanity where national authorities manifestly failed to do so themselves. The Libyan operation was the

---

9 For a fuller discussion of the principles see David Fisher, *Morality and War – Can War be Just in the Twenty-first Century*? (Oxford: Oxford University Press, 2011, pbk., 2012), especially Chapter 4 'The Just War Tradition'. The application of the principles to humanitarian interventions is discussed in Chapter 11.

first time the UN Security Council had implemented the use of force in order to protect civilians in line with the Responsibility to Protect principle. It was also the first time it had done so without the consent and, indeed, operating against the functioning government of the territory concerned.[10] The protection of civilians from massacre furnished a just cause for the Libyan operation.

The next condition of **right intention** is designed to stop political leaders cheating by proclaiming a just cause while in fact being motivated by other factors such as pursuit of territorial gain or oil contracts. There has, therefore, not only to be a just cause but the military operation has to be undertaken for the sake of that cause. This does not preclude a mixture of motives. What it does require is that the primary motive should be furnished by the just cause and base motives, such as greed or cruelty, are excluded. In the case of the Libyan intervention, while motives may undoubtedly have been mixed, there is no convincing evidence that extraneous factors were the dominant motivating factors. On the contrary, the large and motley coalition assembled seems to have been primarily driven by a desire to put an end to the atrocities being perpetrated on the ground by Gaddafi and his forces. It could, therefore, be judged that the operation was undertaken for the sake of the just cause, and so had right intention.

Unlike Iraq, the operation also had wide international support and participation, both regional and international, and was authorised by the UN Security Council. UNSC approval may not be a necessary condition for **competent authority**, where, as with the NATO intervention in Kosovo in 1999, and the Security Council deadlock over Syria, action to prevent a humanitarian catastrophe is blocked, and the UN rendered impotent, by the recalcitrance of individual states, such as Russia, pursuing their own crudely nationalist agenda. But UNSC approval, when it can be secured, is certainly sufficient to confer competent authority. The Libyan intervention had the endorsement of the UN Security Council and was widely supported internationally, despite the misgivings expressed subsequently over its conduct, particularly by Russia, which we shall examine shortly. It, therefore, had competent authority.

The operation was also undertaken as a **last resort** to prevent a humanitarian catastrophe that was already taking place and, if Gaddafi's tanks had been allowed to enter Benghazi, had been about to get a lot worse. The condition of last resort does not require that all other options need to have been first tried before force is resorted to but rather that force should only be used if other

10 R2P had previously been invoked by the UNSCR in its resolution 1706 of August 31 2006, which authorised deployment of a peacekeeping force to Darfur (prior to UNAMID). That deployment did not take place since the Sudan government declined to give its consent.

options are judged unlikely to work. The imposition of sanctions and threatened referral of the actions of his security forces to the International Criminal Court had done little to deter Gaddafi's oppression of his people. It was not an unreasonable judgement that other options were unlikely to work and only military intervention could provide the necessary protection of civilians in imminent danger of attack.

Let us consider now the **principle of proportion.** This principle requires that a military operation should only be undertaken if more good than harm is judged likely to result, taking into account the probability of success. 'Care', Vitoria explains, 'must be taken to ensure that the evil effects of war do not outweigh the possible benefits sought by waging it'.[11] The principle of proportion is usually treated as a separate condition from that of reasonable prospect of success. But assessing the outcome of a military campaign logically requires both a judgement of the balance of good over harm to be achieved and of its probability. So the two conditions are best linked together. Such an assessment of the overall balance of good over harm also requires a weighing up of the likely consequences of military action. The principle of proportion is thus an unashamedly consequentialist principle. This has embarrassed some commentators of an anti-consequentialist persuasion, who omit it from their list of *jus ad bellum* principles, or accord it rather perfunctory attention and low priority.[12] Michael Walzer, for example, has surprisingly little to say about the principle which he dismisses as 'a hard criterion to apply for there is no ready way to establish an independent or stable view of the values against which the destruction of the war is to be measured'.[13]

It is, indeed, a hard principle to apply. Its application is, however, not quite as challenging as Walzer suggests. For it is not open to politicians to cite any good or value as the goal of military action against which its destruction is to be measured. Just war teaching makes clear that the good against which the harm is to be measured is that specified in the just cause, the cause for the sake of which the war is undertaken. Just cause is thus the defining condition. That is an important constraint. It is, nonetheless, notoriously difficult to assess the consequences of our actions because we take moral decisions in conditions of uncertainty and without assured knowledge of the future. But it would be a

11 Vitoria, *On the Law of War*, 3.1., sect17, Anthony Pagden and Jeremy Lawrance (eds.), *Vitoria, Political Writings* (Cambridge: Cambridge University Press, 1991), p. 315.

12 See, for example, Nigel Biggar in David Fisher and Nigel Biggar, 'Was Iraq an Unjust War? A Debate on the Iraq War and Reflections on Libya', *International Affairs*, Vol. 87, No.3, May 2011, p. 696 where proportionality is omitted from the standard just war criteria listed.

13 Michael Walzer, *Just and Unjust Wars – A Moral Argument with Historical Illustrations* (London: Allen Lane, 1978), p. 129.

mistake to excuse politicians who take the fateful decisions on war and peace from making such an assessment because it is difficult, however much some politicians might welcome such exemption. Assessing the likely consequences of military action is a core part of the just war appraisal. It was a task neglected by the political leaders who took us to war in Iraq in 2003 whose planning for what would happen after the initial military operation was woefully inadequate.[14]

Assessing whether military operations in Libya would be likely to bring about more good than harm was very difficult. But, however difficult, it was a key judgement to be made. Given the imminent massacre of innocents and the possession by Western powers of substantial military capability to prevent this, the assessment that more good than harm was likely to result was a not unreasonable judgement to have made at the time. It is also a judgement that appears, on the whole, to have been vindicated by the way events have turned out. The NATO operations did prevent the feared civilian massacres in Benghazi and elsewhere, which was the good to be achieved by military action as specified in the just cause. Nor were Gaddafi's threats idle bluster that could be ignored, as some critics have claimed.[15] Gaddafi had a track record of large scale civilian murders, including the murder of 1270 prisoners in Abu Salim prison in 1996. Such cruelty is a character trait that is not uncommon among dictators, as witness the murderous exploits of President Assad of Syria, including the murder of women and children, in his efforts to suppress the popular uprising against his regime that began in 2011.

Critics of the Libyan intervention have, however, claimed that the NATO operations went far beyond the objective of the prevention of civilian deaths as authorised by UNSCR 1973.[16] It was argued that the protection of civilians had been illegitimately replaced as a goal, as the campaign progressed, by that of regime change. Even a sympathetic report by the UK Royal United Services Institute conceded that 'the operation mutated into a proxy war with regime change as the object'.[17] Critics argued that the change in objective was

14 See Fisher, *Morality and War*, Chapter 10, 'Gulf Wars'.

15 See, for example, Seumas Milne, 'If There were Global Justice NATO Would Be in the Dock', *The Guardian*, 16 May 2012, who claims that, 'there is no evidence that Gaddafi had either the intention or capability to carry out a massacre in Benghazi'.

16 A concern that was quickly voiced by Russia. See, for example, 'Russia Steps Up Criticism of NATO Libya Campaign', Reuters, May 20, 2011, accessed March 4, 2013 at: http://www.reuters.com/article/2011/05/20/us-russia-libya-idUSTRE74J5K820110520

17 Adrian Johnson and Saqeb Mueen (eds.), *Short War, Long Shadow – The Political and Military Legacies of the 2011 Libya Campaign*, Whitehall Report 1–12 (Stephen Austin & Sons for the RUSI, 2012), p. 3.

evidenced by the way the NATO air attacks, by degrading Gaddafi's military capability, thereby assisted the rebel forces in their ground campaign, with a key role played by Special Forces in coordinating the air and ground campaigns. NATO, it was claimed, became the Air Force for the rebels' National Transitional Council. If the life-saving objective of the mission had been replaced during the campaign by that of regime change, this would have called into question the justice of NATO's cause, the rightness of the intention with which the operation was mounted, as well as whether more good than harm was achieved thereby. The Libyan operation would have failed three key requirements of a just war. So was there such a change in objective? Did the NATO operations go beyond the terms of UNSCR 1973?

Some of the criticism made to this effect was clearly disingenuous, suggesting that the UN Security Council resolution had only authorised a very limited operation. That was not true. In authorising member states to use 'all necessary means' to 'protect civilians and civilian populated areas under threat of attack' in Libya, the Security Council was authorising a major and extensive military operation, and not one limited just to Benghazi. This point was underlined by Sir Mark Lyall Grant, the UK's Permanent Representative to the UN, in his evidence to the UK House of Commons Defence Committee. All fifteen members of the Security Council, he claimed, knew from the start that what was envisaged 'was not just a question of flying over Libya imposing a no-fly zone, and even the imposition of a no-fly zone would require strikes on the ground to take out the air defences. In addition, the protection of civilians specifically meant halting Qadhafi's columns and, if necessary ships from attacking Benghazi'. It was, therefore, not reasonable to 'say afterwards that they were misled or that we had over-interpreted the resolution'.[18]

It is also important to recognise that, since Gaddafi was seeking to cling on to power by cowering his population into submission, a NATO operation to save civilian lives would *eo ipso* help thwart Gaddafi's political ambitions. An operation to save civilian lives – without any change in its objective – would necessarily frustrate Gaddafi's efforts to suppress the popular uprising, so contributing to his military defeat and overthrow by the Libyan rebel forces. To that extent there was a natural coincidence between the coalition objectives and those of the rebel forces.

This would suggest, however, that even if there was no change in the primary life-saving objective of the mission, the coalition leaders were at least prepared to accept regime change as a possible outcome of the operation.

---

18 House of Commons Defence Committee (HCDC), *Operations in Libya*, Vol. 1, HC 950 (London: The Stationary Office, 25 January 2012), Answer to Question 6.

The coalition leaders had also made offers to Gaddafi some months into the operation of safe passage to a third party country, so indicating their willingness to pursue regime change not as an objective of the military campaign but rather as a way of avoiding the need for its continuance. Following the referral of the Libyan regime to the ICC by UNSCR 1970, the ICC issued an arrest warrant on 27 June for Gaddafi on the charge of crimes against humanity. If implemented, that too would have required a change of political leadership. So the coalition leaders and broader international community were prepared to pursue regime change, at least as an alternative to military action. But did regime change also become the objective of the military campaign?

It has been argued that some of the special force operations, in particular, the provision of arms to the rebels by French and Qatari forces went beyond the terms of UNSCR 1973 by breaching the arms embargo imposed by UNSCR 1970.[19] That claim is disputed amongst lawyers on the grounds that the terms of UNSCR 1973 had provided some derogation from UNSCR 1970. But arming the rebels could, nonetheless, be considered to depart at least from the spirit of UNSCR 1973. That was perhaps why the UK Government declined to participate in such activities. Arming the rebels could be criticised as at least stretching the terms of the UN resolution. Overall, however, the training and support offered by coalition Special Forces, mainly in the later stages of the campaign, was of a fairly limited kind (in the case of the UK, apart from some assistance with coordinating air operations, a single SAS squadron to train and mentor NTC units). This was hardly in itself evidence that the primary objective of the mission had changed to regime change. Moreover, in so far as the support provided by Special Forces contributed to the effectiveness of the NATO operations, including importantly helping to avoid friendly-fire accidents, such assistance could be regarded as consistent with the primary life-saving objective of the mission.

None of these claims, therefore, furnish compelling evidence that regime change became the primary objective of the campaign, in the sense that regime change replaced saving civilian lives as the goal of the campaign. This charge has always been denied by coalition leaders and would, indeed, have changed the nature of the operation from a humanitarian mission into a brutal exercise of realpolitik, toppling leaders to suit the political and strategic objectives of the West. Such a change in the mission would have fully justified criticism from Russia and others.

19 Jonathan Eyal, "The Responsibility to Protect: A Chance Missed" in Johnson and Mueen (eds.), *Short War, Long Shadow*, pp. 60–61.

But while such a radical change in the primary objective of the mission is implausible, what is plausible is that, as the campaign progressed and the resistance offered by Gaddafi proved stubborn, coalition leaders came to see regime change as likely to be necessary to achieve the objective of saving civilian lives. Hence the offer was made to Gaddafi some months into the campaign of a safe refuge. Hence too the support by Special Forces, albeit late and limited, offered to rebel forces. Once victory has been achieved in a military campaign, it often looks inevitable. But that is seldom how it looks at the time. The Libyan operation was no easy walk over. After initial successes by coalition forces, on 7 April Gaddafi launched his own successful counter-offensive and retook Brega. The Libyan operation took seven months to bring to a successful conclusion. Its scope and pace was not solely in the control of the coalition but was determined at least in part by the strength of resistance offered. Coalition leaders would, no doubt, have been delighted if after a few weeks bombing, Gaddafi had stopped his murderous campaign. He might then have been allowed to stay in office (as Milosevic had been after the 1999 NATO campaign in Kosovo) or at least permitted safe passage to a third country. But Gaddafi did not give up. He resisted strenuously to the bitter end. It is hence hardly surprising that, as the campaign dragged on, regime change may have been perceived as a likely necessary means to stopping the killing of civilians.

So, if regime change had come to be seen as a likely necessary way of achieving the overall life-saving objective of the mission, would that be in breach of just war requirements? The just war tradition adopts a generally restrictive approach to military action undertaken to achieve regime change, weighing its uncertain benefits against the evident costs of the application of force.[20] Regime change pursued as an end in itself – to suit the political and strategic objectives of those seeking the change – would for these reasons not be countenanced by just war teaching. The tradition does, however, recognise that regime change may sometimes be justified if it is the only way to put a stop to a humanitarian catastrophe. In particular, where a humanitarian mission is undertaken to end the brutal oppression of a people by its own government, a change in regime may be a necessary component of the success of the mission and, in particular, of the establishment of a just peace thereafter. For if the government is itself carrying out the massacre, some political reconstitution may be necessary to bring the slaughter to an end and ensure that it does not recur in the future. In such circumstances regime change may be a legitimate objective, not as an end in itself but as a necessary means to put a stop to the

20 For the treatment of regime change by the just war tradition see Fisher, *Morality and War*, especially Chapter 10 'Gulf Wars' and Chapter 11 'Humanitarian Intervention'.

mass killing of innocent civilians. So a change of regime in Libya was not necessarily an illegitimate secondary objective and could be deemed part of the 'all necessary means' to protect civilians authorised by the Security Council.

Overall, therefore, it is reasonable to conclude that there was no change in the primary objective of the NATO operations in Libya. These were intended to save civilian lives and succeeded in doing so. This was the good to be achieved as specified in the just cause. It could, therefore, be argued that more good than harm was achieved and so the principle of proportion was met.

Turning to the conduct of the intervention, NATO operations, on the whole, complied with the *jus in bello* principles of **proportionality** and **non-combatant immunity**. There was criticism of the scale of the operations and, in particular, the number of sorties flown and multiplicity of targets attacked. But such criticism failed to recognise that the application of force, while it should be no more than is necessary, does need to be sufficient to achieve its objective. A hesitant and half-hearted application of force may either fail altogether or require the application of much greater force later. Moreover, considerable efforts were made to ensure that the force used in individual operations was proportionate to the objectives to be secured and that non-combatant casualties were minimised. A Human Rights Watch report assessed that at least 72 civilians died as a result of NATO operations but acknowledged that, 'the number of civilian deaths in Libya from NATO strikes was low given the extent and duration of the bombing campaign'.[21] There were also other lapses. These included – notoriously – the murder on 20 October 2011 of Gaddafi by rebel militia. This took place after he had surrendered and so was no longer a combatant. This was a clear breach of the principle of non-combatant immunity. All of the lapses that occurred are to be deplored. But, overall, the NATO operations could be judged to have complied with the *jus in bello* criteria.

What, however, of ***jus post bellum***? It may seem difficult to claim that a just peace has been established given the messy aftermath of the war, including, as noted earlier, the continuing serious security problems posed by yet to be disarmed militias and the weakness of the central government. It is difficult to predict with confidence quite how and how well events in Libya will turn out.

It has also been argued that the 2011 NATO intervention in Libya was unjust because of the instability in neighbouring Mali brought about by the return there of Tuareg mercenaries, who had been employed by Gaddafi to help bolster his regime and had fled back to their homeland after the regime's

21 'Unacknowledged Deaths: Civilian Casualties in NATO's Air Campaign', Human Rights Watch Report, May 14, 2012, Summary and Recommendations, accessed May 15, 2012 at: http://www.hrw.org/sites/default/files/reports/libya0512_brochure_web.pdf

collapse. Since north-eastern Mali is part of the same Saharan region as southern Libya, weapons and fighters moved easily across Algeria into Mali. Their weapons and expertise, it was claimed, helped fuel the indigenous Islamist insurrection in that country.[22] The grave threat posed by that insurrection in turn prompted the intervention by French forces in January 2013 to assist the Government of Mali to re-establish its control over territory captured by the Islamist rebels and to protect the civilian population from further oppression by the rebels imposing their own harsh version of *sharia* law.[23] That intervention has to date been successful in achieving these objectives. So have such wider consequences, however unintended, of the Libyan intervention, including the many deaths arising from the Mali insurrection, invalidated the claim to justice of the NATO mission in Libya?

In applying the *jus post bellum* condition it is important not to place unreasonable demands on the test. *Jus post bellum* was not included in the classic just war criteria. The rationale for its recent addition to the just war tests is primarily to remind political and military leaders of the need to take the *post bellum* settlement fully into account in the overall reckoning of the balance of consequences to be achieved by war before any decision is taken to go to war. In doing so, they should have and keep up to date, revising as circumstances change, a robust plan for dealing with the consequences of military action and ensuring the prompt restoration of peaceful conditions.

Political leaders can and should be held responsible for the consequences of their actions that are reasonably foreseeable. They are, in particular, responsible for ensuring in the post war settlement that the wrong that occasioned the war, as specified in the just cause, has been righted. Where the international community intervenes, as in Libya, to stop a Government massively oppressing its own people some political reconstitution, including regime change, is, as already noted, likely to be a necessary constituent of any *post-bellum* settlement. What political leaders cannot reasonably be held responsible for are the far distant consequences of their actions that may be influenced by many other factors and may be very difficult, if not, impossible to predict. Here, as elsewhere in our moral life, it is important to impose a sensible cut off point since otherwise the assessment of consequences becomes an impossible and fruitless task, potentially stretching to infinity.

22 Ross Douthat, 'Libya's Unintended Consequences', *The New York Times*, July 7, 2012, accessed July 8, 2012 at: http://www.nytimes.com/2012/07/08/opinion/sunday/libyas-unintended-consequences.html?_r=0

23 For an account of the Operations in Mali see Francois Heisbourg, 'A Surprising Little War: First Lessons of Mali', *Survival*, Vol. 55 No 2, April–May 2013 (Routledge for the IISS, 2013) pp. 7–17.

It would hardly be fair to criticise the 1999 NATO intervention in Kosovo as unjust because in 2013 – fourteen years later – there were still imperfections in the resulting peace settlement, including dispute over the international legal status of Kosovo. The intervention did, after all, successfully achieve its objective of ending the Serbian ethnic cleansing of Kosovar Albanians It would similarly be unfair to criticise the NATO intervention in Libya as unjust because that country's future is still far from assured, still less because of wider regional instability in Mali or elsewhere to which many other factors have contributed. Rather the appropriate *jus post bellum* test is whether the wrong that occasioned the war has been righted and whether political conditions have been established to help prevent its recurrence. On that test the Libyan intervention could be judged a success. The mass slaughter of civilians by an oppressive regime was stopped and a democratically elected moderate government has been installed. Libya's travails are far from over but the people have at least been given a chance to secure a better future. The just peace we seek after war must be just enough to ensure that the wrong that occasioned the war has been righted. But we are not seeking perfect justice nor to right all the wrongs of the world. The bar must not be set so high that it makes it impossible to fulfil our responsibility to protect innocents from mass slaughter.

So despite the *in bello* lapses and messy *post bellum* aftermath, overall, the intervention in Libya met the just war criteria. It was a just intervention.

Libya – A Model for the Future?

Success usually breeds success. So it is curious that only two years after a successful intervention, the international appetite for intervention, far from recovering, still appears to be on the wane. The US, as Obama remarked at the beginning of 2012, is now 'turning the page on a decade of war'.[24] The international community looks on aghast at what is happening in Syria but declines to intervene, even at the lower levels, such as a no fly zone, that have been urged by some as a way to protect civilian lives, while avoiding the difficulties of a full scale military campaign.[25] Indeed, the UN Security Council has found it very

24 Speech by President Obama, 5 January, 2012, 'Obama Unveils New Strategy and "leaner" US forces', accessed on January 6, 2012 at: http://www.bbc.co.uk/news/world-us-canada-16430405

25 A course recommended, for example, by Senator John McCain, see Leigh Munsil 'McCain Urges a No-fly Zone Over Syria' at: http://www.politico.com/story/2013/06/syria-no-fly-zone-92766.html (accessed 6 February 2015)

difficult even to agree on what non-military action should be undertaken, apart from its belated action to enforce the chemical weapons convention after flagrant breaches by the Syrian Government. French forces successfully intervened in Mali at the start of 2013 but other Western countries, including the UK, while applauding the intervention, have been reluctant to join in the operation, preferring to lend logistic, transport and training support. The French Government is itself keen to extract its ground forces as soon as they can be replaced by regional forces.

The declining appetite for intervention reflects in large measure the shadow still cast by the Iraq intervention, widely perceived as unjust, as well as exhaustion from the protracted counter-insurgency operations in Afghanistan.

The Iraq intervention has had two consequences for the wider debate on humanitarian intervention. First, it has had the practical consequence that two of the countries best equipped to undertake military interventions, the US and UK, have been heavily engaged first in Iraq and then in Afghanistan, with few forces to spare for elsewhere and are now anxious to reduce such commitments in the future. The international community has become wearied of the occupation-heavy interventions of the last decade.

But the lesson to be drawn from this is not to rule out all interventions. Rather, 'intervention lite' or 'constrained intervention' of the Libyan variety could point the way towards a more palatable and sustainable model for future humanitarian interventions.[26] French commentators have been quick to claim that the 2013 intervention in Mali 'confirms the responsibility to protect civilian populations that underpinned the earlier intervention in Libya. The first use of the doctrine merely sets a precedent, but the second is case law'.[27] Motives for the Mali intervention, as with other interventions, may have been more mixed than this claim implies. The operation was justified by the French Government under article 51 as offering assistance in response to the request of the interim President of Mali to help defend the country from attack.[28] There was also undoubtedly a concern to protect Western citizens from future

26 'Constrained intervention' was a term first used by Lord Owen in a speech on Oct 5 2011 to the Dublin Institute of International and European Affairs, accessed on March 25, 2013 at: http://www.lorddavidowen.co.uk/constrained-intervention-speech-by-lord-owen-to-the-dublin-institute-of-international-and-european-affairs/

27 Bernard-Henri Levy, 'France to the Rescue: The Good Things about the Mali Intervention', *Newsweek* January 21, 2013 accessed on March 4, 2013 at: http://www.thedailybeast.com/newsweek/2013/01/20/france-to-the-rescue-the-good-things-about-the-mali-intervention.html

28 See Francois Heisbourg, 'A Surprising Little War: First Lessons of Mali', *Survival*, Vol. 55 No 2, April–May 2013 (Routledge for the IISS, 2013) pp. 7–17.

terrorist attacks by denying the territory of northern Mali as a base from which al Qaeda-linked rebels could mount attacks. Such self-defence considerations are, however, not inconsistent with the humanitarian motives that also played an important role in the intervention, which could hence be judged in accordance with the principle of the Responsibility to Protect.

The second consequence of the Iraq intervention was to reinforce the concerns already felt by many non-Western countries that any right of humanitarian intervention would be abused by the great powers, who would be tempted to cloak military actions undertaken for reasons of realpolitik in the guise of humanitarian motives. Humanitarian intervention it was feared would be misused to mask a new form of Western colonial imperialism. This was a concern expressed by the Brazilian Government following the Libyan intervention in underling how important it was that 'the international community, as it exercises its responsibility to protect, must demonstrate a high level of responsibility while protecting'.[29]

Protecting the Responsibility to Protect

Such concerns need to be addressed. But they should not be allowed to undermine the importance or validity of the principle of the Responsibility to Protect. There is no justification for using the injustice of the Iraq intervention as a pretext for preventing humanitarian intervention where gross abuses of human rights are taking place. The Iraq intervention was not a humanitarian intervention. It is illogical to suggest that because one intervention, not undertaken for humanitarian reasons, was unjust, all humanitarian interventions are unjust.

Most importantly, the reasons why the UN Summit modified the doctrine of the inviolability of state borders remain valid. State borders should not be allowed to be impenetrable barriers behind which any atrocity can take place. As the 2001 International Commission on Intervention and State Sovereignty underlined, sovereignty entails responsibilities, as well as rights, including the responsibility of a government to protect its own people.[30] If a government is unable or unwilling to exercise that responsibility, the

---

29 Letter dated 9 November 2011 from the Permanent Representative of Brazil to the United Nations addressed to the Secretary-General, *Responsibility while protecting: elements for the development and promotion of a concept*, General Assembly, Sixty-sixth Session, A/66/551-S/2011/701, November 11, 2011, available at http://www.un.org/en/ga/search/view_doc.asp?symbol=A/66/551 accessed on April 30, 2012

30 *The Responsibility to Protect*, International Commission on Intervention and State Sovereignty (Ottawa: International Development Research Centre, December 2001), p. viii.

international community has a responsibility to do so itself. The Responsibility to Protect remains a valid and important principle governing international relations. It was a belated rediscovery in the twenty-first century of the altruism and universality of the just war principles as taught by Vitoria in the sixteenth century for whom the 'lawful defence of the innocent from unjust death' constituted just cause for war.[31]

The UN Summit's endorsement of the Responsibility to Protect does not, as some had feared, mark the end of the stability and order of the international system. Stability and order are important but so too is the protection of citizens from mass slaughter. What is proposed is not the abolition of state sovereignty but rather some rebalancing of the rights of states to grant greater recognition to the rights of individuals. State sovereignty remains important but it does not have an absolute status. The choice posed by opponents of intervention between order and justice is an unreal one. It is possible to have both.

The international community's endorsement of the Responsibility to Protect does, however, mark an important shift in the way the onus of proof is established in favour of humanitarian intervention. For, where a massacre is taking place which a domestic government is failing to prevent or is itself perpetrating, then the international community has a responsibility to take action to prevent this. If it fails to do so, the onus of proof is on the international community to explain why it is failing to fulfil its responsibility. This shift in the burden of proof has important implications for the current debate on Syria. For, even if, because of the complexity of the geo-political situation, a full-scale military intervention in Syria is judged likely to cause more harm than good and so fail the just war tests, that does not remove the international community's obligation urgently to explore other options to fulfil its responsibility to protect the Syrian people. This is an obligation that the international community, divided amongst itself, has been too slow and hesitant to recognise. The priority at the end of 2013 is to make a success of the Geneva peace conference planned for January 2014. But, if that process fails, other options, including military, will need to be considered if that obligation is to be fulfilled.

The case for humanitarian intervention remains, therefore, valid. But if we are to address the legitimate concerns of its opponents, it is essential that the criteria for a just intervention should be clearly defined and agreed in advance and rigorously and consistently applied in practice. It was a weakness of the 2005 Summit that it failed to include the just war criteria in the Summit

31 Vitoria, *On the American Indians*, Question 3, Article 5 in Pagden and Lawrance (eds.), *Vitoria, Political Writings*, p. 286.

declaration even though they had featured in the preceding high level reports and despite the urging of the UK Government. Their inclusion was opposed on somewhat inconsistent grounds by: the US, fearing it would constrain its freedom of action; and by Russia and China, fearful it might encourage action bypassing the Security Council.[32] Their exclusion was a mistake, for it is not enough for a humanitarian intervention to have a just cause. All the other just war criteria have also to be met, which, taken together and mutually reinforcing each other, are designed to try to ensure that intervention only takes place if it is judged likely to bring about more good than harm.

An ethical foreign policy needs to be underpinned by robust and soundly-based ethical reasoning. Experience in Iraq and Afghanistan has reminded us of the difficulties and limits in the use of force, so underlining the importance of the careful application of the just war criteria before an intervention is embarked on. The just war criteria are not optional extras that can be readily dispensed with. They furnish essential ethical guidance for governments and the international community to determine when interventions may legitimately be undertaken; and when they may not. They emphasise the need for rigorous analysis before interventions are undertaken. They impose crucial constraints on the behaviour of states, including their ability to take pre-emptive action. The criteria are thus an important restraint on the abuse of power by states and so furnish the necessary reassurance for those fearing that humanitarian intervention might be used to mask such abuse.

But the criteria also provide guidance on when interventions should take place. For if the criteria are met and the scale of suffering to be averted is very great, we may have not merely a right but a duty to intervene, as the Responsibility to Protect doctrine underlines. The just war criteria provide the basis not only for criticising interventions by states that fail to meet them, such as that in Iraq, but also for criticising the United Nations for its failure to intervene, for example in Rwanda.

Conclusion

Looking back on the past two decades of liberal intervention by Western states the record is decidedly mixed. There have been unjust interventions, as in the

32 The respective position of the Chinese, Russian, UK and US Government on the inclusion of criteria in the Summit declaration are noted in Alex J. Bellamy, 'The Responsibility to Protect and the Problem of Military Intervention', *International Affairs*, Vol. 84 No 4, July 2008, p. 625.

2003 invasion of Iraq, and interventions, such as in Afghanistan, that, while undertaken for honourable motives, have proved more difficult in execution than originally supposed. It is important, however, to underline that neither of these was a humanitarian intervention. There have been successful humanitarian interventions. These include the NATO operation to end ethnic cleansing in Kosovo (1999), the British intervention in Sierra Leone that removed the rebel threats to President Kabbah's incipient democracy (2000), the NATO operation in Libya in 2011 and the 2013 French intervention in Mali. There have also been some very costly failures to intervene, above all in Rwanda in 1994 where the failure of the international community cost the lives of nearly a million people. Non-intervention in Syria has cost more than 110,000 lives by September 2013.[33] Over 2 million refugees have fled the country.[34]

It is thus far too simplistic to conclude from the failure of intervention in Iraq or the difficulty of the intervention in Afghanistan that all intervention is mistaken. The case for humanitarian intervention remains as strong as ever. But any intervention must be guided and constrained by the just war principles and only undertaken where these can be met. The international realm is not, as the realists proclaimed, a moral-free zone. The UN Summit's recognition of an international Responsibility to Protect and the legitimacy of humanitarian intervention was an important victory for morality, rediscovering the altruistic vision of the just war thinkers of the sixteenth century. It is crucial that the concessions re-won for morality in 2005 are not lost. For it remains our responsibility to ensure that another genocide like that in Rwanda does not take place and that the world will not, as it did in 1994, stand idly by while a million people are slaughtered. We should, therefore, try to ensure that: humanitarian intervention - if undertaken in accordance with the just war criteria – does have a future; the Libyan intervention is not the last of its kind; and the principle of the Responsibility to Protect is itself protected.

---

33 'Syria Death Toll: More than 110,00 Dead in Conflict, NGO says', Agence France Presse, 1 September 2013 accessed November 29, 2013 at http://www.huffingtonpost.com/2013/09/01/syria-death-toll_n_3851982.html

34 'Number of Syrian refugees top 2 million mark' according to UN Refugee Agency 3 September 2013 accessed on November 29, 2013 at http://www.unhcr.org/522495669.html

CHAPTER 3

Object Lesson or Subject People: On the Receiving End of the Responsibility to Protect

Robert Wilton

Robert Wilton was the Chief of the European Mission in Kosovo. He spent ten years working for the UK Government in the Ministry of Defence, Cabinet Office and Foreign Office. He increasingly specialised in the Balkans, covering amongst other things events in Kosovo (1999), Serbia (2000) and Macedonia (2001). He was involved with OSCE mission to oversee the elections there in 2001 and 2002. In 2006 the UK Government asked him to become independent security advisor to the new Prime Minister of Kosovo, at the latter's request. His work included reviewing the capacity of the Prime Minister's Office, helping design the future defence and security sector, and advising the Kosovo team during their negotiations for the recognition of independence. This chapter, written from the perspective of a practitioner who was intimately involved with events as they unfolded and continued to develop long after most of the international attention had drifted away, reviews the Kosovo intervention as an apparently clear example of 'force for good': the threat and use of force, with limited actual commitment of material and relatively limited human cost, to remedy a clear example of human suffering and to bring stability and democracy, a mission that had some immediate success in 1999 and subsequently reached a new point of achievement with the recognition of a democratic, multi-ethnic independent state. The chapter reviews the ways in which the success was achieved. It also suggests various aspects of the intervention which were not, arguably, so successful. The exploration of the apparent successes and the consideration of the possible failures offer a new synthesis of argument on what makes for effective intervention, and on the limits to the good that force can do.

Introduction: The Accidental Guests

Ten years and more after the international intervention in Kosovo in 1999, spring was still pock-marked with anniversary events reflecting the international role in the country. The year would begin with the commemoration of the 15th January 1999 Racak massacre, which swung the balance of international perception against the Milosevic regime thanks to the Kosovo Verification

 | DOI 10.1163/9789004280380_004

Mission's rapid arrival in the aftermath. On March 24th would come the anniversary of the start of the NATO bombing campaign. In the first half of June Kosovo's liberation would be remembered, date by date and town by town, marking the advance of NATO troops northwards from Macedonia and spreading out through the country.[1]

Ten years and more afterwards, some of the guests at these occasions were still international representatives, from the diverse international organizations that continued to play a significant role guiding the country. None of the dates of 1999 proved truly conclusive for Kosovo's constitutional status. Liberation in 1999 was followed not by independence, but by more than a decade of internationally-managed constitutional uncertainty and improvisation; by dependence. Even after Kosovo's formal declaration of independence in 2008, co-ordinated with key international players and followed by a steady stream of bilateral recognitions, there remained in the country international officials and officers with executive powers and significant capacity to influence. An armed intervention to stop a humanitarian crisis became a protracted constitutional and tutelary arrangement.

The persistence of an international role in the administration and guidance of Kosovo more than a decade after its liberation is significant not only to any study of Kosovo, but also to a study of the concept and nature of international intervention. One aspect of such a study concerns the theory and practice, the legitimacy and success, of intervention as a means to achieving international ends. Another aspect is what the intervention means in reality for those on the receiving end of it – what it means for their national aspirations, and also what it means for their everyday lives and their very status as citizens.

Kosovo and the Responsibility to Protect

There was a legitimate – and perhaps predominantly – humanitarian justification for the international community's decision to intervene in Kosovo in 1999. Kosovo has no oil. Whatever crimes were being committed within its borders, when the bombing started in March 1999 Kosovo did not present a significant stability or even refugee issue for Western Europe or the United States. The world had emerged from one epochal confrontation and had not recognized

1 This analysis is a development of a lecture to Euro-ISME at the UK Defence Academy on June 15th 2012, the opportunity and the stimulating discussion of which are gratefully acknowledged. June 15th is also the anniversary of the liberation of the town of Gjilan, centre of a region still dominated in 2012 by the US base at Camp Bondsteel.

the first symptoms of the next. Instead, the Kosovo intervention was arguably a response to three human factors. The first was the immediate and worsening humanitarian situation on the ground. However blame might be ascribed, and even accepting for the sake of argument the contention that it was only with NATO's bombing that widespread oppression truly became ethnic cleansing, by the beginning of 1999 the security situation in Kosovo was clearly out of any one of the participants' control, having a direct impact on the civilian population, and threatening worse. The second factor was the shadow of previous failures to respond adequately to extreme humanitarian crises. Most notoriously, over Rwanda in 1994 and Srebrenica in 1995, the international community seemed to have failed catastrophically to address a situation before it degenerated into horror. These failures were felt strongly and explicitly, especially in the Clinton Government in the United States.[2] It was also the Clinton Government especially that felt the impact of the third factor: the sense of unfinished business with the government of Yugoslavia.[3]

Kosovo in 1999 was an emotional intervention, led by two western leaders in whom emotion and politics overlapped unusually. President Bill Clinton became revered in Kosovo, his poster smiling down over the boulevard named in his honour, and as the poster began to fade it was reinforced by a statue.[4] Prime Minister Tony Blair's apotheosis came in the refugee camps of Albanians

2 Clinton delivered his public apology for the failure to intervene in Rwanda at Kigali in March 1998. He said that he was 'directing my administration to improve, with the international community, our system for identifying and spotlighting nations in danger of genocidal violence…we must as an international community have the ability to act when genocide threatens'. (Text available at http://www.cbsnews.com/2100-202_162-5798.html retrieved on 2/2/13.)

3 'Bill Clinton was still President; he appointed as his special envoy for Kosovo Richard Holbrooke, who had been the chief negotiator of the Dayton Accords. In Brussels the Supreme Allied Commander Europe – NATO's military chief – was US General Wesley Clark, who had been with Holbrooke at Dayton and had been notoriously embarrassed in 1994 by Bosnian Serb General Ratko Mladic, subsequently indicted for war crimes. For them, the developing crisis in Kosovo was a confirmation of what they expected from the Serbian regime, and an opportunity to take the fight from the proxy war in Bosnia to the heart of nationalism in Belgrade'. Wilton, 'The beginning and the end of humanitarian intervention: Kosovo 1999' *Defence & Security Analysis, Volume 24 Issue 4*, Taylor & Francis, 2008. US Secretary of State Albright vowed in early 1998 that 'We are not going to stand by and watch the Serbian authorities do in Kosovo what they can no longer get away with doing in Bosnia'. (Steven Erlanger, "Albright Warns Serbs on Kosovo Violence," New York Times, March 8, 1998).

4 Almost certainly the only statue in Kosovo of a living subject and – among the figures of Skenderbeu, Mother Theresa and various martyrs of the liberation war – the only non-Albanian so honoured.

expelled from Kosovo.[5] It was only a month into the NATO bombing campaign against Yugoslav regime and military targets, with little sign of progress and continued resistance (including in the US) to the idea of a land campaign, that Kosovo acquired a theoretical justification. Blair's speech to the Chicago Economic Club on 22nd April 1999 articulated the humanitarian justification for intervention, drawing a tenuous but straight line between foreign humanitarian crises and domestic security: 'We cannot turn our backs on conflicts and the violation of human rights within other countries if we want still to be secure. ... If we can establish and spread the values of liberty, the rule of law, human rights and an open society then that is in our national interests too'.[6]

The motivation for the Chicago speech may have been pragmatic rather than intellectual: to couch the Kosovo intervention in more broadly palatable terms, at a moment when commitment and certainty were faltering and more were needed. But the Kosovo intervention and its aftermath were followed by the UN's report on its own performance over Srebrenica,[7] UN Secretary-General Annan's call for a new consensus on humanitarian intervention, and the Canadian International Commission on Intervention and State Sovereignty (ICISS)'s December 2001 report 'The Responsibility to Protect'. The Chicago speech, with its five principles to justify intervention, took on the characteristics of a timely first sketch of what Blair himself – cynically but presciently – called 'a new doctrine of international community'.[8] Kosovo was its stimulus, and retrospectively its exemplar.

---

5 Perhaps the high-water mark of his reputation, when his genuine moral sense found a cause with some genuine validity, causing him to make a promise which he kept. His ceremonial visit to an independent Kosovo in July 2010, addressing the nation and meeting children named for him, was – after Iraq and Afghanistan had taken the lustre off the Kosovo precedent – nostalgia. 'I did what was right. I did not regret it then. I do not regret it now'. (See http://www.bbc.co.uk/news/10576544, retrieved on February 1, 2013.)

6 Full speech available at http://www.pbs.org/newshour/bb/international/jan-june99/blair_doctrine4-23.html (retrieved on February 1, 2013). The blunt claim that 'This is a just war, based not on any territorial ambitions but on values' was at least half-right, if not more; Blair also recognized 'a more subtle blend of mutual self interest and moral purpose in defending the values we cherish'.

7 Distributed on November 15th, 1999, and available at http://www.un.org/en/ga/search/view_doc.asp?symbol=A/54/549 (retrieved on February 2, 2013)

8 http://www.pbs.org/newshour/bb/international/jan-june99/blair_doctrine4-23.html 'Blair's Chicago speech...became the theological underpinning for the Kosovo intervention (and for anticipated future interventions), and the Kosovo intervention became the archetype for the policy'. (Wilton *op.cit.*) This chapter does not attempt to give a full picture of the evolution of the Responsibility To Protect doctrine. A general sense of the Chicago speech in that context can be found at http://www.opendemocracy.net/globalization-institutions_government/article_1857.jsp

The ground intervention – the column of 50,000 NATO troops that entered Kosovo from Macedonia in June 1999, and whose 5,000 descendants were still in the country in 2013 – was even more clearly a protective intervention. The air campaign destroyed with the aim of protecting. The ground force – 'KFOR' – entered the country unopposed, on the basis of an agreement signed with Yugoslav forces under which they would pull out in front of it. KFOR's mission was initially and notionally to protect Kosovo and its citizens from further oppression or any armed Yugoslav attempt to re-enter. But once Milosevic's army, police and paramilitaries were out – and as it became clear that there was no likelihood of the latter threat being realized – KFOR's focus shifted. While theoretically responsible for the security of Kosovo, its work was entirely security within Kosovo. It guarded Serbian cultural and religious sites (until this responsibility was handed on to the Kosovo Police, under a managed transition from 2010). It was the more substantial force for public order, behind the nascent national police force. Its commander was one of the two or three most senior international voices offering advice, and occasionally caution, to the new Kosovo authorities. Kosovo's Albanians felt that it was their only guarantee against a Serbian invasion; Kosovo's Serbs felt – perhaps with fractionally more justification – that it was their only guarantee against attacks on their property, heritage and even selves.[9]

Ability to Protect?

At the start, the Kosovo intervention was fundamentally about protection. The administrative aspect was an afterthought, an unavoidable side-effect of the military neutralization and diplomatic defeat of Milosevic. The escalation of ethnic cleansing by Serbian forces after the start of the NATO bombing showed the riskiness and fragility of the decision to intervene to protect; the

(retrieved on 4/2/13), which also notes: 'Kosovo is a flawed application of the "Blair doctrine"; Afghanistan and Iraq are clear violations of it'. Cynical – even conspiratorial – interpretations of the intervention have been offered; see e.g. http://www.globalresearch.ca/the-u-s-nato-military-intervention-in-kosovo/1666 (retrieved on 10/2/13)

9 KFOR also took on – with a willingness that varied with commanders and with attitudes in NATO headquarters – roles relating to the decommissioning of the Kosovo Liberation Army, its transition to the 'Kosovo Protection Corps', and the eventual establishment of a Kosovo Security Force. Given the threat to stability (internally and even regionally) that would have been posed by uncontrolled or frustrated guerrillas, this was a logical embellishment of the role – however much the establishment of the new Security Force discomfited some NATO capitals.

withdrawal of those forces two and a half months later vindicated it.[10] By moving into Kosovo in June 1999, on armoured vehicles and diplomatic passports, the international community took on a new – broader, more vague and longer – responsibility to protect.

Put simply, a large international intervention justified by the need to protect Kosovo's Albanians became, three months later, an intervention to protect Kosovo's Serbs. The military alliance that had spent two and a half months assaulting Serbian military and regime targets became the only protection for the Serb civilians left behind when soldiers and paramilitaries withdrew. Their monasteries, churches and in some cases villages were protected by NATO troops.

There have been two significant tests of KFOR's protection of Kosovo's Serbs. Although explanations and caveats may be offered, both are seen as failures. In the summer of 1999, Kosovo's Albanians came out of hiding or exile and, in individual cases, took private revenge on Serbs for what they had suffered; a large number of Serb civilians fled in anticipation of reprisals. The Independent International Commission on Kosovo, reporting in 2000, noted that "KFOR was evidently unable, during the early days of its deployment, to avert Albanian acts of revenge. The killings of Serbs and other minorities, as well as the destruction of their homes, under the very noses of armed international soldiers represented a profound failure of the international community to uphold the principles that had been hailed as the driving force behind the war effort."[11] KFOR did not have the anticipation, plan, coverage or political clarity to prevent what would turn out to be, not least in numbers of humans affected,

10 Recognizing the bigger achievement, Kosovo's Albanians were phlegmatic about the losses they themselves suffered in the bombing, including the bombings of refugees on April 14th and May 14th 1999.

11 http://reliefweb.int/sites/reliefweb.int/files/resources/F62789D9FCC56FB3C1256C1700303E3B-thekosovoreport.htm (retrieved on 10/2/13). The statistics are as volatile as the issue, and figures for Serb flight vary from tens to hundreds of thousands of people. The Independent International Commission on Kosovo gave a figure of around 100,000. A US Army history of its part in the intervention – likely if anything to be playing down rather than exaggerating the negative effects of the intervention – recalls that, "No one in Task Force Falcon anticipated the level of violence and lawlessness, sometimes within minutes, following the departure of the Serbian security forces and preceding the arrival of NATO forces. The task force entered the province prepared to protect ethnic Albanians only to discover that the tables had turned: Ethnic Serbs now required the protection. Thousands of Serbs fled Kosovo within days of the end of Operation Allied Force. One municipality went from a population of ten thousand Serbs to fewer than twenty." (http://www.history.army.mil/brochures/Kosovo/Kosovo.pdf (retrieved on 10/2/13).)

its greatest failure to protect.[12] Then, in March 2004, pent-up Kosovo Albanian frustration at the stagnation of the international engagement and Kosovo Serb nervousness at their own vulnerability were ignited into two days of rioting that resulted in nineteen deaths, and further Kosovo Serb flight and destruction of religious sites. In its report on the violence, Amnesty International described complacency by the UN administration in Kosovo and "eye-witness accounts and other reports which indicate that in some instances KFOR troops signally failed to discharge the duties assigned to them."[13] Anecdotal descriptions of incidents show KFOR trying sometimes to exercise riot control, and helping those in danger – including Serb clergy – to safety; but the overall impression of KFOR was of organizationally chaotic and inflexible, tactically under-prepared bystanders. Kosovo's Serbs, and the viability of minority existence in Kosovo, did not feel protected.

On January 17th 2010, the North Atlantic Council approved the 'unfixing' of a first tranche of Serb patrimonial sites in Kosovo – places of religious and cultural significance, including the three monasteries that comprise a UNESCO World Heritage site, and which KFOR had been protecting since its arrival. Unfixing meant the managed, stepped handover to Kosovo Police protection. Among that first tranche was the Gazimestan monument to the 1389 battle of Kosovo, central to Serb mythography and the place where exactly six hundred years later Slobodan Milosevic held the rally that confirmed the centrality of nationalism to his political approach. The unfixing continued steadily, step-by-step for each site, and tranche-by-tranche of sites, based on an assessment of the relative lack of threat and of the readiness of the Kosovo Police to assume responsibility. As of three years later, at least, the assessment seemed accurate:

---

12 "Given the Bosnian experience, however, KFOR should have prepared itself for this type of violence. More should have been done to stop the rampage. The KFOR troops should had been alerted and told what to do before they entered Kosovo, and they should have been mandated and instructed to use military force against those who were aggressively threatening other people's lives. But during the early days of attacks KFOR troops and infrastructure were not yet fully in place, and KFOR's own security was its chief concern." (Independent International Commission on Kosovo report at http://reliefweb.int/sites/reliefweb.int/files/resources/F62789D9FCC56FB3C1256C1700303E3B-thekosovoreport.htm (retrieved on 10/2/13).)

13 '*The March Violence:* KFOR *and* UNMIK*'s failure to protect the rights of the minority communities*', Amnesty International report Index EUR 70/016/2004, 8th July 2004, available at http://miris.eurac.edu/mugs2/do/blob.pdf?type=pdf&serial=1089282359991 (retrieved on 10/2/13). Figures from Amnesty International (who also cite the UN, and are consistent with other sources): nineteen killed (of whom eleven were Kosovo Albanian), over 950 injured, 51,000 people involved in 33 incidents, over 4,000 people forced to flee.

no unfixed site had suffered attack – and, indeed, there were efforts by the Serbian Orthodox Church and by civil society to improve popular understanding of some sites. But unfixing was driven equally by KFOR's need to shed tasks, as NATO members continued to withdraw troops. Perhaps as a result of KFOR's having stood up to violent Serb extremists in the north of Kosovo in Summer 2011, and in the context of a sense that after a period of stagnation there was new momentum in the consolidation of Kosovo's statehood and territorial integrity, Kosovo Serb satisfaction with KFOR in the March 2012 iteration of the regular UNDP attitude survey was the lowest it had been since Summer 2004.[14]

For obvious reasons, the Kosovo Albanian experience of the international responsibility to protect has been opposite to that of the Kosovo Serbs. KFOR came as liberators and stayed as guests – and employers, and trainers. Yet it is shortcomings in the international performance as perceived by Kosovo's Albanians, rather than Kosovo's Serbs, that illustrate a subtler and arguably more significant doubt about the responsibility to protect.

Kosovo Albanian satisfaction with KFOR has held consistently high. It has been the most popular of the international institutions in Kosovo, and often more popular than indigenous institutions.[15] In Summer 2011 KFOR made arguably its most significant contribution to the consolidation of territorial integrity when, following a precipitate attempt by the Kosovo authorities to establish police controls at their northern border with Serbia, KFOR intervened to protect the Kosovo Police and – confounding a tradition of international

14 Between June 2011, just before KFOR's confrontations with armed Serbs in the north, and November 2011 satisfaction dropped from 36% to 1% (UNDP Public Pulse Report III, Prishtinë/Pristina March 2012, p. 26, also at http://www.kosovo.undp.org/content/dam/kosovo/docs/PublicPulse/PP3/Public_Pulse_3_eng_web.pdf accessed March 9, 2013). An ironic and telling point was the Kosovo Serb attitude towards the International Civilian Office. As the one explicitly the 'status-positive', pro-independence international organization, the ICO had traditionally been seen as antipathetic to the Kosovo Serb interest as traditionally and crudely presented (certainly as represented by Belgrade); yet some of the most vocal concern about the impending closure of the ICO in 2012 was expressed by the Serbian Orthodox Church in Kosovo, because the ICO had been the only international organization to offer an explicit plan and legal framework for the protection of cultural and religious heritage in Kosovo, rather than just aspiration.

15 For the March 2012 UNDP survey which showed the further decline in Kosovo Serb satisfaction with KFOR to almost zero, Kosovo Albanian satisfaction was 84%, almost exactly what it had been in Summer 2004; in the intervening period it had fluctuated between the mid-70s and mid-90s. Kosovo Albanian satisfaction with their own police force was 85%; with the EU rule of law mission police 35% (UNDP Public Pulse Report III, Prishtinë/Pristina March 2012, p. 25, also at http://www.kosovo.undp.org/content/dam/kosovo/docs/PublicPulse/PP3/Public_Pulse_3_eng_web.pdf retrieved on March 9, 2013)

appeasement of provocations in and around Kosovo – held firm against armed Serb extremists. Had KFOR, under consecutive German Commanders, not acted as resolutely the situation could have been a substantial setback for Kosovo's aspirations.

But the wider story of the international intervention has been of Kosovo Albanian frustration, and the north of Kosovo is the sharpest focus of this. Kosovo's Albanians can have little complaint about the international community's physical protection of them (with one significant exception); but they might complain about the way in which their aspirations and expectations have been treated.

Outstaying a Welcome

Kosovo's Albanians believed that they won a war in 1999, with NATO help, and that the implication and reward of victory was independence from Serbia. The immediate manifestations of the international settlement – the expulsion of Belgrade's forces, and the establishment of a UN administration to administer the province pending the emergence of a final settlement of constitutional arrangements – seemed to reinforce this. However, the international missions in Kosovo proliferated and grew, and a final and irrevocable settlement never seemed quite to materialize. Rather than an immediate achievement, real independence – full sovereignty, in an agreed territory – turned out to be a long and winding road, without a map, along which Kosovo moved sluggishly. This sluggishness was desired by some of the interveners, and exacerbated by the presence of the intervention itself.

Superficially, much of the intervention was demonstrably about the development of a functioning and distinct Kosovo. Despite its studied neutrality about Kosovo's present and future status, the UN Mission In Kosovo (UNMIK) oversaw and supported the development of the skeleton of the Kosovo state, executive, legislative and judicial.[16] Other international organizations officially neutral about status – the European Union, the Organization for Security and Co-operation in Europe – contributed through their capacity-building programmes to the self-confidence and effectiveness of that state.

But for more than a decade after liberation, Kosovo endured a constant deferral of clarity and finality. UNMIK settled into its administrative role with

16 Kosovo posterity will revile UNMIK for delaying independence for so long, and will forget that much of what would become the independent state developed under and thanks to the mission.

increasing comfort, and the part of its task concerned with facilitating a political process to determine the status of Kosovo, complicated and controversial, was quietly forgotten. The violence of March 2004 was in part the result. The subsequent report by the Norwegian diplomat Kai Eide urged a more robust effort to establish a settlement. In protracted negotiations and discussions, such a settlement was developed under UN authority by an expert international team led by former Finnish President Martti Ahtisaari, and presented to the Secretary-General in Spring 2007. The 'Ahtisaari Plan' was both a compromise package and the one credible model of a functioning Kosovo thus far offered: it gave 'the I-word' in return for an exhaustive package of minority protections, including decentralization of central power to new and reinforced municipalities defined on a substantially ethnic basis. It was unveiled and finalized in February and March 2007 and, in an echo of the manoeuvring over the proposed Rambouillet agreement exactly eight years before, the Kosovo representatives were pushed to accept the package and Serbia refused.[17] The next step was for the Plan to be submitted to the UN Security Council for approval. Behind the scenes, the US and Kosovo's friends in Europe were gauging the true level of Russian, and to a lesser extent Chinese, objections. Each month, the Kosovo Government was encouraged by friendly diplomats to accept just one more month's delay, while they waited for a more clement diplomatic climate and a more favourable Chairmanship of the Security Council. Once it became clear that the Security Council model was not going to work, attention shifted to a forthcoming summit meeting between Presidents Bush and Putin, where the buck would stop and a pragmatic acceptance be agreed. They did not. Instead Kosovo and Serbia were pushed into a further round of talks, a series of face-to-face meetings overseen by a 'Troika' of EU, US and Russian diplomats.[18] These confirmed what had been entirely clear to Ahtisaari and his expert UN team – that there was no negotiated middle ground to be found between the Serbian and Kosovan positions. That had been, in effect, the objective of the further delay: to demonstrate to the 'don't knows' in the international community that there really was no negotiated solution awaiting just one more push, and thereby to encourage them to tolerate Kosovo's February

17 Except that this time there was no international will or force to try to compel Serbia to accept compromise. Instead the European Union had moved into a phase were its need to sustain the impression that the states of eastern and south-eastern Europe were all on a steady path towards membership, and its desire to demonstrate diplomatic effectiveness, made alienating Serbia undesirable.

18 The author was present in a number of the diplomatic and Troika meetings involving the Kosovo Government.

2008 declaration of independence, stage-managed by the country's international patrons.

Even before independence, Kosovo was a functioning state – just one with some unusually powerful visitors limiting its freedom of action. Within the constellation of a Kosovo President, a Kosovo Parliament and a Kosovo judiciary, a Kosovo Government raised and spent taxes; there was already a Kosovo Police Service and Kosovo Customs. But the police were overseen by UN police. KFOR remained deployed across the country. The Special Representative of the UN Secretary-General (the SRSG) had the power to over-rule or impose laws.

Independence in 2008 began Kosovo's *de jure* international validation, as states began individually to recognize the new country. But Kosovo's *de facto* independence did not substantially improve; clarity and finality were further postponed. To oversee the implementation of the Ahtisaari Plan, an International Civilian Representative was established in Kosovo with powers to appoint or approve certain key officials and 'executive powers' to intervene if the Kosovo institutions went significantly astray. A European Union rule of law mission, EULEX, took on much of UNMIK's role in selected areas of police activity, and in mentoring and monitoring the Kosovo Police Service. KFOR remained. So, in a rump and increasingly bizarre form, did UNMIK.

The International Civilian Representative and his Office departed in 2012, declaring the Ahtisaari Plan substantially implemented; but although this gave an opportunity for yet another Government celebration of milestone progress, the euphoria was becoming muted. The other *ad hoc* international missions – all of them neutral on Kosovo's status – lingered. In a press conference on the day of the formal ending of international supervision of Kosovo's independence, the leader of the Vetëvendosje Movement – Albin Kurti, the most consistent critic of Kosovo's international limbo – declared that the commemoration was "a farce organized with the people's money, against the people. ... The visible external supervision is being removed, only to become an internal supervision, hidden within the laws itself. An office has merely been closed. Nothing else has changed. KFOR, EULEX, and even UNMIK are here without recognizing us, without being accountable to us, with an executive power over us and immunity over the law."[19]

19 In a letter to the Ambassadors of France, Germany, Italy, the UK and the US (available at http://www.vetevendosje.org/?cid=2%2c2%2c4973 retrieved on March 16, 2013), Kurti wrote "After September 10, 2012, Kosova's institutions will continue to be subordinate to international missions that claim executive powers, above those granted through the democratic process to Kosova's Parliament and Government. Kosova will continue to host within its borders, international missions based upon a UN Resolution which recognizes Serbia's sovereignty over Kosova, and at best is defined as 'status neutral'."

The reality of liberation was constitutional stagnation – and with it stagnation in economic development and popular faith in their democracy – and the international intervention became part of the stagnation. As of 2012 and the ending of supervised independence but the continuation of the intervention by NATO and others, in reality there was no danger of Serb invasion, and arguably had not been since summer 1999.[20] In reality, the threat of widespread internal unrest remained limited. In any case, KFOR had not always handled it well, such unrest as there had been was fuelled by the international stagnation of which KFOR's posture was a part, and the main factors for insecurity and discomfort in the lives of Kosovo people had been outside KFOR's control.

What were those international missions achieving? In Summer 2011 KFOR had at last found a way to make its studied neutrality resilient and constructive, but this was in a scenario that had largely been created by the international failure to deal decisively and finally with Belgrade over Kosovo's status. EULEX still had formal dominance in selected areas of law-enforcement, and substantial influence in the judiciary. But any low-level capacity-building seemed obscured by perceived failures and humiliations at the strategic level; a mission intended to advance the rule of law in Kosovo and boost the EU's diplomatic and peace-building credentials was in danger of seriously damaging them instead. In its 2012 review of EULEX effectiveness, the European Court of Auditors found that EULEX "assistance has not been sufficiently effective. Although the EU helped to build capacity, notably in the area of customs, assistance to the police and the judiciary has had only modest success. Levels of organised crime and corruption in Kosovo remain high. The judiciary continues to suffer from political interference, inefficiency and a lack of transparency and enforcement. Kosovo's limited capacity to protect key witnesses and the difficulties relocating witnesses abroad are important shortcomings. There has been almost no progress in establishing the rule of law in the north of Kosovo."[21] By this point UNMIK had charismatic and experienced leadership

---

20 In preparation for the June 2012 Euro-ISME discussion, the author conducted an extremely small and informal survey of attitudes in Kosovo; it put Serbia as a much lower threat to Kosovo than economic problems and corruption.

21 Press Release ECA/12/41, 30 October 2012, available at http://europa.eu/rapid/press-release_ECA-12-41_en.htm retrieved on March 16, 2013. A report by the KIPRED think-tank in January 2013 suggested a misdirection of effort, noting that of the international personnel first deployed with EULEX "around 60% were allocated to the Police Component and only 13% to the Justice Component. This was done besides that at the time the justice sector was not only one of the weakest links in rule of law but also one of the least trusted among the public. Kosovo Police at the time was one of the highest ranking." (*A Comprehensive Analysis of EULEX: what next? – KIPRED Policy Paper No. 1/13*,

but no obvious function; yet it could not die because it remained Russia's way of demonstrating that neither independence nor the European Union was fully the centre of gravity for Kosovo policy.

The security challenges to and from Kosovo – organized crime, porous borders, corruption – are consistently recognized, and yet after more than a decade of intervention they have not been decisively tackled, nor have robust Kosovo structures been fostered to do the tackling. NATO has mentored the new Kosovo Security Force, but parked the KFOR Commander's recommendation that it be declared operationally capable. EULEX was intended to mentor and monitor a growing Kosovo capability, but allowed its prosecutorial function to be hijacked – prosecutions like that against the Governor of the Central Bank appeared to be pursued for political reasons; the prosecution of one powerful Government figure in particular failed – while it oversaw a weakening of the public credibility of justice rather than the opposite, most notoriously in the case of 'Witness X', who committed suicide before he could testify against a former Minister. In taking a passive stance, especially in the north of Kosovo, EULEX was reflecting the lack of consensus among its sponsors and a fastidious effort at even-handedness in Brussels. But – with Brussels blocking other channels of political progress in the north, and EULEX setting the limits to Kosovo Police activity and treating the north as essentially a no-go area – the north of Kosovo went backwards during the first four years of the European rule of law mission, and arguably because of it.

A decade or more in, there were two ways of perceiving the prolonged international intervention in Kosovo. In one, an immature state was securely on a track that both locked it into a stable future within the global institutional framework, principally the EU, and also gave it the training and support necessary to mature to that end. In the other, Kosovo was trapped in a stagnation defined by the competing global manoeuvring of the US and Russia, with Serbia taking every opportunity it got to maintain the abortive status quo, helped by other states who remained unconvinced of Kosovo's validity as a state; the EU meanwhile preached the mantra of European perspective, while its practical engagement had been distracted into areas that attempted to develop Brussels' institutional strength but were neutral, or even negative, for Kosovo's development.[22]

Pristina, 2013, p.12, available at http://www.kipred.org/advCms/documents/56243_A_Comprehensive_Analysis_of_EULEX.pdf (retrieved on March 16, 2013).)

22 By 2012, the sole focus of international Kosovo policy had become the 'EU-facilitated dialogue' between Kosovo and Serbia. This was Brussels's chance to demonstrate its potential as a diplomatic player in its own neighbourhood; all of Kosovo's EU member state friends

Kosovo's prolonged constitutional limbo looked like a clever diplomatic balance – giving the people of Kosovo enough to keep the lid on their frustrations while not alienating Serbia from the Euro-Atlantic sphere, bridging the various strands of feeling within the European Union, and parking a second- or third-tier difference between the US and Russia. The international intervention became part of this limbo: the missions' continuing, executive roles in Kosovo demonstrated it and exacerbated it. The impact on the ground was in many ways negative: the failure to resolve Kosovo, and the maintenance of the limbo, froze international investment, distracted Kosovo's communities from a meaningful effort to establish a *modus vivendi*, left the north of Kosovo a security vacuum satisfying no-one but organized criminals, and prolonged the state of uncertainty that made Kosovo's citizens wary of long-term commitments or a sincere effort to come to terms with their own past. The original responsibility to protect was rapidly out of date in Kosovo; the evolving international occupation that followed, while in some ways well-intentioned and constructive, also did some harm to the interests of most if not all of Kosovo's citizens.[23]

The responsibility to protect is clearly a different obligation to the fulfilment of the political ambitions of one group of the population, however much of a majority they form and whatever the validity of their claims. It is understandable that the collective – or lowest common denominator – interest of the international interveners is likewise different. It could even be argued that the responsibility to protect Kosovo's Serbs has on occasion necessitated the frustration of some Kosovo Albanian ambitions. Yet the growing feeling among ninety per cent of Kosovo's citizens that they have welcomed an international mission

were pushing participation, as was the US, which recognized both that Kosovo's future was in Europe and that Washington's own global interests required a competent EU diplomatic capacity. As a result, Brussels effectively dominated Kosovo's foreign policy, such as it was, with the Prime Minister alternating between dutiful appearances at the talks and belligerent or grumpy comments to his domestic press.

23 For the interveners, the intervention has been costly but not without benefit: NATO might rather be out, but KFOR has been for much of its life a relatively small, low-tech mission which has been a training ground for new members and mainly staffed by personnel who would not be on the front line in Afghanistan anyway. EU political and economic realities mean that real progress on Kosovo's EU membership is a safe distance away; in the meantime, Kosovo has been recruited to the EU project and providing a testing ground for the common foreign and security policy and the new European External Action Service. Even Belgrade could be happy with a scenario that continued to fuel the nationalist flame of the Kosovo issue, without requiring either the administration of the troublesome province or the admission of its loss.

under false pretences conceivably weakens the moral legitimacy of that mission.

The Irresponsibility of Protection

Intervention is an assertion of moral superiority and practical competence. Given the chaos in Kosovo in 1999, the regime's loss of moral authority over its citizens, and the demonstrable frailties of the new Kosovo institutions since, such an assertion was plausible. But it can only be validated by the subsequent performance of the intervention. Those among whom the intervention happens, and those whose taxes sustain it, are entitled to count the cost.

For more than a decade, the people of Kosovo did not exist in the world community. Their representative and voice in the UN was a UN official appointed by the UN, with no formal obligation to consult Kosovo in any way about what he said. Kosovo was a problem to be reported on, not a population to be represented. Even with the EU taking over more responsibility from the UN, the ability of Kosovo's leadership to articulate the interests of their people internationally has been limited. The fragile relationship between the people of Kosovo and the world has exacerbated the fragility of their relationship with their own Government. "Over the past 12 years, authorities in Kosovo have been primarily accountable to the international community, instead of their own community. Up until today, international actors have had a mandate to overrule decisions of the Kosovo Government, or at least to influence them substantially, often from behind the scenes. Financial revenue from international assistance is core to Kosovo's budget. The prospect of EU accession strengthens this: the Kosovo Government is more meticulously reporting to the European Union about its policy intentions than to its own population. The EU uses the preconditions for accession as a policy tool to push for certain reforms, even if they are not popular with the broader community (for example, reforms related to minority rights), reinforcing the lack of trust between citizens and the state."[24]

24 *The EU as a Peacebuilder in Kosovo*, IKV Pax Christi report, Utrecht, August 2011, p. 6. If Kosovo has been essentially a colony, the question is 'whose?' The US has had much the most powerful direct influence on Government, and through advisors and the strategic significance of a highway project has secured a substantial role in steering the Kosovo economy; the EU, through the institutional requirements of its annual Progress Report, began to acquire an important influence in shaping policy and longer-term reform, and through the EU-facilitated dialogue with Serbia took over the main plank of Kosovo foreign policy. Most respondents in the author's informal survey, asked where the most

As late as 2012, more than a decade after the intervention, international officials of various kinds were still a numerous, and disproportionately powerful force in Kosovo. KFOR still involved more than 6,000 personnel; EULEX had a ceiling of 1,950 foreigners, until a cut in 2012; UNMIK was still surprisingly large, relative to its negligible role and influence; the International Civilian Office was moving towards closure but still included dozens of foreigners. These were in addition to a variety of other international personnel, including those of the EU office, the OSCE and various UN agencies – on top of the foreign embassy staff typical of any capital city. These international personnel – at the roughest estimate 9,000 of them – enjoyed status and conditions explicitly different from routine foreign visitors and from Kosovo citizens. Depending on the status of their organization and their status within it, they were likely to have diplomatic immunity or similar protection, private health care, a car with a distinct licence plate, and a salary substantially higher than a comparable professional in a Kosovo institution – and higher than Kosovar colleagues in their own institution.[25]

This has a series of impacts. The financial cost of the missions is a matter for the budgetary priorities of participating states.[26] The presence of the missions has been a massive injection to the Kosovo economy, amongst other things in salaries and institutional and personal consumption. Even this positive impact created its distortions, however. A young Kosovar working as a political officer

---

important decisions affecting Kosovo were taken, said Washington D.C., some said New York (UN Headquarters) and some said Brussels, while very few said Prishtina.

25 Foreigners working for EU missions would be either on contract – with a salary paid by the mission – or seconded by an EU member state, in which case a salary paid by their own government would be supplemented by the mission with a daily allowance of €100 or more. Contracted staff in EU missions could earn between 1,800 and 7,875 euros per month, depending on experience and responsibility http://www.consilium.europa.eu/uedocs/cmsUpload/Annex%202%20salary%20international%20staff.pdf (retrieved on March 16, 2013)

26 Up to June 2012, the EU had committed 614 million euro from the EU General Budget to support EULEX – the mission's annual budget was around 10% of Kosovo's. As of the end of 2011 member states were also paying for 1,087 seconded staff; a not implausible average salary of 50,000 euros would mean a collective annual wage bill of around 50 million euros, with the EU paying more than 100,000 euros every day in allowances to those staff. (June 2012 and staff number figures from European Court of Auditors Special Report No 18 2012, 'European Union assistance to Kosovo related to the rule of law', para. 14, available at http://www.eca.europa.eu/Lists/ECADocuments/SR12_18/SR12_18_EN.PDF retrieved on March 16, 2013. The proposed budget for UNMIK for the 2012/13 period was $47 million, the 2011/12 figure of $44.9 million http://www.un.org/press/en/2012/gaab4029.doc.htm (retrieved on March 16 2013)

in one of the international organizations in Pristina – or as a driver, interpreter, or logistician indeed – could expect to earn better than older, more experienced professionals working in the Kosovo public sector. Back in 1999 Kosovo's 'Minister of Information' was "critical of UNMIK's pay scale, noting that the UN mission's pay for a concierge is $2,000 a month, while educated Kosovars with doctorates earned only $200 a month."[27] Kosovo doctors protested in February 2010 over average salaries of 250 euros per month, when an interpreter for an international organization would be earning at least twice as much.[28]

More uncomfortable, particularly in the context of a developing state, is the moral effect of this relationship. "The real colonizer is almost of necessity a man of strong character, a creator rather than an accepter of relationships, at least at the outset. It is only later that he becomes colonial. The typical colonial, on the other hand, finds the relationship ready made; he takes it up, adapts himself to it, and very often exploits it. And in any case, whether he accepts it passively or seizes upon it greedily, the relationship changes him more than he it."[29] The role of the international mission official in Kosovo is essentially colonial: away from home, with substantially higher disposable income and purchasing power, with looser legal restraint, and among a population who in many cases are instinctively welcoming, and who in most cases judge that they need to be more accommodating to internationals than they would be to fellow-citizens, and over whom the official may have financially-transformative power of employment.[30] However well-intentioned the international official, this scenario can not be healthy for either colonizer or colonized.

On top of the effects on individual attitudes, foreign and Kosovar, the practical effects for the development of the Kosovo state are negative. International officials supposed to be reinforcing the practices of a functioning state instead undermine it: their privileged access to Government officials short-circuits the proper channels of democratic access; their disproportionate influence confirms that personal contacts are more important than personal ability or validity of case. Ambassadors on first-name terms with the Prime Minister can

27 http://www.monitor.net/monitor/9910a/copyright/klacomplaint.html retrieved on March 16, 2013

28 More than a decade of international consumption has helped to stimulate a surprising quality of restaurants and supermarkets in Prishtina; as of 2013, and as with the property rental market, the bubble was continuing to expand.

29 Mannoni, transl. Powesland, *Prospero and Caliban – the psychology of colonisation* (University of Michigan 1990), p. 97.

30 Many 'internationals' have access to their own shops – on the NATO or UN bases – and there are certain bars and residential areas which have tended to be 'international'.

reach him more easily than can some Ministers or party leaders. Middle-ranking diplomats can influence Ministers more easily than can officials. The totemic power of an international opinion had more weight than formally-raised complaints by Kosovan citizens and parties in deciding whether there should be re-runs of contested election results in the winter of 2010/11. State-building is an exercise in short-term anti-democratic practice with the hope of establishing democratic practice in the longer-term, but it does not take long for the wrong habits to be learned.[31]

Some of the side-effects of intervention are starker. One of the ancillary justifications for intervention and state-building in the Balkans has been the desire to tackle the trans-national organized crime that has benefited from the region's weak states and porous borders. But the large-scale trans-national movement of peace-keepers, combined with the failure actually to address Kosovo's border weaknesses, makes some problems worse. According to an Amnesty International report "Following the arrival of KFOR in July 1999, by late 1999 the United Nations Development Fund for Women (UNIFEM) had reported significant concentrations of organized prostitution, involving trafficked women, in four locations close to major concentrations of KFOR troops, with the military making up the majority of clients, some of whom were allegedly also involved in the trafficking process. KFOR and UNMIK were publicly identified in early 2000 as a causal factor by the International Organization for Migration… In May 2000, Pasquale Lupoli, Chief of Mission, alleged that KFOR troops and UN workers in Kosovo had fed the 'mushrooming sex trade in which

31 This section of analysis is clearly subjective, based on the author's experience and perception. Part of the work of the International Civilian Office was managing the establishment of the legal framework necessary for democratic institutions. This habitually involved unelected foreigners, with an authority assumed from their superiors and the nebulous constitutional basis of the international role in Kosovo, applying a degree of pressure on elected Kosovars that ranged, depending on how controversial the issue, from gentle persuasion to aggressive brow-beating. A ruling by Kosovo's Constitutional Court that the selection of a new President in spring 2011 had been invalidated by incorrect procedure was a positive demonstration of the independence of the judiciary and the Presidency's willingness to abide by its rulings (he stepped down), and left Kosovo's political parties needing to find a compromise; the first reaction of part of the international community was to try to pressure the Court into reversing its decision, and the second was to try to pressure selected parties into a solution. The departure of the ICO was facilitated by a package of Constitutional Amendments that enshrined further protections of Ahtisaari Plan principles, including special protections for minority community voices in the Assembly; minority representatives tried to secure extra protections in return for their necessary assent to the Amendments, but were pushed by international diplomats to abandon their effort so as not to jeopardize the international timetable.

young girls are being forced into prostitution by criminal gangs', which he attributed 'largely [down] to the international presence there'."[32]

Not only does the colonial status of the intervention bring some negative side-effects, but also its representatives sometimes fail to demonstrate the unimpeachable standard-setting that could be its only possible moral justification. UN investigation from 2002 revealed the theft of $4.3 million from Kosovo's Energy Corporation by the senior UNMIK official in charge of it. Investigation into other UNMIK-managed utilities suggested widespread fraud, theft and malpractice at Prishtina airport.[33] On February 10th, 2007, two demonstrators were killed when UN police used out-dated rubber bullets with inappropriate tactics.[34] In 2010, sixteen policemen from the EU's rule of law mission were caught smuggling alcohol and cigarettes. In three consecutive surveys in 2010 and 2011, Kosovo citizens believed EULEX police almost twice as corrupt as Kosovo police.[35]

The colonial perspective – the irresponsibility of interveners living temporarily and with special status in a place not fully sovereign – was perhaps best demonstrated by the UNMIK response to the UN investigators into Prishtina airport: "the Special Representative conveyed the message that – in most instances – no administrative action against airport managers would be taken, citing reasons such as that 'staff in peacekeeping missions, including UNMIK,

32 *Serbia and Montenegro (Kosovo): the legacy of past human rights abuses*, Amnesty International Document available at http://www.amnesty.org/en/library/asset/EUR70/009/2004/en/643cb425-d5f0-11dd-bb24-1fb85fe8fa05/eur700092004en.html (retrieved on March 17, 2013)

33 See e.g. A/60/720 of 14 March 2006, at http://www.un.org/en/ga/search/view_doc.asp?symbol=A/60/720 and http://www.bartstaes.be/articles.php?id=2999 both retrieved on March 17, 2013; UN press release GA/AB/3613 of 4 May 2004, available at http://www.unis.unvienna.org/unis/en/pressrels/2004/gaab3613.html retrieved on March 17, 2013. The latter reported that "no verification had been carried out of Trutschler's curriculum vitae. Mr. Trutschler had provided $200,000 to another UNMIK staff member as an investment in the singing career of that staff member's daughter. There had been a general lack of supervision of Mr. Trutschler. He had also made other fraudulent travel claims during his employment with UNMIK" – item by item these are the kinds of faults that the international community would typically ascribe to the immature, unreconstructed Kosovo system.

34 Amnesty International was continuing to push the issue six years later: http://amnesty.org/en/library/asset/EUR70/003/2013/en/1b5273a8-54ae-4696-9647-d5a68e18c515/eur700032013en.html retrieved on March 17, 2013

35 UNDP Public Pulse Report III, Prishtinë/Pristina March 2012, p. 18, also at http://www.ks.undp.org/content/dam/kosovo/docs/PublicPulse/PP3/Public_Pulse_3_eng_web.pdf retrieved on March 16, 2013

are transient'."[36] After the airport scandal, one editor commented: "Kosovo citizens have expected much more from UNMIK, as they assumed that the international community would know how to build a democratic society. What happened in the last couple of years was far from the expectations and hopes of the citizens."[37]

Conclusion: In the Laboratory of Intervention

It is unlikely that the NATO and UN officials and the international leaders hurrying to establish an intervention in 1999 could have foreseen that the shape or even the continued existence of that intervention a decade and more later. Much good had been done in Kosovo by the international community. Her people were almost all enjoying a life fundamentally more secure and promising than they had been in the 1990s. For all the delays and obstacles, the country was enjoying the unquestionable benefits of a closer relationship with the EU and of the prospect of eventual membership. But any analysis of intervention, the general or the specific, should recognize the reality of the phenomenon, especially as it mutates over time, and the negative effects that it brings. The definitive humanitarian intervention, the birthplace of 'responsibility to protect' doctrine, has seen the interveners under the microscope as well as the intervened.

A responsibility to protect was perceptible in the spring of 1999. As soon as the intervention happened, this responsibility swung 180 degrees – almost inevitably, given that the intervention took the form of guaranteeing the victory of the 'protected'; the same was seen in Libya, and to an extent in Iraq, and (at the time of writing) might yet be seen in Syria. The initial humanitarian cause, seductively universal in appeal, was short-lived. Different objectives and inclinations were apparent from the start in Kosovo – whether US-Russia, US-EU, or intra-EU.[38] The defining factors in Kosovo's development have been

36 A/60/720 of 14 March 2006, at http://www.un.org/en/ga/search/view_doc.asp?symbol=A/60/720 retrieved on March 17, 2013

37 Blerim Shala, *Zeri*, April 2006.

38 Rival intervener objectives have tended to cause stagnation. Rival intervener approaches have tended to cause confusion. Kosovo has been subject to the influence of both American and European models in the development of its judiciary: the international judges on the Constitutional Court came from Bulgaria, Portugal and the US; EULEX included prosecutors from the very different British and French systems, amongst others; one major case was ham-strung by different approaches to parliamentary immunity.

less to do with peace-building among ethnic communities and more to do with international sphere of influence politics, individual state calculations and prejudices about self-determination, and Brussels's determination to be a diplomatic heavyweight in a world where its own stakeholders cannot always establish a coherent policy.

It is understandable, particularly if seen from the perspective of taxpayers supporting the costs of intervention by their states, that interventions become more about the interests of the intervener than the intervened-on. The Kosovo intervention was motivated by genuine humanitarian concern, but was prolonged – and hampered – by concerns of security (the potential effect of regional instability and state weakness) and more importantly politics (intervener relationships with Serbia as well as Kosovo, the prioritisation of Brussels's development over Kosovo's). EULEX is valued not for its effect on Kosovo, but for its effect on the development of a more powerful common foreign and security policy.

The intervention provokes a number of frustrations among those on the receiving end of it. On the surface, they are impatient at the slow achievement of real sovereignty and self-determination; they are reluctant to participate whole-heartedly in reconciliation initiatives while the nature and even shape of their state seem up for negotiation; they are irritated by the international community's short-term concern for 'stability' rather than development.[39]

Perhaps it is churlish of Kosovo to complain about an intervention that returned a million refugees to their homes, has pumped billions of euros into the country, and continues to manage a transition from a grim past to a promising future. But at the very least those planning and doing the intervening should be aware of its side-effects and the essentially colonial relationship that can evolve – to try to see the intervention a decade in the future, and to try to see it from both ends.

Kosovo has had, to all intents and purposes, the status of a League of Nations Mandate; progress might have been simpler and quicker had it had only one Mandate power over it.

39 "the EU is signaling that it is more interested in propping up current leaders and stability than in promoting sustainable change in Kosovo. Again, this is not only prolonging he problem, it is exacerbating it." *The* EU *as a Peacebuilder in Kosovo*, IKV Pax Christi report, Utrecht, August 2011, p. 14.

CHAPTER 4

Tony Blair and Military Intervention: Protector or Provocateur?

Peter Lee

In 1994, genocide made front page news across the world as neighbour turned upon neighbour in the East African State of Rwanda, ethnic tension erupting into a brutal and sustained massacre that would cost almost a million lives. The following year, genocidal violence returned to Europe for the first time since the Second World War when 8,000 Bosnian Muslim men and boys were massacred in Srebrenica at the hands of a Serbian paramilitary unit. In both cases, small and ill-equipped contingents of UN peacekeepers were forced to observe – impotently – as humanitarian catastrophes unfolded before them.

Against the backdrop of these atrocities in Rwanda and Serbia, Tony Blair – as the new Leader of the Opposition in the British Parliament – was setting out the policies that would shape his Premiership when he was elected Prime Minister in 1997. Key to his foreign policy was the belief that responsible, capable states should be prepared to use force to preserve the lives of innocents, like those in Rwanda and Bosnia, faced with mass displacement or extermination. By the time the Serb leader Slobodan Milosevic escalated violence against Kosovar Muslims in 1998–9, Blair's outlook was fixed, viewing the Kosovo emergency primarily as a moral issue.[1]

For Blair, military intervention was, and would remain, a matter of humanitarian concern based on a moral responsibility to protect innocent victims of state-sanctioned violence: pre-dating Kofi Annan's announcement of the UN's adoption of the doctrine of Responsibility to Protect in 2005.[2] In his now-famous Chicago Speech of 24 April 1999 Blair proposed a new Doctrine of the International Community. There he set out the global political context in which states should be willing to interfere across internationally recognised borders – violating the sovereignty of degenerate or failing states – to prevent genocide, ethnic cleansing or other crimes against humanity. The questions he asked himself as he considered his response to a number of international political crises included: 'should this be allowed to happen or not? Should this

1 Tony Blair, *A Journey* (London: Hutchinson, 2010), p. 228.

2 Kofi Annan, 14 September 2005, 'Secretary-General's address to the 2005 World Summit', located at http://www.un.org/sg/statements/?nid=1669 accessed 5 August 2013

 | DOI 10.1163/9789004280380_005

regime remain in power? Should these people continue to suffer injustice?'[3] These questions, and many others besides, have been addressed or at least touched upon in numerous ways.

John Kampfner provides a journalistic overview of Blair's foreign policy through the prism of the five interventionist operations or wars into which the UK was led by the then Prime Minister.[4] Kampfner prioritized the political aspects of Blair's military interventions, interviewing more than forty key actors. However, apart from recognising that there was a moral dimension to Blair's actions Kampfner offers no analysis of the moral basis of Blair's arguments. David Coates and Joel Krieger focus on the 2003 Iraq War, exploring whether he was justified in doing so.[5] While emphasizing US strategic aims and linking those to Blair's response to 9/11 and his commitment to stand shoulder-to-shoulder with the US, they also address the moral argument in terms that belong to the just war tradition – though this is not explicitly invoked by the authors – asking whether there was a just cause and legitimate international authorisation, and whether military action was a last resort and pursued with honest intentions (rather than for the strategic aim of securing mineral resources). Philippe Sands provides a coruscating critique of the legal basis of the Iraq invasion.[6] With the insight of a QC Sands identifies the flaws in the legal arguments of both the Bush and Blair administrations, though the focus of this paper will be on Blair's declared *moral*, as opposed to legal, motivations and arguments. Examples from the academy include Paul Hoggett's analysis of 'the security case, the global strategic case and the modernising case for war', which sets aside the moral dimension.[7] David Fisher and Nigel Biggar use just war criteria to assess the morality of the 2003 Iraq War.[8] However, in arguing the humanitarian aspect of the justification of intervention Biggar refers solely to Saddam's historical atrocities and not the contemporary (at that time) threat to the civilian population. In contrast, Oliver Daddow begins from Blair's moral imperative before arguing the significance of domestic politics in shaping the then prime minister's foreign policy. Elsewhere, I have explored Blair's moral justification of the 2003 Iraq War at

---

3 Blair, *A Journey*, p. 229.

4 John Kampfner, *Blair's Wars* (London: The Free Press, 2004).

5 David Coates and Joel Krieger, *Blair's War* (Cambridge: Polity Press, 2004).

6 Philippe Sands, *Lawless World*, 2nd Edn. (London: Penguin Books, 2006).

7 Paul Hoggett, 'Iraq: Blair's Mission Impossible', *The British Journal of Politics & International Relations*, 7, 3 (2005): p. 418.

8 David Fisher and Nigel Biggar, 'Was Iraq and Unjust War? A Debate on the Iraq War and Reflections on Libya', *International Affairs*, 87, 3 (2011): pp. 687–707.

length.[9] In contrast to the foregoing, this chapter will focus on a specific, and narrow, aspect of the moral reasoning Blair used to underpin his military interventions in Kosovo (1999) and Iraq (2003), assessing the extent to which he can be considered to be either a protector of the innocent from atrocities – contributing to the moral basis of the subsequent R2P – or a political provocateur.

The criteria for military, or humanitarian, intervention to protect the innocent which will be explored in this assessment are three of those proposed by Blair as part of his 1999 Doctrine of the International Community. There he set out the conditions under which the principle of the inviolability of state sovereignty might be set aside: specifically, in the cases of genocide, oppression leading to population displacement and regional instability, and illegitimate regimes. He stated: 'we need to bear in mind five major considerations: First, are we sure of our case? ...Second, have we exhausted all diplomatic options? ...Third, on the basis of a practical assessment of the situation, are there military operations we can sensibly and prudently undertake? Fourth, are we prepared for the long term? ...And finally, do we have national interests involved?[10] In these five criteria for intervention Blair invokes and conflates – in a way typical of his New Labour, Third Way politics – two potentially competing narratives: the *realpolitik* of national self-interest and moral arguments that correspond remarkably closely to several key *jus ad bellum* criteria of the just war tradition (just cause, last resort, reasonable chance of success, proportionality and right intention).[11]

For the purposes of this chapter, analysis of the Kosovo (1999) and Iraq (2003) interventions will focus on two areas of the moral argument put forward by Blair: first, the existence of a real and imminent threat to the indigenous

9 Peter Lee, *Blair's Just War: Iraq and the Illusion of Morality* (Basingstoke: Palgrave Macmillan, 2012).

10 Tony Blair, 'Prime Minister's Speech: Doctrine of the International Community at the Economic Club, Chicago', 24 April 1999, http://webarchive.nationalarchives.gov.uk/20061004085342/http://number10.gov.uk/page1297 accessed 20 February 2013. On 18 July 2010 it was confirmed by Professor Lawrence Freedman of King's College London that he penned this text for Blair on 16 April 1999.

11 For further explication of just war criteria – as understood more broadly within the just war tradition – see Richard Norman, *Ethics, Killing and War* (Cambridge: Cambridge University Press, 1995), p. 118, and; Alex J. Bellamy, *Just Wars: From Cicero to Iraq* (Cambridge: Polity Press, 2006), pp. 121–123. For a more substantial treatment of the provenance and application of the moral imperatives contained in Blair's 1999 Chicago speech on the Doctrine of the International Community, see Lee, *Blair's Just War: Iraq and the Illusion of Morality*, 15ff.

civilian populations as a humanitarian case (just cause) for military action; and second, the extent to which military force was used as a last resort after exhausting all diplomatic options. Rather than attempt to specify definitively what constitutes a 'real and imminent threat' to the indigenous populations of Iraq and Kosovo, this chapter will view them as contested concepts, as they surely are in the messy domain of political discourse in the build-up to any war. However, Alex Bellamy identifies a number of factors that can be considered when assessing such a threat. 'A threat is imminent only immediately before the hammer is about to fall: when the enemy has displayed an intention to attack, has armed itself, and deployed its forces into an offensive position and is about to strike'.[12] Furthermore, the notion of 'exhausting all diplomatic options' is similarly contested in pre-war discourse between protagonists. It will be used here in the sense that Blair himself set out in 1999, namely: 'We should always give peace every chance'.[13] Finally, running through this analysis will be an assessment of Blair's intentions[14] in pursuing his chosen courses of action.

Kosovo

For almost 1,000 years Kosovo has held deep significance for the Serbs who have controlled it for much of that time. Several centuries of rule by the Ottoman Empire failed to dull the Serbian claim on the region, leading to Kosovo's eventual reintegration in the reconstituted Serbia early in the twentieth century. Serb claims were sustained through decades of disruption brought about by two World Wars and the Cold War. In contrast, throughout this time the Kosovars – who increasingly identified themselves ethnically, culturally

12 Bellamy, *Just Wars*, p. 168.

13 Blair, 24 April 1999.

14 The concept of 'right intention' has been disputed within the just war tradition. Where Aquinas, in *Summa Theologica*, II-II, Q. 40, A. 1, 1813–4, deemed good intentions to be an essential part of a just war, Grotius, in *The Rights of War and Peace* II.XXII.XVII, 1113–4, rejected its essentiality. Aquinas referred to the intentions of individual rulers, where Grotius focused on the state which, he argued, could not have intentions in the same way as an individual. Vattel, in *Law of Nations*, II.IV.56. pp. 290–291, would later argue, even as states and state sovereignty were more firmly established, that 'every sovereign power has a right to succour an oppressed people who implore their assistance'. However, the *intention* of the intervening Prince towards neighbouring oppressed people would have to be honourable. It is in the context of such a reading of individual intentions and intervention that I will assess Blair's intentions with regard to Kosovo and Iraq.

and religiously with their Albanian Muslim neighbours – aspired to a different and separate future. From 1987, Milosevic's nationalistic hard line on Kosovo's place within a greater Serbia bought him the support of Kosovo Serb nationalists on his way to attaining the Presidency of Serbia in 1989. His subsequent rescinding of Kosovo's autonomy within greater Serbia, together with moves towards independence by Slovenia, Croatia and Bosnia, contributed to the violent collapse of Yugoslavia. In Kosovo itself, escalating violence pitted Serb police, military and civilian militia against separatists, in particular the Kosovo Liberation Army (KLA). By 1998 increasing numbers of Kosovo Albanians being killed at the hands of Serbs or forced from the lands they had occupied for centuries.

By this stage, Blair's evolving foreign policy increasingly stressed the importance of human rights and the need for them to be defended, even where that ideal clashed with the rights of states, as set out in the UN Charter, to non-interference.[15] Setting out a case that would shape his premiership and subsequent UK military interventions under his leadership, Blair challenged the limitations of international law:

> But the principle of non-interference must be qualified in important respects. Acts of genocide can never be a purely internal matter. When oppression produces massive flows of refugees, which unsettle neighbouring countries, then they can properly be described as "threats to international peace and security." When regimes are based on minority rule they lose legitimacy – look at South Africa.[16]

There are two ways in which war can be entered into legally under international law as expressed in the UN Charter. The first is through the right to self-defence and the Charter states: 'Nothing in the present Charter shall impair the inherent right of individual or collective self-defence if an armed attack occurs against a Member of the United Nations', though it should be remembered that this is only a temporary right, 'until the Security Council has taken measures necessary to maintain international peace and security'.[17] The second way to pursue a legal war is through an appropriate resolution passed by the Security Council: 'The Security Council shall determine the existence of any threat to the peace, breach of the peace, or act of aggression and shall make recommendations, or decide what measures shall be taken…to maintain or restore

15 Charter of the United Nations, Article 2.

16 Blair, 24 April 1999.

17 Charter of the United Nations, Article 51.

international peace and security'.[18] The Security Council has a wider remit to preserve peace and can choose to act as it sees fit to promote peace and maintain stability in a region.

In setting out his case for intervention in Kosovo Blair went beyond a desire – or perceived need – to conform to international law, relying extensively on moral arguments instead. This approach is reflected in his comments about NATO's action to stop Slobodan Milosevic's Serbian Army and militia from conducting ethnic cleansing in Kosovo:

> This is a just war, based not on any territorial ambitions but on values. We cannot let the evil of ethnic cleansing stand. We must not rest until it is reversed. We have learned twice before in this century that appeasement does not work. If we let an evil dictator range unchallenged, we will have to spill infinitely more blood and treasure to stop him later.[19]

Blair invoked the language of just war as a means of confronting 'the evil of ethnic cleansing'. The horrors of ethnic cleansing in Bosnia-Herzogovina between 1992 and 1995, as well as Rwanda in 1994, were still fresh in the memory and both Blair and President Clinton were determined that force should be used to ensure that such an atrocity would not be repeated. In setting out the barbarous actions of the Milosevic regime against Albanian Kosovars Blair sought to establish his case for military intervention. In so doing he even went beyond the codified morality of the just war tradition, referring to Milosevic as 'an evil dictator' who needed to be challenged and opposed in order to prevent ethnic cleansing by his Serbian regime. Blair's position was straightforward: 'I saw it essentially as a moral issue. And that, in a sense, came to define my view on foreign and military intervention'.[20]

Kosovo – Real and Imminent Threat to the Civilian Population

Blair's moral indignation – and his case for intervention – was prompted by fast-moving events on the ground in Kosovo. The carnage inflicted of the village of Ivaja on 9 March 1999 played out in microcosm the wider ravages of violent nationalism and ethnic intolerance that was promoted and sustained by Milosevic. As Anthony Loyd reported in an article in *The Times* on 11 March

18 *Ibid.*, Article 39.
19 Blair, 24 April 1999.
20 Blair, *A Journey*, p. 228.

1999, the five hundred ethnic Albanian occupants of the village came under sustained bombardment, followed by a ground assault that culminated in the remaining buildings being burned as the population fled. When combined with similar attacks in the area that week alone, more than 4,000 ethnic Albanians were displaced from their homes, with many women, children, elderly, sick and injured left to fend for themselves in nearby forests outside Kacanik while men and boys were detained for interrogation.

Blair later wrote of his outrage as this and many similar events unfolded: 'Here were ordinary civilians being driven from their homes and turned into refugees, killed, raped, beaten up with savagery and often sadism, whole families humiliated or eliminated'.[21] In addition to the immediate atrocities that were being committed by Serbian forces against Kosovo Albanians – the results of which were reported daily on television news bulletins as well as in print media – Blair was also concerned that such ethnic cleansing could escalate and extend into neighbouring countries. With the war in Bosnia and Herzegovina still fresh in the minds of political leaders and members of wider society alike, the motivation to prevent similar carnage, or worse, was strong: Western Europe had recently seen genocide, murder, mass rape and concentration camps for the first time since 1945.

Just over a week later, on 23 March 1999, Blair described to the UK parliament the scale of the attacks that were taking place in Kosovo:

> Let me give the House an indication of the scale of what is happening. A quarter of a million Kosovars – more than 10 per cent of the population – are now homeless as a result of repression by Serb forces; 65,000 people have been forced from their homes in the past month, and no fewer than 25,000 in the four days since the peace talks broke down; and only yesterday, 5,000 people in the Srbica area were forcibly evicted from their villages.[22]

In terms of making a case for intervention, the figures were highly persuasive. Against the backdrop of continued negotiations – which will be addressed in the next section – Blair was also making final preparations for military action: action that would take the form of a sustained aerial campaign designed to coerce Milosevic into stopping the ethnic cleansing and establishing some

---

21 *Ibid.*

22 Tony Blair, 'Parliamentary Debate on Kosovo', 23 March 1999, *Hansard*, Vol. 328, p. 161, http://hansard.millbanksystems.com/commons/1999/mar/23/kosovo accessed 1 March 2013

kind of peace in the region. In the previous 48 hours the Kosovo Verification Mission (KVM) – deployed under the auspices of the Organization for Security and Co-operation in Europe (OSCE) – abandoned its monitoring role as violence escalated and military action against Milosevic and his regime became increasingly imminent.

As military intervention approached, the UN Secretary-General reported to the UN Security Council, in much greater detail, many of the atrocities that were taking place in Kosovo:

> The humanitarian and human rights situation in Kosovo remains grave. The general insecurity, combined with continuing and unpredictable outbreaks of violence, has resulted in a cycle of displacement and return throughout Kosovo. During the reporting period, targeted killings of civilians, summary executions, mistreatment of detainees and new abduction cases were reported almost daily. Since 20 January, the Office of the United Nations High Commissioner for Human Rights (UNHCHR) has registered more than 65 cases of violent death, including one in custody. The Office's background investigations of targeted violence further confirmed the observations expressed in my previous report that the nature of violent activity in Kosovo, which has now spread to urban areas, has increased the number of persons who live in fear of being directly affected by violence or arbitrary treatment.[23]

That atrocities were taking place on a large and growing scale is beyond dispute, given not only the many mutually reinforcing journalistic accounts but also the verification of OSCE monitors. What is not so obvious, and was even less so at the time, were some of the underlying complexities of the violence and the identities of the perpetrators. The majority of the acts of violence, particularly the larger-scale incidents involving established military units, were being committed by the Serb authorities against Kosovo Albanians. This is reflected in the preponderance of Serb commanders being indicted and convicted by the International Criminal Tribunal for the Former Yugoslavia (ICTY).[24] However, members of the KLA were also guilty of atrocities: Haradin Bala, for example, was found guilty of cruel treatment, torture and murder and

23 Kofi Annan, 'Report of the Secretary-General Prepared Pursuant to Resolutions 1160 (1998), 1199 (1998) and 1203 (1998) of the Security Council', III. p. 4, 17 March 1999, http://www.un.org/ga/search/view_doc.asp?symbol=S/1999/293 accessed 23 February 2013

24 A full list of ICTY cases – ongoing and completed – can be found at http://www.icty.org/action/cases/4 accessed 23 February 2013

sentenced to 13 years' imprisonment by the International Criminal Tribunal for the Former Yugoslavia (ICTY) on 27 September 2007.[25]

Furthermore, as Alan Kuperman argues persuasively, it was the policy of the KLA in the 1990s to escalate violence against Serb forces to provoke a reaction, the purpose of which would be to incite NATO – or some of the states thereof – into launching a humanitarian intervention on their behalf: ultimately leading to Kosovo's independence. Kuperman interviewed Emrush Xhemajli, a co-founder of the KLA and joint architect of this policy, on 9 August 2000. Xhemajli told him: "When we took the decision to start the war in 1993... We thought it was essential to get international support to win the war. You could not stand against the world... We thought that with the international community on our side, we could win the war. But otherwise we would plan for a 10- to 15-year war, with a strategy to get the international community on our side."[26] Kuperman refers to this as the moral hazard of humanitarian intervention: the very willingness of NATO leaders to conduct military, or so-called humanitarian, intervention actually prompts the very violence that they eventually seek to stop.

At the time, however, Blair did not explore these subtleties in his public discourse – his focus was on the actions of Milosevic and the Serb forces. The challenge Blair faced in gaining sufficient political support for military intervention was difficult enough, if he had attempted to be more subtle in his descriptions of events they would probably not have had the same emotional impact and, consequently, weakened his case. One month into the bombing campaign Blair described events in his Chicago speech:

> Unspeakable things are happening in Europe. Awful crimes that we never thought we would see again have reappeared – ethnic cleansing, systematic rape, mass murder...the tear stained faces of the hundreds of thousands of refugees streaming across the border...their heart-rending tales of cruelty.[27]

None of the aforementioned crimes against humanity however, neither their immediacy nor their severity, had translated into UN Security Council-sanctioned

25 During the trial of KLA member Lahi Brahiminaj, the ICTY was satisfied beyond any reasonable doubt that multiple murders and cases of cruel treatment and torture were committed by members and affiliates of the KLA. However, in the majority of these cases it proved impossible to attribute specific crimes to specific perpetrators for the purpose of securing convictions. See case details at http://www.icty.org/action/cases/4 accessed 7 August 2013

26 Alan J. Kuperman, 'The Moral Hazard of Humanitarian Intervention: Lessons from the Balkans', *International Studies Quarterly* 52 (2008), p. 69.

27 Blair, 24 April 1999.

legal authority for NATO's military action. Russia's historical political, religious and cultural links with Serbia ensured that there would be no UN Security Council Resolution to provide that legal basis for military intervention. Yet Blair still managed to successfully cajole, pressurize and persuade NATO and European Union leaders into action using humanitarian arguments. Furthermore, motivated in significant part by the religious dimension of the atrocities committed against Kosovar Muslims by Serbs, the League of Arab States supported the intervention.

None of these expressions of support equated to a basis in international law for the intervention but they did provide a degree of legitimacy to Blair's morally-driven agenda. While there is not the scope to adequately explore it here, this case highlights a crucial tension between legal sanction – in the shape of positive law as defined by the UN Charter – and the moral imperative to protect the innocent from atrocities: a tension that has not been resolved by the UN's subsequent adoption of the Responsibility to Protect.[28] As Blair would later state: 'in relation to Kosovo…we took military action because I thought it was the right thing to do.Because you could not allow in the case of Kosovo ethnic cleansing and genocide to happen right on the doorstep of Europe and do nothing about it.[29] Note that Blair claimed, 'it was the right thing to do', rather than, 'it was legally sanctioned'. He clearly prioritized the former over the latter throughout this and all his interventions. He later recalled: 'We had acted without UN authority in Kosovo …I never even thought about it for Sierra Leone. Yet it would be hard to argue that, morally, in each of those situations, we should not have intervened'.[30] In making this moral assessment of Blair's actions, the discussion now moves on to consider whether or not – as Blair himself advocated in his Chicago speech of 24 April 1999 – all diplomatic options had been exhausted prior to the launching of air strikes against Milosevic and his regime.

Kosovo – Last Resort after Exhausting All Diplomatic Options

Although violence by Serb police, military and paramilitary forces escalated in 1998 the warning signs had been present for several years. Despite, or perhaps

28 Jennifer M. Welsh and Maria Banda, 'International Law and the Responsibility to Protect: Clarifying or Expanding States' Responsibilities?' *Global Responsibility to Protect*, 2, 3 (June 2010): pp. 213–231.

29 Tony Blair, 'Prime Minister's Press Conference at Sedgefield', 3 September 2002, http://webarchive.nationalarchives.gov.uk/20061004051823/http://number10.gov.uk/page3001 accessed 12 May 2012

30 Blair, *A Journey*, p. 433.

because of, events elsewhere in the Balkans the administration of President H.W. Bush took seriously the increasingly belligerent language used by Milosevic towards Kosovo: threats made credible by the renunciation of Kosovo's autonomy and stronger direct control from Belgrade. As early as December 1992 President Bush warned Milosevic and his military commander, General Zivota Panic, not to escalate violence in Kosovo, despite the declaration of Kosovan independence by its unofficial President, Ibrahim Rugova. David Binder quoted the President in a *New York Times* article on 28 December 1992: 'In the event of conflict in Kosovo caused by Serbian action, the United States will be prepared to employ military force against the Serbs in Kosovo and in Serbia proper'. The US had yet to suffer the ignominy of withdrawal from Mogadishu, Somalia the following year so Bush's threat held some weight. However, Milosevic would go on to observe the hesitancy and indecision of the UN and key states during the Bosnia War from 1992 to 1995, emboldening him to resist the inevitable diplomatic manoeuvres that emerged in response to the 1998 escalation of force against Kosovo.

The UN Security Council responded swiftly – at least in diplomatic, non-military terms. On 31 March UN Security Council Resolution 1160 (1998) condemned 'the use of excessive force by Serbian police forces against civilians and peaceful demonstrators in Kosovo, as well as all acts of terrorism by the Kosovo Liberation Army'.[31] Apart from proscribing the sale of arms to the Federal Republic of Yugoslavia (FRY), including Kosovo, the resolution offered no ultimatum to Milosevic and called only for further monitoring. The Contact Group – comprising the US, UK, France, Germany, Italy, and Russia – continued with diplomatic engagement as 1998 wore on and the fighting gained greater ferocity. For all the efforts of the Contact Group, no progress was being made on the ground. A further Security Council Resolution on 23 September upped the diplomatic *ante*, condemning 'all acts of violence by any party', and expressing concern at the reports of continuing violations of the prohibitions imposed by resolution 1160 (1998)'.[32] This second resolution went further than the first, warning both parties – but Milosevic in particular – that the Security Council would 'consider further action and additional measures to maintain or restore peace and stability in the region'.[33]

31 United Nations Security Council Resolution 1660, 31 March 1998, http://www.un.org/ga/search/view_doc.asp?symbol=S/RES/1160(1998) accessed 15 January 2013

32 United Nations Security Council Resolution 1199, 23 September 1998, http://www.un.org/en/ga/search/view_doc.asp?symbol=S/RES/1199(1998) accessed 15 January 2013

33 *Ibid.*

For Blair, it was not until the end of 1998 that Kosovo became a personal priority, with the massacre of forty-five Kosovo-Albanian civilians at Račak on 15 January 1999 focusing attention on the escalating number of deaths and displacements.[34] Behind the scenes Blair was communicating regularly with President Bill Clinton and the European leaders of NATO member states, the culmination of which were the international conferences held at Rambouillet, France from 6–23 February and Paris from 15–18 March. All of the above activities suggest that all diplomatic options – to use Blair's phrase – were being exhausted, with the US making significant efforts to bring together the opposing sides.

Complicating any assessment of the diplomatic efforts was the nature of some of the conditions to which Milosevic and the Serbs would be required to accept. One of the most controversial demands concerned the access of NATO personnel and equipment to the sovereign territory of the Federal Republic of Yugoslavia. Appendix B of the Rambouillet text stated:

> NATO personnel shall enjoy, together with their vehicles, vessels, aircraft, and equipment, free and unrestricted passage and unimpeded access throughout the FRY including associated airspace and territorial waters. This shall include, but not be limited to, the right of bivouac, maneuver, billet, and utilization of any areas or facilities as required for support, training, and operations.[35]

The extent to which Milosevic would be required to surrender control of FRY sovereign territory resulted in the withdrawal of his representatives from the peace talks, making the signature of the opposing Albanian representative an irrelevance. In addition, while the US and UK signed up to the agreement Russia did not: thereby emboldening Milosevic as the split between the permanent members of the Security Council became more apparent. While diplomacy appeared to be taking place, the severity of the demands placed on Milosevic calls into question the degree to which it could be viewed as a genuine attempt to avoid war. In a *Daily Telegraph* article on 28 June 1999 Henry Kissinger famously denounced the Rambouillet demands, stating:

> The Rambouillet text, which called on Serbia to admit NATO troops throughout Yugoslavia, was a provocation, an excuse to start bombing.

34 Blair, *A Journey*, pp. 225–227.

35 'Appendix B: Status of Multi-National Military Implementation Force', Rambouillet Interim Agreement for Peace and Self-Government in Kosovo, http://www.theguardian.com/world/1999/apr/28/balkans12 accessed 29 January 2013

> Rambouillet is not a document that an angelic Serb could have accepted. It was a terrible diplomatic document that should never have been presented in that form.

In addition to the surrender of sovereignty to NATO personnel and equipment, Milosevic would also have had to accept much greater, and for him unacceptable, freedoms and autonomy for Kosovo and its people. The peace talks finally broke down on 23 March 1999 amidst claim and counter-claim about bad faith, underhand negotiating tactics and unreasonable demands. Milosevic ordered an escalation of violence and the ethnic cleansing of Kosovo, which led to the huge numbers – hundreds of thousands – of displaced refugees. Blair told the British Parliament:

> On the assumptions that [final talks] produce no change in President Milosevic's position and that the repression in Kosovo by Serb forces continues, Britain stands ready with its NATO allies to take military action. We do so for very clear reasons. We do so primarily to avert what would otherwise be a humanitarian disaster in Kosovo.[36]

In summary, analysis of two key elements of Blair's moral case for intervening in Kosovo – the existence of a real and imminent threat to the indigenous civilian population, and the extent to which military force was used as a last resort after exhausting all diplomatic options – highlights ambiguities that were not always made clear in Blair's intervention discourse at the time. Diplomatic efforts clearly took place before the onset of military intervention – in the form of aerial bombardment – to stop the killing and ethnic cleansing of ethnic Albanians from Kosovo. Those who participated on the NATO side would probably maintain that those efforts were exhaustive. Certainly Blair expended significant political capital in achieving the necessary support, though he admits to being unable to win over President Yeltsin – whom he labelled 'unpredictable' – and Russia to his and NATO's position.[37] Even if further diplomatic efforts were theoretically possible, with Milosevic escalating the level of violence after the failure of the March peace talks the calculation shifted towards taking action. The massacres in Rwanda in 1994 had demonstrated how rapidly huge numbers of people could be killed – time was now of the essence. Political and military realities exposed the limits to which moral concerns could, or should, delay the onset of the use of force. To use Bellamy's expression while

36 Blair, 23 March 1999, *Hansard*, Vol. 328, p. 161.

37 Blair, *A Journey*, p. 243.

assessing the imminence of the threat to Kosovar civilians, Milosevic's 'hammer'[38] was not only falling, but pounding. Milosevic will therefore bear the brunt of history's judgement for events in Kosovo in 1998–9 but it should not be forgotten that NATO's intervention also marked the culmination of the KLA's strategic aim of winning external support against Serbia. Blair even received support from some unlikely quarters with the Archbishop of York, David Hope, encouraging both sides "to open up new avenues of mediation in the hope that sooner or later opposing factions will return to the negotiating table with serious intent towards a genuine and just resolution."[39] The Archbishop of Canterbury, George Carey, went further: "In the Balkans, the evil of ethnic cleansing is leading to the crucifixion of Kosovo as the refugee crisis continues. Military action thus far is recognition that the civilised world cannot stand idly by and accept that evil should triumph."[40] Blair's memoirs state simply that he 'had enunciated the new doctrine of a "responsibility to protect" ...I had put it into effect in Kosovo'.[41] Despite the frequently overlooked complexities of the Kosovo intervention, on balance Blair made a strong moral case for taking action to protect the lives, freedoms and homes of Kosovo Albanians.

Iraq

On the surface, Blair's position from 2002 until 2010 and beyond seems unequivocal: his case for invading Iraq was based on Saddam's possession of weapons of mass destruction (WMD). He confirmed as much several months after the March 2003 invasion of Iraq when, on 8 July 2003, he was questioned by the House of Commons Liaison Committee and told its members: 'I accept entirely the legal basis for action was through weapons of mass destruction'.[42] However, from the 1999 Kosovo intervention to the 2003 Iraq War Blair was entirely consistent in proclaiming that his primary concern was with the morality of potential action rather than the legality. As he told an earlier

38 Bellamy, *Just Wars*, p. 168.

39 David Hope, 'Sermon at York Minster, 2 April 1999', *The Church of England Newspaper*, 9 April 1999, p. 1.

40 George Carey, 'Sermon at Canterbury Cathedral 3 April 1999' *Ibid.*

41 Blair, *A Journey*, p. 400.

42 Tony Blair, 'Select Committee on Liaison Minutes of Evidence', 8 July 2003, http://www.publications.parliament.uk/pa/cm200203/cmselect/cmliaisn/334-ii/3070804.htm accessed 14 April 2012

meeting of the Liaison Committee about how he came to decisions concerning the use of military intervention: 'The two most important [questions] are is it right and is it do-able?'[43] This statement is consistent with the arguments put forward in the first half of this chapter, with Blair's actions being guided by the moral imperative: 'Is it right'. However, in 2002, during the long build-up to the Iraq invasion, his private views cast a different light over his priorities:

> From a centre-left perspective, the case should be obvious. Saddam's regime is a brutal, oppressive military dictatorship. He kills opponents, has wrecked his country's economy and is a source of instability and danger in the region...a political philosophy that does care about other nations – eg Kosovo, Afghanistan, Sierra Leone – and is prepared to change regimes on its merits, should be gung-ho on Saddam.
>
> So why isn't it? Because people believe we are only doing it to support the US; and they are only doing it to settle an old score. And the WMD problems don't seem obviously worse than 3 years ago.
>
> So we have to re-order our story and message. Increasingly it should be about the nature of the regime.[44]

In this minute, Blair comes across as an ardent and committed regime changer: he had demonstrated his credentials previously in Kosovo, Sierra Leone and Afghanistan and advocated a 'gung-ho' approach to Saddam Hussein and his regime. Furthermore, he acknowledged that the WMD threat had apparently not changed for at least three years. On the matter of intention, Blair's message to his chief of staff suggests that he was motivated primarily by regime change, with WMD and other moral arguments playing a secondary role in his political calculation.[45] Reinforcing this view of Blair's motivation – his 'intentions', to use the vocabulary of just war moral reasoning – was a further exchange of notes with his Chief of Staff on 19 July 2002 which spoke of a 'road map for getting rid of Saddam': incorporating the release of documents 'on human rights abuses, WMD etc.', all as

---

43 Tony Blair, 'Select Committee on Liaison Minutes of Evidence', 21 January 2003, http://www.parliament.the-stationery-office.co.uk/pa/cm200203/cmselect/cmliaisn/334-i/3012102.htm accessed 28 February 2013

44 Tony Blair, 'Minute to Jonathan Powell, 17 March 2002', Evidence to the Iraq Inquiry, http://www.iraqinquiry.org.uk/media/50751/Blair-to-Powell-17March2002-minute.pdf accessed 24 January 2011

45 For a comprehensive analysis of Blair's motivations and intentions regarding his support for the 2003 Iraq War see Peter Lee, *Blair's Just War: Iraq and the Illusion of Morality* (Basingstoke: Palgrave Macmillan, 2012).

part of a 'Rolls Royce information campaign'.[46] It is against this backdrop that Blair's own moral arguments for military intervention featured in this chapter will be examined. Namely, the extent to which there was a real and imminent threat to Iraqi civilians and the degree to which all diplomatic options were exhausted.

Iraq – Real and Imminent Threat to the Civilian Population

On 18 March 2003 Blair stood before the British Parliament and set out his case for war against Iraq and Saddam Hussein. Consistent with his communication strategy over several years as Prime Minister, Blair's speech sought to engage emotionally as much as intellectually with his listeners both in the House of Commons and beyond. One particular characteristic of Blair's speeches across a range of policy issues was his use of the representative individual whose example was projected as the generalised embodiment of whatever point Blair was trying to make at the time: in this case the need to support military action. He told the listening MPs and his television audience:

> The brutality of the repression – the death and torture camps, the barbaric prisons for political opponents, the routine beatings for anyone or their families suspected of disloyalty are well documented. Just last week, someone slandering Saddam was tied to a lamp post in a street in Baghdad, his tongue cut out, mutilated and left to bleed to death, as a warning to others…
>
> I recall a few weeks ago talking to an Iraqi exile and saying to her that I understood how grim it must be under the lash of Saddam. "But you don't," she replied. "You cannot. You do not know what it is like to live in perpetual fear." And she is right. We take our freedom for granted. But imagine not to be able to speak or discuss or debate or even question the society you live in. To see friends and family taken away and never daring to complain. To suffer the humility of failing courage in face of pitiless terror. That is how the Iraqi people live. Leave Saddam in place and that is how they will continue to live.[47]

---

46 Jonathan Powell, 'Minute to Prime Minister, 19 July 2002', Evidence to the Iraq Inquiry, http://www.iraqinquiry.org.uk/media/50772/Powell-to-Blair-19July2002-minute.pdf accessed 7 July 2011

47 Tony Blair, 'Statement to Parliament Opening the Iraq Debate', 18 March 2003, *Hansard*, p. 760, http://www.publications.parliament.uk/pa/cm200203/cmhansrd/vo030318/debtext/30318-06.htm accessed 1 March 2013

Few could hear or read these words without a measure of sympathy for the victims of Saddam Hussein's victims: beatings, mutilations, death, fear and terror. Whether these particular examples were rhetorical devices created by Blair and his speech makers or actual individuals, there was little doubt that Saddam had led a brutal regime for many years. The pertinent question in relation to this aspect of Blair's moral case for military intervention is this: Was the regime's violence against civilians imminent or ongoing, severe enough and widespread enough to justify going to war? In the examples mentioned by Blair, above, the violence was ongoing and severe – at least for the individuals involved. However, the extent to which such a degree of violence was co-ordinated and widespread was less clear. In the year prior to the invasion of Iraq on 19 March 2003, one of the consistent themes of Blair's attempts to achieve political support for military intervention – domestically and internationally – was the need to protect Iraqi civilians form the tyrannical rule of Saddam Hussein and his regime. Consider the following statements from Blair's speeches and Parliamentary statements and the scale of the threat that he suggests:

> The regime of Saddam is detestable. Brutal, repressive, political opponents routinely tortured and executed.[48]
>
> Saddam has used these [chemical] weapons against his own people, the Iraqi Kurds. Scores of towns and villages were attacked. Iraqi military officials dressed in full protection gear were used to witness the attacks and visited later to assess the damage. Wounded civilians were normally shot on the scene. In one attack alone, on the city of Halabja, it is estimated that 5,000 were murdered and 9,000 wounded in this way. All in all in the North around 100,000 Kurds died, according to Amnesty International. In the destruction of the marshlands in Southern Iraq, around 200,000 people were forcibly removed. Many died.[49]
>
> There is no doubt at all in our mind that Saddam has been trying to rebuild that arsenal of chemical, biological and potentially nuclear capability, and he is someone who has actually used it, used it in respect of his own people.[50]

48 Tony Blair, 'Speech at the George Bush Senior Presidential Library', 7 April 2002, http://webarchive.nationalarchives.gov.uk/20041109040811/http://number10.gov.uk/output/Page1712.asp accessed 2 March 2013

49 Tony Blair, 'Speech to the TUC Conference in Blackpool', 10 September 2002, http://webarchive.nationalarchives.gov.uk/20041109040811/http://number10.gov.uk/page1725 accessed 21 January 2013

50 Tony Blair, 'Press Conference', 13 January 2003, http://webarchive.nationalarchives.gov.uk/20061004051823/http://number10.gov.uk/page3005 accessed 21 January 2013

> Saddam is a leader who...has used weapons of mass destruction against other countries, against his own people.[51]

In numerous speeches, press conferences and public statements Blair consistently referred to Saddam's use of WMD – chemical weapons specifically – against his own people. The nature of these weapons and the extensive, inhumane suffering and deaths they can cause suggested a humanitarian catastrophe that needed to be averted. On closer inspection however, no evidence was put forward by Blair that suggested the ongoing and severe treatment of civilians was *widespread* during the build-up to the 2003 war. His speech on 10 September 2002, above, implied a level of death, suffering and displacement that at least matched or exceeded that which took place in Kosovo prior to NATO's intervention in 1999: 5,000 murdered and 9,000 wounded in Halabja; 100,000 Kurds killed; and 200,000 Marsh Arabs forced from their lands. The problem for Blair was that these actions took place more than a decade earlier – something he never made explicit in his speeches where he sought to discursively co-locate ongoing but small-scale brutality with widespread, historical, chemically-induced deaths and ethnic cleansing.

It was in March 1988, as the Iran-Iraq War was approaching its conclusion, that Saddam ordered chemical weapons to be used against Iraqi Kurds in Halabja. The numbers who died at that time were fairly accurately reported by Blair in his 2002–3 speeches. What Blair did not mention was that in the 1980s Iraq was supported by the West, led by the US and UK, in its fight against Iran. Ironically – given all that Blair would say later – when the world became aware of the Halabja massacre, diplomatic opprobrium did not rain down on Saddam. Contrarily, when the UN's response eventually came two months later in Security Council Resolution 612 (1988) it merely called on both sides to refrain from the future use of chemical weapons in accordance with their obligations under the Geneva Protocol.[52]

In addition, following his defeat in the 1991 Gulf War and the withdrawal of Iraqi forces from Kuwait, in response to what he viewed as their disloyalty Saddam ordered the draining of the Southern Marshes, the ancestral home the Shia Marsh Arabs: thereby displacing in excess of 100,000 people. In either 1988 or 1991 when these events took place – or the hammer fell, to use Bellamy's

51 Tony Blair 'Select Committee on Liaison Minutes of Evidence', 21 January 2003, http://www.parliament.the-stationery-office.co.uk/pa/cm200203/cmselect/cmliaisn/334-i/3012102.htm accessed 28 February 2013

52 United Nations Security Council Resolution 612 (1988), 9 May 1988, http://daccess-dds-ny.un.org/doc/RESOLUTION/GEN/NR0/541/39/IMG/NR054139.pdf?OpenElement accessed 27 May 2012

expression once more – there may well have been a case for military intervention on moral grounds to protect civilians.

Despite extensive research there appears to be no public record of Blair calling for military action against Iraq on humanitarian grounds in either 1988 or 1991. So a situation emerged in the lead-up to the 2003 Iraq War where Blair called upon historical acts of barbarity in making his case for military action to protect Iraqi civilians in the present. The ongoing level of violence against civilians in 2002–3 – horrific though it would have been for the individuals, families and communities involved – did not reach a level that would have prompted intervention in the way that Milosevic's actions in Kosovo did.

In his testimony to the Iraq Inquiry in 2010 Peter Goldsmith, Attorney General during the period when Blair was making his case for intervention, stated his position in 2002: 'The self-defence [argument] didn't work, the humanitarian crisis [argument] didn't work. Put in those terms, there wasn't a basis for military action'.[53] This view was supported by Robin Cook, Cabinet Minister and Leader of the House of Commons until his resignation on 17 March 2003, two days before the US/UK-led force launched its assault on Iraq. He specifically raised the humanitarian issue in his resignation speech to the House of Commons the following day:

> The legal basis for our action in Kosovo was the need to respond to an urgent and compelling humanitarian crisis. Our difficulty in getting support this time is that neither the international community nor the British public is persuaded that there is an urgent and compelling reason for this military action in Iraq.[54]

While Blair's case clearly went far beyond the humanitarian argument, the specific element being discussed here – the need to protect Iraqi civilians – fell significantly short of a *casus belli* in 2003 and was explicitly rejected by two key members of Blair's own government. This argument was more than 10 years out of date. There had been definite, documented widespread and severe brutality against Iraqis by Saddam's regime in 1988 and 1991. We can also be reasonably confident that there was also imminent, ongoing and severe brutality to a much smaller number of Iraqis in the years leading up to the eventual military

53 Peter Goldsmith, 'Evidence to the Iraq Inquiry', 27 January 2010, http://www.iraqinquiry.org.uk/media/45317/20100127goldsmith-final.pdf accessed 12 May 2012

54 Robin Cook, 'Resignation Speech to the House of Commons', 17 March 2003, *Hansard*, 726, http://www.publications.parliament.uk/pa/cm200203/cmhansrd/vo030317/debtext/30317-33.htm#30317-33_spnew0 accessed 21 May 2012

intervention in 2003. However, as the time for military action drew closer there was not the imminent, ongoing, severe and *widespread* barbarity that was seen in Kosovo and which prompted the intervention in 1999.

The chapter now turns to the final point of comparison between Kosovo and Iraq in the context of protecting civilians and Blair's criteria for military intervention: were all diplomatic options exhausted before the invasion was launched?

Iraq – Last Resort after Exhausting All Diplomatic Options

In the summer of 2002 when the UK Attorney General pointed out to Blair that the self-defence argument and the humanitarian case were both insufficient to justify military action, he also identified the only remaining legitimate approach to be taken: 'If there was going to be a basis for military action, it had to be as a result of the new United Nations Security Council Resolution'.[55] This may have been the case from a legal perspective but for Blair, who justified his intervention in Kosovo on moral, not legal grounds, the UN approach would be adopted purely out of political expediency: 'We had acted without UN authority in Kosovo…I never even thought about it for Sierra Leone. Yet it would be hard to argue that, morally, in each of those situations, we should not have intervened'.[56]

Reinforcing this interpretation of events was Blair's testimony to the Iraq Inquiry in January 2011:

> So in a sense what I was saying to America was "look" – and by the way I am absolutely sure this is how George Bush took it – "Whatever the political heat, if I think this is the right thing to do I am going to be with you. I am not going to back out because the going gets tough. On the other hand, here are the difficulties and this is why I think the UN route is the right way to go."[57]

As has been mentioned previously, Blair was already committed to working with the Bush administration in 'getting rid of Saddam', with a legal case 'based on WMD' providing the means through which to achieve UN authorisation and,

55 *Ibid.*

56 Blair, *A Journey*, p. 433.

57 Tony Blair, 'Statement to the Iraq Inquiry', 21 January 2011, http://www.iraqinquiry.org.uk/media/50865/20110121-Blair.pdf accessed 14 April 2012

consequently, public support.[58] From September to 8 November 2002 when United Nations Security Council Resolution (UNSCR) 1441(2002) was passed, intense negotiations took place between the permanent five members of the Security Council. The Council was split throughout this period, and afterwards, with the US and UK taking an aggressive approach and calling for automaticity – a clause that would trigger military action if certain conditions were not met by Saddam. France, Russia and China took the opposite view and would not countenance any resolution with an in-built trigger clause. What emerged was a diplomatic compromise that allowed each side in the disagreement to claim that they had achieved what they wanted. In the wording of UNSCR 1441, the Security Council:

> 12. *Decides* to convene immediately upon receipt of a report in accordance with paragraphs 4 or 11 above [where Iraq fails to meet its disarmament or inspection obligations], in order to consider the situation and the need for full compliance with all of the relevant Council resolutions in order to secure international peace and security;
> 13. *Recalls*, in that context, that the Council has repeatedly warned Iraq that it will face serious consequences as a result of its continued violations of its obligations.[59]

For France, Russia and China, a diplomatic victory was seen to have been achieved because UNSCR 1441 did not include the accepted diplomatic phrase that authorised war: 'all means necessary'. The US and the UK chose to interpret the resolution somewhat differently, in particular the phrase 'serious consequences'. Jack Straw, the then Foreign Secretary, described his understanding at that time:

> This resolution contains, if you like, an ultimatum. I mean, it talks about the final opportunity. It then in OP13 talks about serious consequences, which as Stephen Pattison [Head of the UN Department in the Foreign and Commonwealth Office] explains everyone knows means military action if there was non-compliance. So it contained its own ultimatum.[60]

---

58 Powell, 'Minute to Prime Minister', 19 July 2002.

59 United Nations Security Council Resolution 1441, 8 November 2002, http://www.un.org/Depts/unmovic/documents/1441.pdf accessed 20 May 2012

60 Jack Straw, 'Evidence to the Iraq Inquiry', 2 February 2011, http://www.iraqinquiry.org.uk/media/53031/Straw%202011-02-02%20S1.pdf accessed 25 April 2012

Complicating matters for Straw and Blair were the legal interpretations of the document by Britain's two most senior International Lawyers in the Foreign and Commonwealth Office, Sir Michael Wood and his deputy, Elizabeth Wilmshurst. Supporting the interpretation of UNSCR 1441 by France, Russia and China, Sir Michael informed the Foreign Secretary on 23 January 2003 that regardless of Saddam's actions – that is, even if he did not cooperate with the UN weapons inspectors – a further vote and resolution by the Security Council would be necessary before the UK could legally use military force against Iraq. Elizabeth Wilmshurst held the same opinion and would later resign on the eve of the invasion on the basis that she believed the UK to about to commit the international crime of aggression.[61] Consequently, there was a fundamental contradiction at the heart of Blair's case for war in Iraq based on his own morally-driven, 1999-stated conditions for humanitarian intervention: the need to exhaust all diplomatic options. If Blair shifted his position on what 'all diplomatic options' meant – and he did – how can his actions be assessed?

Blair's position was inconsistent at best and disingenuous at worst. He repeatedly stated that he would get a second UN resolution before undertaking military action. As he told the House of Commons Liaison Committee on 21 January 2003: 'The fact is we are going to have a second UN Resolution'.[62] However, in February and March 2003 as the invasion neared and it became clear that no Security Council follow-up to Resolution 1441 was likely in the near future, Blair backtracked. On 11 March 2003 he cleared the way for a change of approach:

> if there was a veto applied by one of the countries with a veto or by countries that I thought were applying the veto unreasonably, in those circumstances we would [proceed without one] but we're fighting very hard to get a second resolution through and, as we speak now, I still believe we will get that second resolution.[63]

At the same time, with the pressure of a huge invasion force readying itself across the border in Saudi Arabia and a vast naval armada forming up off the Iraqi coast, Hans Blix's team of UN weapons inspectors were finally getting full

61 Elizabeth Wilmshurst, 'Evidence to the Iraq Inquiry', 26 January 2010, http://www.iraqinquiry.org.uk/media/43719/document2010-01-27-100908.pdf accessed 25 April 2012

62 Blair, 21 January 2003.

63 Tony Blair, 'PM Answers Iraq Questions at MTV Forum', 11 March 2003, http://webarchive.nationalarchives.gov.uk/20050301192918/http://number10.gov.uk/page3250 accessed 25 April 2012

cooperation from Saddam's regime. Problematically for Blair, Blix's inspectors were not finding any weapons of mass destruction. As a result, the likelihood of obtaining a further Security Council Resolution authorising military action receded. At the same time, Blair's *casus belli*, WMD, similarly receded (recall that the Attorney General had already ruled out the humanitarian case and the self-defence argument, leaving only Security Council approval for war as a legitimate option).

In what now looks somewhat like an act of desperation Blair, advised by his Attorney General who had in turn been 'advised' by members of the US administration, 'resurrected' UNSCR 678 (1990), which had authorised the use of military force in the 1991 Gulf War. It is perhaps ironic that one of the reasons the US-led force that liberated Kuwait from Iraqi forces in 1991 did not subsequently march on Baghdad and topple Saddam Hussein at that time is because Security Council Resolution 678 (1990) did not sanction such action. Such detail did not stop Blair from using the unilaterally revived Resolution 678 (revived that is, without a vote of the Security Council in 2003) as the basis for military action.

The final act to be considered in assessing the extent to which all diplomatic options were exhausted concerns Blair's dismissal of a French initiative in the week the invasion eventually took place. In his eve-of-war statement to Parliament on 18 March 2003 Blair told his audience that France intended to 'veto a second Resolution whatever the circumstances'.[64] Evidence that emerged at the Iraq Inquiry shows that Blair was being less than fully honest in the way he represented the French position. Dominique de Villepin, the French Foreign Minister, had contacted Jack Straw on 13 March, to offer one final diplomatic initiative. The French government was open to any suggestion that did not involve 'automaticity' – the trigger clause that the US and UK wanted.[65] The French government told Blair, via Jack Straw: 'France could work on any mechanism which contained an ultimatum as long as it was the Security Council which took full responsibility at the end of any deadline'.[66] Blair clearly rejected the offer, which would have resulted in further weapons inspections,

64 Tony Blair, 'Statement to Parliament Opening the Iraq Debate', 18 March 2003, *Hansard*, 760, http://www.publications.parliament.uk/pa/cm200203/cmhansrd/vo030318/debtext/30318-06.htm accessed 1 March 2013

65 Jack Straw, 'Memo to No 10, Conversation between Himself and the French Foreign Secretary', submitted in evidence to the Iraq Inquiry, 13 March, 2003, http://www.iraqinquiry.org.uk/media/51625/13%20March%202003%20FCO%20telno%2053%20'Iraq%20-%20ForeignSecretarysconversationwithFrenchForeignMinister.pdf accessed 25 April 2012

66 *Ibid.*

misrepresenting France's true position to the British Parliament. Blair had little choice. Had Hans Blix's team been given several more weeks or months and continued to find no WMD, Blair's legal basis for involvement in the war – such as it was – would have disappeared.

In sum, the two aspects of Blair's moral justification for military intervention in Iraq discussed here – a real and imminent threat to the civilian population, and the extent to which military force was used as a last resort – fall far short of the degree of legitimacy he achieved in relation to Kosovo. The most serious humanitarian crises, in Halabja and in the southern marshes, had occurred more than a decade earlier, with no public record demonstrating that a younger Tony Blair advocated military intervention in either case. Further, Blair's use of the diplomatic process in the build-up to the 2003 invasion appears to be more politically self-serving than a genuine attempt to find a peaceful solution to the Iraq crisis. His co-operation with the US-led rush to war in February and March 2003 curtailed the efforts of Hans Blix and his weapons inspectors just as they were becoming most effective. It is a matter of considerable convenience for Blair that Blix and his team were not granted sufficient time to establish that Saddam's regime did not possess WMD, thereby removing Blair's *casus belli* in the process.

Conclusion

Reflecting on the military interventions to which he had committed British forces, Blair wrote in 2010 that while moral questions regarding protection of the innocent from atrocities did not necessarily lead to military intervention, they did set out a framework for doing so.[67] Throughout his Premiership Blair was entirely consistent in prioritising the moral case for military intervention, with the stated aim of protecting the weak who suffered injustice at the hands of brutal dictators. The criteria that he set out on 24 April 1999 in Chicago were – given the legal constraints of the UN Charter and the complexities of international relations – both persuasive and practical. Furthermore, those suggestions would later be encapsulated in large part in the UN's subsequent Responsibility to Protect doctrine.[68]

---

67 Blair, *A Journey*, p. 229.

68 United Nations 2005 World Summit Outcome, 'Responsibility to Protect Populations from Genocide, War Crimes, Ethnic Cleansing and Crimes Against Humanity', 24 October 2005, http://www.un.org/en/preventgenocide/adviser/pdf/World%20Summit%20Outcome%20Document.pdf#page=30 accessed 20 February 2013

Having analysed Blair's military interventions in Kosovo (1999) and Iraq (2003) in light of two of Blair's criteria – the existence of a real and imminent threat to the civilian population as a humanitarian case for military action and the extent to which military force was used as a last resort after exhausting all diplomatic options – a mixed picture emerges. In Kosovo there was an ongoing, severe and increasingly widespread threat to civilians as the ethnic cleansing and killing of Kosovo Albanians spread, all broadcast live on global media. Questions remain about the extent to which the diplomatic negotiations at Rambouillet were entered into in good faith by all of the parties involved. However, once the killings escalated in March 1999, it is difficult to see many viable alternatives to the swift NATO action that took place.

By the time Blair turned his sights on Saddam Hussein and Iraq, he appeared increasingly reliant on the certainty of his own moral rectitude and judgement, deaf to dissenting voices and selective in his regard for the evidence, or lack of evidence, before him. His commitment to the Iraq intervention was politically driven in a way that the Kosovo intervention had not been. The arguments that had been so successfully applied to protecting civilians in Kosovo failed when transposed to the situation in Iraq: there was no imminent or ongoing, widespread *and* severe brutality taking place. This chapter therefore concludes that Tony Blair's moral justification of the Kosovo intervention – despite the complexities that were not always adequately addressed – successfully cast him in the light of protector of the innocent. In contrast, the shortcomings of his moral justification of the 2003 Iraq intervention has resulted in his being widely viewed as a provocateur who, at least to some degree, misled the British people about his true intentions and went to war on a false prospectus.

CHAPTER 5

Ten Myths about the Responsibility to Protect: A Realist Critique

Jean-Baptiste Jeangène Vilmer

The concept of "responsibility to protect" (R2P) is one of the most cited on the international stage in the early twenty-first century, and its popularity is often at the expense of accuracy. More often cited than understood, R2P gives rise to a number of misconceptions. This chapter exposes the main ones.[1]

1 R2P is Not a Novel Concept

Contrary to a widespread assumption, the idea of a "responsibility to protect" does not date from the eponymous report of the International Commission on Intervention and State Sovereignty (ICISS), which made it renowned in 2001.[2] It has several origins. The first is the idea of conditional sovereignty, previously theorised by lawyers during the late nineteenth century. The principle of non-intervention only protects the states 'truly worthy of the name', warned Rolin-Jaequemyns in 1876.[3] 'Sovereignty must be respected when it is respectable, yet it is not when it violates international obligations', added Fauchille in 1922.[4] They spoke of 'intervention for abuse of sovereignty' or 'corruption of sovereignty'.[5]

---

1 A previous and shorter version of this chapter has been published in Portuguese (Brazil): "Dez mitos sobre a Responsabilidade de Proteger," *Política Externa*, 21:4, 2013, pp. 47–58. I also developed this argument in Chapter 2 of J.-B. Jeangène Vilmer, *La Guerre au nom de l'humanité. Tuer ou laisser mourir*, preface by Hubert Védrine (Paris: PUF, 2012). I would like to thank the two anonymous reviewers for their insightful comments on a previous version of this English version.

2 ICISS, *The Responsibility to Protect* (Ottawa: International Development Research Center, 2001).

3 G. Rolin-Jaequemyns, "Le droit international et la phase actuelle de la question d'Orient," *Revue de droit international et de législation comparée*, 8, 1876, p. 369.

4 P. Fauchille, *Traité de droit international public*, 8th ed. (Paris: Rousseau & Cie, 1922), p. 565.

5 A. Rougier, "La théorie de l'intervention d'humanité," *Revue générale de droit international public*, 17, 1910, p. 495.

 | DOI 10.1163/9789004280380_006

Other provenances date from the 1990s, and were made possible by the end of the Cold War. It was then possible for the major powers to intervene without the risk of triggering a world war and for national liberation struggles and other secessionist tendencies to take place, as demonstrated by the Yugoslav example. Added to this are the efforts of French diplomacy to promote the right of assistance, the development of humanitarian action, the growing role of media and the consecration of the so-called "CNN effect," the development of a global discourse on human rights and the multiplication of available legal instruments, and finally globalization, which lessens the divide between the victim and the potential observer-intervener.

During this period, marked by the 'inhumanitarian non-interventions'[6] in Rwanda and Srebrenica, and the intervention in Kosovo in 1999, at least three ideas led to R2P. The first is the concept of "human security." Initially too broadly defined by UNDP as the sum of seven elements (economic security, food security, health security, environmental security, personal security, collective security and political security), it was narrowed down at the end of the decade to the human cost of violent conflict.

The second is the redefinition of sovereignty as responsibility made by Francis Deng, then Representative of the Secretary-General on internally displaced persons. Developing Reisman's observation that "in order to qualify for the name of government, a government now has to meet certain standards, all of which involve restraints on the use of power,"[7] Deng thinks that 'these principles impose on the international community a correlative responsibility for their enforcement'.[8]

The third is what is sometimes called the "Annan doctrine," that sovereignty is no longer a barrier behind which one can commit abuse. In 2000, Annan noted, on the one hand, that 'no legal principle – not even sovereignty – can ever shield crimes against humanity'[9] and, on the other, that 'in essence the problem is one of responsibility: in circumstances in which universally accepted human rights are being violated on a massive scale we have a responsibility to act'.[10] At the turn of the millennium, he clearly articulated the

---

6 S. Chesterman, *Just War or Just Peace?* (Oxford: Oxford University Press, 2002).

7 M.W. Reisman, "Through or Despite Governments: Differentiated Responsibilities in Human Rights Programs," *Iowa Law Review*, 72, 1987, p. 391.

8 F. Deng et al., *Sovereignty as Responsibility: Conflict Management in Africa* (Washington D.C.: Brookings, 1996), p. 6. See also F. Deng, "From 'Sovereignty as Responsibility' to the 'Responsibility to Protect'," *Global Responsibility to Protect*, 2, 2010, pp. 353–370.

9 K. Annan, We the Peoples: *The Role of the United Nations in the 21st Century* (New York, 2000), §219.

10 Report of the Secretary-General on the work of the Organization, General Assembly Official Records, 55th session, Supplement n 1, UN Doc. A/55/1 (30 August 2000), §37, p. 5.

question by showing the limits of the traditional concept of "humanitarian intervention" and the relevance of a reformulation in terms of responsibility.

2 R2P is Not Equivalent to the French *"droit d'ingérence"*

The concept of "*droit ou devoir d'ingérence*" (right or duty to intervene) was popularized in the French-speaking world by Bernard Kouchner and Mario Bettati from the late 1980s. Although it appeared as a legitimate extension of the idea of "failure to assist a person in danger," extrapolated at the international scale (failure to assist *peoples* in danger), against a background of crisis in Biafra, it has been widely criticised, and rightly so. The formula is ambiguous, as "right" and "duty" are used interchangeably even though they do not mean at all the same thing: right allows, but duty requires. It also confuses *ingérence* with assistance.

In French, the word *ingérence* literally refers to an illegal interference and the paradoxical expression *droit d'ingérence* literally means *right to do what we don't have the right to do* – this logical inconsistency being the reason why it is rejected by the *Académie française*.[11] In the context of an international crisis, *ingérence* is an intervention without the consent of the target state, hence violating its sovereignty, and *droit d'ingérence* is an alleged right to do so on humanitarian grounds – while assistance implies its consent, and is therefore legal.

However, there is no *droit d'ingérence*, as President Mitterrand told his Minister Kouchner,[12] while defending at the UN the "duty of humanitarian assistance." What the French-initiated General Assembly resolutions often cited by proponents of this *droit d'ingérence* (43/131, 45/100, 46/182) are actually helping to create is a duty of assistance. They do not authorise the use of force on a foreign territory without the consent of the target state (that would be *ingérence*): rather, they authorize humanitarian assistance with its consent – and the so-called *droit d'ingérence* grew by taking advantage of this ambiguity.

There is disparity between the representation of the *droit d'ingérence* in France and reality, which shows the extent with which we are dealing with a mythological construction for which the French media has to bear some responsibility. They impart upon this idea a nation (France), fathers (Kouchner and Bettati, systematically presented as its "inventors"), a date of birth

11 For a discussion of this, see the *Dictionnaire de l'Académie française*, http://www.academie-francaise.fr

12 B. Kouchner, *Ce que je crois* (Paris: Grasset, 1995), p. 50.

(the 1980s), a founding myth (Cassin opposing "Goebbels claiming to the League of Nations that 'a man is master in his own home'") and an excessive influence (a 'theory that changed international relations').[13] These tales were created to impregnate the national imagination – and they actually succeeded. However, they are false. The idea of a right to intervene is neither recent nor French; the term *droit d'ingérence* has existed for at least a century and a half.[14] Cassin certainly opposed Goebbels but no more so than his Polish, Norwegian and Czechoslovakian colleagues; and, far from drastically changing the world affairs, this notion of *droit d'ingérence* remained very French. In the English-speaking world, where it causes the greatest suspicion, one mocks 'the heavily personalised, apparently insular, indeed incestuous, nature of much Parisian intellectual debate which underpinned [this] idea'.[15]

In 2001 the R2P appeared. Facing this new competition, what do the French proponents of the *droit d'ingérence* do? They take all the credit. They argue that R2P is nothing other than the replacement term for the *droit d'ingérence*. This has been France's official stance for years. It has not only been the opinion of Bettati[16] and Kouchner,[17] but also of the Ambassador of France to the UN when invoking R2P for military intervention in Burma in 2008[18] and, three years later, that of President Sarkozy and his minister Alain Juppé in the case of Libya. All of them concur that France invented the notion of R2P, because it is merely a renaming of the *droit d'ingérence*. In so doing, they commit two errors. Firstly, they confuse two different things. On the one hand, R2P is much broader than the notion of *ingérence* used to describe a military intervention. R2P is nothing

13 *Le Monde*, 24 September 2011, p. ARH5 et ARH1.

14 See P. Colletta, *Histoire du Royaume de Naples*, translation of the 4th ed. (Paris: Ladvocat, 1835), t. I, p. 194; Revue des deux mondes, 12, 1837, p. 778; P. Fiore, Nouveau droit international public: suivant les besoins de la civilisation moderne, 2nd ed. (Paris: Durand et Pédone-Lauriel, 1885), t. I, p. 511; J. Baak, "Hegel et le droit des gens," Revue de droit international, 2, 1928, p. 276; J. Guerrero, "La question de l'intervention à la VIe Conférence Panaméricaine (Janvier 1928)," Revue générale de droit international public, 36:1–2, 1929, p. 44.

15 T. Allen et D. Styan, "A Right to Interfere? Bernard Kouchner and the New Humanitarianism," *Journal of International Development*, 12:6, 2000, p. 826.

16 M. Bettati, in Société française pour le droit international (SFDI), *La responsabilité de protéger*, Actes du colloque de Nanterre (Paris: Pedone, 2008), p. 10 and *Libération*, 3 mars 2011, p. 2.

17 See the joint press conference of Bernard Kouchner and Heidemarie Wieczorek-Zeul, 7 May 2008 and the press release of B. Kouchner, of the 8 May 2008, at the Permanent Mission of France to the United Nations Office and other international organizations in Geneva.

18 J.-M. Ripert, press conference, 7 May 2008.

but an attitude facing a humanitarian crisis – a sense of "responsibility" to protect the victims, which can be embodied in various ways. It not only comprises intervention but, insisted the ICISS, it should also play a role in prevention and reconstruction. If a military intervention is necessary, it should only be considered as a last resort. In his 2009 report on the implementation of R2P, the Secretary-General identifies three "pillars," with military intervention only considered in the third.[19] One cannot say that R2P is the "replacement term" for the *droit d'ingérence* when they do not actually have the same semantic extension.

On the other hand, and this is the most obvious difference between the two, R2P is legalist: in its 2005 UN version, a military intervention cannot take place without the authorisation of the UN Security Council. However, this is not an issue for the *droit d'ingérence*.

Secondly, R2P has been constructed not only without the aid of the *droit d'ingérence*, but even to thwart it and the other traditional expression, "humanitarian intervention." Its purpose is neither to honour them nor extend them, but to replace them (e.g. 'shifting the terms of the debate', a 'change in terminology' for the ICISS).[20] Ramesh Thakur, one of the authors of the ICISS report, says Kouchner 'is one of the unrepentant "humanitarian warriors" who gave humanitarian intervention such a bad name that we had to rescue the deeply divisive idea and repackage it into the more unifying and politically marketable "responsibility to protect"'.[21] That the proponents of the *droit d'ingérence* appropriate the paternity of a concept built specifically against them is somewhat ironic.

3 The 2005 UN Version is Not a Consecration, but a Devaluation of the Concept

The operational R2P, the one states are presently referring to, is not that of the 2001 report but that of the articles 138–139 of the 2005 UN World Summit Outcome Document. States acknowledge that 'each individual State has the responsibility to protect its populations from genocide, war crimes, ethnic cleansing and crimes against humanity' (art. 138) and that 'we are prepared to take collective action, in a timely and decisive manner, through the Security Council, (...) should peaceful means be inadequate and national authorities

19 UN Doc. A/63/677, 12 January 2009.

20 ICISS, *op. cit.*, §2.28–2.29, pp. 16–17.

21 *The Globe and Mail*, 8 May 2008.

manifestly fail to protect their populations from genocide, war crimes, ethnic cleansing and crimes against humanity' (art. 139).[22]

Proponents of R2P often present these articles as a consecration. In fact, the passage from the 2001 report to the 2005 World Summit is the opposite of a promotion: it is a devaluation of the concept. Several states, including China, Russia, states from the G77 and the Non-Aligned Movement, but also the United States in particular did everything in negotiations to reduce its scope. John Bolton, the US ambassador to the UN, was very clear in his letter: 'the obligation/responsibility discussed in the text is not of a legal character... We do not accept that either the United Nations as a whole, or the Security Council, or individual states, have an obligation to intervene under international law'.[23]

And the fact is there is no obligation to intervene under international law. It does not mean there is no obligation at all, one can argue there is a moral obligation, some kind of Kantian imperfect duty (see 7. *infra*); and it does not mean either that being legally binding would have made a real difference since dozens of Security Council resolutions are already violated without any consequence; but it does mean that the acknowledgement of the R2P by the UN does not make it a "legal" norm and does not necessarily strengthen it. On the contrary, the price for such a consensus is a weakening of the concept.

According to Articles 138–139, this responsibility primarily rests with the state on whose territory the crimes potentially take place (art. 138). Thus far, nothing innovative: this internal responsibility, that of the state to protect its own citizens, has existed in international human rights law for decades (for instance in the 1948 Convention against Genocide). The responsibility we are looking for is the external or international one that would "require" other states to act. In article 139, states 'are prepared to take collective action', under certain conditions. But *being prepared* to do so something is not *having* to do it. Where is the announced 'responsibility' to protect? When firefighters or police have the responsibility to protect the population, it does not mean they can do it if they wish, but that they have a professional obligation to do so.[24] They cannot fail to act. States can and, most of the time, they do.

Was all this agitation really necessary to affirm what we have known for a long time – that the Security Council can authorise an intervention under Chapter 7? There is nothing original in these two paragraphs that is not already

22 UN Doc. A/60/L.1 (2005).

23 Letter from John Bolton to the United Nations, 30 August 2005.

24 A. Hehir, *The Responsibility to Protect: Rhetoric, Reality and the Future of Humanitarian Intervention* (Basingstoke: Palgrave Macmillan, 2012), p. 138.

found in the existing UN Charter.[25] One could even say that they devalue and undermine the concept of R2P, being less bold than the 2001 report. Firstly, the idea of a "code of conduct" – reasoned or limited use of the veto in the case of a humanitarian disaster – as proposed by the ICISS in 2001[26] and the UN High-level Panel on Threats, Challenges and Change in 2004,[27] is abandoned. Secondly, the initial objective was that R2P is activated when the state on whose territory the humanitarian disaster occurs cannot or will not act. In the English version of the UN document, the term used is "manifest failure" – a much more forceful description. Raising the threshold at which the international responsibility is activated leads to a weakening of the concept. Thirdly, in the 2001 version, the responsibility was "collective." In 2005, it is only that of the UN's through the Security Council, thus excluding any alternative – which the ICISS did not completely exclude. In practice, however the question arises, and the articles 138–139 ignore it whole-heartedly: what is to be done if the Security Council has neither the capacity nor the will to act, as is the case in Syria today? Finally, the explicit reference to Chapter 7 adds weight to the text but at the same time implies that it is not a human rights violation by a state which in itself triggers the use of force, rather the fact that it threatens peace and security.[28] This reduces the chances for these articles to be applied since they require not only a humanitarian catastrophe, but also one which is a threat to peace and security.

Welsh concludes that 'R2P as it was formulated at the Summit weakens that commitment in significant ways, contains important ambiguities and reinforces submissive deference toward the Security Council. These concessions were the price to be paid for a minimum consensus among member states'.[29] In consequence, some have described this UN version as 'R2P lite'.[30]

---

25 L. Boisson de Chazournes et L. Condorelli, "De la 'responsabilité de protéger', ou d'une nouvelle parure pour une notion déjà bien établie," *Revue générale de droit international public*, 110:1, 2006, p. 13 and O. Corten, *Le droit contre la guerre. L'interdiction du recours à la force en droit international contemporain* (Paris: Pedone, 2008), p. 777.

26 ICISS, *op. cit.*, §6.21, p. 56.

27 *A more* secure *world*: *Our shared responsibility*, UN Doc. A/59/565 (2 December 2004), §256.

28 J. Welsh, "The Responsibility to Protect: Securing the Individual in International Society," in B.J. Goold et L. Lazarus (eds.), *Security and Human Rights* (Portland: Hart Publishing, 2007), p. 379.

29 *Ibid.* p. 380.

30 T. Weiss, *Humanitarian Intervention: Ideas in Action* (Cambridge: Polity, 2007), p. 117.

4 Libya is Not Its Baptism of Fire

Contrary to another widespread assumption, the Security Council did not wait for R2P to justify military intervention on humanitarian grounds, and the intervention in Libya is not the first of its kind. The Council intervened in Somalia (res. 794 of 1992), Haiti (res. 940 of 1994), Rwanda (res. 929 of 1994), Bosnia-Herzegovina (res. 836 of 1993, 1031 of 1995, 1088 of 1996), Albania (res. 1101 of 1997) and East Timor (res. 1264 of 1999) – each time authorizing the use of 'all necessary means' to deliver humanitarian assistance, ensure the implementation of a cease-fire or a peace agreement. From this vantage point, the emergence of the R2P concept made little difference as this has been a recurring pattern for the past 20 years.[31] One finds it more recently in the cases of Ivory Coast (res. 1933 of 2010 and 1975 of 2011), where the Security Council authorized the ONUCI and the French forces to use 'all necessary measures' to protect civilians, and of course of Libya (res. 1973 of 2011).

If these post-R2P responses are the same as the pre-R2P ones, one may question what the added value of this concept is.[32] Hehir is correct in stating that 'despite the ICISS report, the 2005 World Summit Outcome Document and the 2009 General Assembly Debate, the manner in which an intra-state humanitarian crisis will be, and legally can be, dealt with today is exactly the same as was the case in 1990'.[33] However, Resolution 1973 seems unique for one particular reason: it is probably the first time that the Security Council has authorized a military intervention for humanitarian purposes without the consent of a functional state.[34] In previous cases, either the state consented, was not in existence or, if in existence, did not have a functional capacity to consent. However, from a legal perspective, though, this specificity makes no difference because the consent of the target state is indifferent to a Chapter 7 resolution.[35]

31 O. Corten and B. Delcourt, "L'intervention militaire en Libye: une avancée du droit international?" *Politique, revue de débats*, 70, 2011, pp. 5–7.

32 D. Chandler, "Understanding the Gap between the Promise and Reality of the Responsibility to Protect," in P. Cunliffe (ed.), *Critical Perspectives on the Responsibility to Protect: Interrogating theory and practice* (London: Routledge, 2011), p. 23.

33 A. Hehir, *The Responsibility to Protect*, p. 85.

34 P. Williams, "The Road to Humanitarian War in Libya," *Global Responsibility to Protect*, 3, 2011, p. 249 and A. Bellamy, "Libya and the Responsibility to Protect: The Exception and the Norm," *Ethics & International Affairs*, 25:3, 2011, p. 263.

35 S. Chesterman, "'Leading from Behind': The Responsibility to Protect, the Obama Doctrine, and Humanitarian Intervention after Libya," *Ethics & International Affairs*, 25:3, 2011, p. 280.

This fact is neglected by those who describe this resolution as historic.[36] They usually do so because they are R2P promoters and they believe that this resolution plays a role in the construction of this standard.

Much has been said that Resolution 1973 was based on R2P and even represented its 'baptism of fire'[37] and was 'a test for the doctrine'.[38] This is how it is often presented, but rarely quoted. And for good reason: the sole responsibility referred to in this resolution is the internal responsibility 'of the Libyan authorities to protect the Libyan population' (preamble), and not the external responsibility of the so-called "international community" to intervene. The part of the R2P mobilized in Resolution 1973 is that which has existed in international law since the 1948 Convention against Genocide.[39] If R2P, understood as an external accountability of the "international community," was the norm as purported by its supporters, the Security Council would have invoked it explicitly. However, it did not.

The intervention in Libya had little to do with R2P: it was rather the result of a coincidence of factors.[40] The first was the clarity of the threat. Since Rwanda, the intention to commit crimes against humanity has never been stated so clearly as when Gaddafi publicly announced that "officers have been deployed in all tribes and regions so that they can purify all decisions from these cockroaches," that "any Libyan who takes arms against Libya will be executed" and, the same day the Security Council resolution was passed, when he called his supporters to "cleanse the city of Benghazi."[41] The threat was certainly credible, given Gaddafi's record of human rights violations for decades and the fact that the violence had already created between 1000 and 10 000 victims in a few weeks. The *mens rea* is rarely so clear. The second factor was the unpredictable and precipitous nature of the abuses. Paradoxically, identified and monitored crises mobilize less action because they are less surprising. Nobody expected that mass crimes could take place in Libya in such a short time, and the Security Council voted the resolution authorizing the intervention under the pressure of an impending attack announced on Benghazi. The third factor was the

36 A. Bellamy, "Libya and the Responsibility to Protect," pp. 263–264.

37 *Le Monde*, 22 April 2011, p. 16.

38 J. Pattison, "Introduction to Roundtable: Libya, RtoP, and Humanitarian Intervention," *Ethics & International Affairs*, 25:3, 2011, p. 252.

39 *Idem* in Resolution 1996 (8 July 2011): the only "Responsibility to Protect Civilians" evoked is the one of "The Government of the Republic of South Sudan."

40 A. Bellamy, "Libya and the Responsibility to Protect: The Exception and the Norm," pp. 265–266.

41 Aljazeera, 'No Let Up in Gaddafi Offensive', 17 March 2011. http://www.aljazeera.com/news/africa/2011/03/2011317645549498.html

consensus, and in particular the support of the states of the Gulf Cooperation Council, the Organization of Islamic Cooperation and the Arab League.

The exceptional nature of the Libyan case stems from the improbability that these three factors were reunited. And even if they were to do so again, the political situation, the interests of potentially intervening states and the risks caused by the intervention would be different, and would thus motivate a different reaction, as evidenced by the Syrian case.

5 R2P is Not a Legal Norm

R2P proponents sometimes present it as a legal norm. It is increasingly rare to do this because the consensus is rather that R2P is *not* a legal norm – as the 2009 UN debate and Ban Ki-moon's preliminary report[42] showed – but it is still a widely held belief among its most zealous defenders. For instance, Ernesto Zedillo, director of the Yale Center for the Study of Globalization, termed it "a revolution in international law," when he was introducing Gareth Evans at Yale Law School in 2009.[43]

Yet, as requested by US Ambassador John Bolton, there is no legal obligation to act. If R2P was a legal concept, R2P should be understood in the light of the Articles on Responsibility of States for internationally wrongful acts (2001) and the absence of such action in the face of a responsibility would itself be illegal. This is not the case. R2P is an "obligation" without any ramifications should it not be fulfilled. That is why it cannot be characterized 'as an emerging international *legal* norm – there are no identified consequences for the failure to fulfill the R2P, by either the subject state or the P5, and there is no will to enforce commitment to it'.[44]

However, between the naive liberals labelling it a legal norm and the cynical realists not calling it a norm at all, there is an alternative route, acknowledging that R2P is not a legal norm in the strictest sense, since it imposes no binding obligation on states, but believing that the notion is not 'devoid of legal content' either.[45] While recognising that R2P 'does not impose any new obligations

42 B. Ki-Moon, Implementing the R2P: Report of the Secretary General, A/63/677, 12 January 2009.

43 Yale Law School, 20 February 2009 (this author was present).

44 A. Kapur, "'Humanity as the A and Ω of Sovereignty': Four Replies to Anne Peters," *European Journal of International Law*, 20:3, p. 562.

45 A. Bellamy et R. Reike, "The Responsibility to Protect and International Law," *Global Responsibility to Protect*, 2, 2010, p. 269.

upon states or the UN to take action in situations of humanitarian crisis' and is therefore 'not a form of law that imposes duties on subjects', Orford argues that it nevertheless 'represents one of the most significant normative shifts in international relations since the creation of the UN in 1945'.[46]

She explains that 'the vocabulary of "responsibility" works here as a language for conferring authority and allocating powers rather than as a language for imposing binding obligations and commanding obedience'.[47] But is it not, then, a diversion of the term? Why speak of 'responsibility' if it does not designate any obligation – whether it be legal or merely moral? We cannot, on one hand, use this word to give the impression that the international community has made a significant step forward in committing, in giving itself the moral obligation to intervene if necessary, and, on the other hand, devoid this word of its ordinary meaning to replace it with a vague discourse on authority. That would be falsification.

It is of course possible to recognize that R2P has a normative effect – in the sense that it is one more layer in the slow construction of an interventionist norm – but one of two changes should be made: we persist to call it "responsibility" and must then specify the nature of what is, by definition, an obligation or a duty. There is no need to be legalistic here; we may well consider a nonlegal obligation, but it must be explained. Alternatively, we devoid this concept of its meaning, claiming that it is not a discourse on obligation or duty but another entity, in which case, to be consistent, we should give up calling it "responsibility." In the meantime, we can have the impression that, as Hehir commented in another setting (the discourse of prevention in Bellamy): 'there is a desire to maintain the brand name 'responsibility to protect'/'R2P' while radically changing its content'.[48]

R2P's normative effect is well summarised by the Brazilian ambassador to the UN in 2009: R2P 'is not a principle proper, much less a novel legal prescription. Rather, it is a powerful political call for all States to abide by legal obligations already set forth in the Charter, in relevant human rights conventions and international humanitarian law and other instruments'.[49] Such a normative effect is of course limited by the diffuse nature of the obligation and of the question to know who exactly has the responsibility to protect.

46 A. Orford, *International Authority and the Responsibility to Protect* (Cambridge: Cambridge University Press, 2011), p. 25 and 41.

47 *Ibid.*, p. 26.

48 A. Hehir, "The Responsibility to Protect: 'Sound and Fury Signifying Nothing'?" *International Relations*, 24:2, 2010, p. 227.

49 Brazil, Plenary Meeting of the General Assembly on the R2P, 23 July 2009.

6 R2P is an Imperfect Duty, or Rather a Discretionary Right

In principle, a responsibility is an obligation. It does not imply that we can intervene when we see fit (the right to intervene), but that we must do so (the duty to intervene). So where does this duty lie? To begin with, it is completely absent from the 2001 report. ICISS chose the ambiguous term "responsibility" as a euphemism to avoid speaking of duty. But is it not one and the same thing? What would a responsibility to protect be, if not a duty to do so?[50] The ICISS report, whose title refers to a *Responsibility*, does not explain or justify anywhere why intervening would be an obligation rather than a simple permission, a duty rather than a right.[51]

With the exception of a minority speaking of a "duty to intervene," and those in France confusing the duty and right of "*ingérence*," most interventionists defend a right, a permission rather than an obligation. This has several advantages, including the justification of selectivity, that is being able to intervene in Kosovo but not in Chechnya, in Timor but not in Tibet, in Libya but not in Syria. If the intervention was a duty, it would be difficult to explain the reasons driving intervention in one place but not another, when two situations appear similar.

From this angle, speaking of a "responsibility to protect" is much more problematic, since it moves the debate into the field of duty. It is still possible to qualify this difficulty by using Kant's perfect and imperfect duties: some believe that the duty to intervene is perfect, that is to say really mandatory in the sense that it is forbidden not to accomplish it[52]; others that it is imperfect, that is to say desired but not required, as for example the duty of charity.

Those defending a strong duty assume that there is a legal obligation to intervene. This is false, as we have just seen. R2P is, at best, a weak duty, reduced to its meritorious dimension: accomplishing it is commendable, but not necessary because, like the Kantian duty of beneficence,[53] agents enjoy some latitude in deciding when and how performing beneficent acts – here, saving strangers.

50 D. Rodin, "The Responsibility to Protect and the Logic of Rights," in O. Jütersonke et K. Krause (eds.), *From Rights to Responsibilities: Rethinking Interventions for Humanitarian Purposes* (Geneva: Programme for Strategic and International Security Studies, 2006), p. 58.

51 K.-C. Tan, "The Duty to Protect," in T. Nardin et M.S. Williams (eds.), *Humanitarian Intervention*, Nomos XLVII (New York: New York University Press, 2006), p. 88.

52 C. Bagnoli, "Humanitarian Intervention as a Perfect Duty: a Kantian Argument," in T. Nardin et M.S. Williams (eds.), *Humanitarian Intervention*, *op. cit.*, pp. 117–140.

53 See I. Kant, *Doctrine of Virtue*, §386–394 and 448–454.

It poses a problem of enforceability, and this is precisely the reason why this imperfect duty does not scare anyone: it is a charity we can choose to give to or not, depending on the circumstances, even if we feel obliged to adopt the general principle. What states want to avoid – what they actually managed to avoid in negotiating the articles 138–139 – is a perfect duty to intervene, which therefore does not exist.

One of the reasons why the duty to intervene is only imperfect is that it is not assigned. The intervention, says Walzer, "is an imperfect duty – a duty that doesn't belong to any particular agent. Somebody ought to intervene, but no specific state in the society of states is morally bound to do so."[54] This issue of agency, that some believe "insurmountable,"[55] is serious because to be effective, to be real, a duty needs an agent. If R2P is a duty, it is a duty without an agent.

Articles 138–139, however, assign the duty to protect to the 'international community'. The problem is that it does not *really* exist. It exists only when some states decide to act on its behalf. Speaking of international community, even of United Nations, is more expressing a wish (to form a community, to be united), than describing a reality.

A duty not clearly assigned is also dangerous because it can be claimed by anyone at any time to intervene when not needed or, conversely, because it can be avoided by those who would like not to intervene when they should do so. One of the perverse effects of this diffuse responsibility is actually to encourage inaction. The corollary, from the point of view of the victims, is that they do not have a "right" to be protected and they cannot ask for help invoking an obligation of the international community.[56] R2P generates no strict duty to intervene: at best it provides a right to do so, 'a discretionary entitlement',[57] which is a 'liberty right on the part of international agencies and international states to intervene or not intervene as they see fit'.[58]

This discussion should not give the impression that I assume that a duty, a right or a norm only *exist* if they are enforceable. That would be a controversial claim, and the goal of this chapter is not to deal with such difficult metaethical

54 M. Walzer, "Preface to the Third Edition," in *Just and Unjust Wars*, 3rd ed. (New York: Basic Books, 2000), p. xiii.

55 P. Cunliffe, "A Dangerous Duty: Power, Paternalism and the Global 'Duty of Care'," in P. Cunliffe (ed.), *op. cit.*, 2011, p. 52.

56 J. Welsh and M. Banda, "International Law and the Responsibility to Protect: Clarifying or Expanding States' Responsibilities?" *Global Responsibility to Protect*, 2, 2010, p. 219.

57 F. Berman, "Moral versus Legal Legitimacy," in C. Reed and D. Ryall (eds.), *The Price of Peace* (Cambridge: Cambridge University Press), 2007, p. 161.

58 D. Rodin, "The Responsibility to Protect and the Logic of Rights," p. 57.

questions. What I rather assume, from a realist point of view in international relations theory, is not a claim about existence, but efficiency: a duty, a right or a norm are *efficient* in international relations – an anarchic environment (in the sense that there is no world government able to prevent recourse to armed violence) where actors struggle for power – only insofar as they are enforceable. Therefore, R2P may exist in the minds of many well-intentioned people, and there may be many good ethical reasons why we should feel responsible to protect others, but as long as such a responsibility has no way of being implemented, from rhetoric to action, it will stay what it is: a dead letter.

7 R2P is Not Progress, It is an Admission of Failure

R2P is nothing but a political call and, from a realist perspective, this is a great weakness since it depends entirely on the good will of states, whom do not choose to exhibit it when it is not in their interest to do so. R2P assumes that moral pressure has the ability to change the behaviour of states. A belief that may seem naive as evidenced by the numerous political calls of this kind since 1945 – particularly the vibrant slogan "never again!" – which have never been very effective. Darfur, for example, gave rise to global outrage and considerable pressure from the so-called "global civil society," in vain. That demonstrates that these efforts are insufficient to actually change the inclination of states, which primarily base their decisions to use force on considerations of national interest.

However, both of them are not necessarily incompatible, as the national interest also includes the self-image that states would prefer to project on the domestic and international scenes. This image, for reasons both identity and instrumental, can include the defence of human rights. To some extent, moral pressure has the ability to change the behaviour of states because they understand it is in their interest to appear ethical. For Aron, realism 'would be unrealistic if it considered the moral judgments men pass on the conduct of their rulers as negligible'.[59] It would be unrealistic not to take morality into account, not so much because the actors *are* really ethical than because they must *appear* so on the international stage. 'They cannot follow their interest without claiming to do so in obedience to some general scheme of values' as Niebuhr previously observed more than half a century ago.[60] However, this

59 Raymond Aron, "What Is a Theory of International Relations?" *Journal of International Affairs*, 21:2, 1967, p. 205.

60 Reinhold Niebuhr, "The Moral Issue in International Relations," in N. Guilhot (ed.), *The Invention of International Relations Theory* (New York: Columbia University Press, 2011), p. 269.

incentive is limited, as offset by other material interests (the cost of the intervention *versus* the potential gains).

The existence of R2P is precisely the evidence that states do not honour their commitments because, if they did, we would never have needed this new concept: the existing legal framework, the international human rights law, would have sufficed. For many decades, the overwhelming majority of states have already committed to protecting their people in conventions and treaties, declarations and promises. Such wishful thinking has prevented nothing, though.

The fact that it is now necessary to add an international responsibility, implicitly recognises that such an internal responsibility (that of the state towards its own population) failed. But if states are unable to protect their own people, despite their international commitments, why should we believe that in the name of another – and even less binding – international commitment they would now be able to protect people in other states?[61] This is the R2P paradox: it is based entirely on the political will, but its very existence is evidence of the lack of political will. It is therefore an admission of failure.

8 R2P is Not Immune to the Charge of Neocolonialism

As an imperfect duty, R2P is a *responsibility* without *accountability*. The intervening state under R2P is responsible without being accountable. This is the logic of paternalism.[62] And it should remind us that the best advocates of a duty to intervene were the 19th-century interventionists invoking messianic reasoning: the great powers claimed not only the right to intervene, but a duty to do so, and this responsibility was incumbent upon them because they were the only repositories of "civilization."

Use of the term "responsibility to protect" implies that some countries – incidentally the same powers that intervened in the 19th century – still feel invested with a mission, not of civilization but of rescue. The distinction may not be clear and could evoke grim memories in these potential target states. During negotiations at the 2005 World Summit, many developing countries opposed the concept precisely because of its neo-colonialist connotations.[63] During the 2009 General Assembly debate, however, the argument that R2P is a Western Trojan horse was widely rejected by the developing countries, which recognised that the principle previously in the Article 4 (h) of the Constitutive

61 A. Hehir, *The Responsibility to Protect*, pp. 144–145.

62 P. Cunliffe, "A Dangerous Duty," p. 62.

63 J. Welsh, "The Responsibility to Protect," p. 367.

Act of the African Union (2000) for instance, was not specifically Western. But the neocolonialist argument is not so much about the principle as its implementation through the use of force (military intervention).

The fact that very few states are opposed to the principle – even North Korea acknowledged that the international community had the right to 'encourage and assist sovereign States in their efforts to fulfil their responsibility to protect their own people'[64] – should not mislead us. There is indeed a global consensus, which makes R2P an emerging norm. But we need to be specific about the content of this collective belief. *What is almost universally shared is the sole principle of non-indifference*: in the cases of genocide, ethnic cleansing, crimes against humanity or war crimes, all states recognise that they must act. Not all of them accept that such action should entail military intervention – and that is the very important difference between R2P and humanitarian intervention. However, in practice, one observes that it is the same recurring powers, since the 19th century, claiming the right to intervene in always the same target states.

So herein lies another paradox: R2P was built as an alternative to the concept of humanitarian intervention, accusing it of having colonialist connotations inherited from the 19th-century interventions; and of allowing abuses, that is to say invoking humanitarian reasons only to dissimulate the national interest.

But R2P is no more impervious to abuse: the fact that it should not be exercised without the authorisation of the Security Council did not prevent Russia from using it to justify its invasion of Georgia in August 2008, claiming to prevent atrocities against South Ossetians, and France's willingness to use force to deliver humanitarian aid to Burma in May of the same year. Both argued that a military intervention was justified by R2P. Two episodes which for various reasons – one factual (Georgia did not commit mass atrocities in South Ossetia), the other of applicability (R2P does not apply to natural disasters, like cyclones) – reflect a diversion of the principle. Not only does R2P not avoid the abuses it claims to get round but as a responsibility or a duty, it also evokes nuances reminiscent of the "white man's burden" of colonization.[65]

9 Selectivity is a False Problem

The problem of selectivity, or "double standards," is based on a moral intuition, which is the most minimal principle of justice: similar cases should be treated

---

64 UN Doc A/63/PV.100, p. 17.

65 M. Ayoob, "Humanitarian Intervention and State Sovereignty," *International Journal of Human Rights*, 6:1, 2002, pp. 84–85.

similarly. Then, why Libya and not Syria? Why Kosovo and not Chechnya? The question is legitimate since, on one hand, one professes to act on behalf of a universal rule – the protection of human rights – yet on the other hand, one does not apply it universally. Are there worthy victims, who deserve to be rescued, whilst others are deemed unworthy, and thus allowed to die? How can we justify this moral asymmetry?

As valid as it may appear, the double standards critique is a false problem, arising only to those with two convictions. First, that intervention is purely humanitarian or altruistic, and second, that there is a duty, not just a right, to intervene. If intervention is not mandatory, it is selective *per se*. Intervening in Libya, for reasons that are unique to this particular situation, does not imply having to intervene in Syria or elsewhere. It is rather ironic that the same people who denounce the US, the UK, France or NATO as a "world police" also criticize these countries for intervening selectively, as if they were in charge of enforcing egalitarianism.

Also, the selectivity critique can worsen the situation. What exactly do those who are indignant over intervention in Libya and Kosovo, over Syria and Chechnya, actually propose? Probably not that we intervene everywhere, because they know there are prudential reasons not to declare war on Russia, nor to throw the entire Middle East into unrest. Do they then ask that we intervene nowhere? That out of logical consistency, we leave certain victims to die on the ground because we cannot save them all? Such a view borders on absurdity. Just because we cannot intervene everywhere, does not mean we should not intervene where it is possible to do so.

The principle of universalizability – similar cases should be treated similarly – makes perfect sense but, in this instance, how similar are the actual cases? In the words of the just war doctrine, we would have the same *just cause* to intervene, and even more incentive to do so in Syria because the number of victims and the atrocities committed are much worse than in Libya. But this criterion is not sufficient. It should be balanced against another criterion: the *likely consequences* of the intervention – because the rationale of humanitarian intervention is not for it to occur whenever it is justified, but when it can have a positive effect, or a "reasonable chance of success."

Even in these 'elementary situations' that, for Kalikowski, make inconsistency inconsistent, even in cases of 'open aggression, genocide, torture, mistreatment of the defenceless',[66] we should remain consequentialist. 'The non-perfectionist cannot escape the conclusion that circumstances may

66 Leszek Kolakowski, *Marxism and Beyond* (London: Pall Mall Press, 1969), p. 240.

justify what superficially appears to be the most despicable kinds of human conduct'.[67] This is where realism becomes tragic.[68]

Now, if we compare Libya and Syria, the different contexts in which these two conflicts are situated are reason enough to concur that the consequences of any military intervention would also differ. In Libya, the opposition had effective control over a part of the territory, while the regular army was weak, and the risk of regional escalation was almost negligible. That is not to say the intervention had no regional impact – today we understand its consequences on the Western Sahel, particularly Mali – but Libya's isolation precluded an extension of the war to neighbouring countries. In Syria, the opposite holds true: as of mid 2014, elements of the opposition are brave and getting stronger, but they still lack permanent control over important cities. More importantly, they are divided and the West is more afraid of certain of the Islamic factions than of Assad. Hence the absence of real support. The regular army, equipped with modern Russian weaponry, is strong and above all, the country's location in the heart of an explosive region renders a very high risk of conflagration.

We have prudential reasons not to intervene, because we are afraid of doing more harm than good, and this attitude is both realist and moral. It does not mean, however, that we should do nothing. We can and we should bring war to a speedier end. For the longer it lasts, the more the opposition will radicalise, and the harder it will become to handle the post-Al-Assad era. In this context of limited options, I believe the 'best moral choice that circumstances permit'[69] is to arm the rebels, back them with our special forces, and wage war by proxy.[70]

10 Conclusion: Criticising R2P Does Not Imply Renouncing Interventionism

R2P offers 'nothing new', as Francis Deng himself recognizes.[71] Its zealous proponents, talking about a new norm, need to be reminded of this, as do its

67 Arnold Wolfers, *Discord and Collaboration* (Baltimore: Johns Hopkins University Press, 1962), p. 50.

68 Toni Erskine and Richard N. Lebow (eds.), *Tragedy and International Relations* (Basingstoke: Palgrave Macmillan, 2012).

69 Arnold Wolfers, *Discord and Collaboration*, p. 50.

70 J.-B. Jeangène Vilmer, "Il faut armer les rebelles syriens," *Le Monde*, 8 December 2012, p. 15, and "Armer les rebelles syriens, un 'moindre mal' pour accélérer l'issue du conflit," *LeMonde.fr*, 29 May 2013.

71 Interview with A. Hehir, "The Responsibility to Protect and International Law," in P. Cunliffe (ed.), *op. cit.*, p. 93.

anti-interventionist critics who consider it as a new danger. R2P cannot be the 'expansion of the right of military intervention', as Jackson deplores.[72] It does not expand anything, and is merely a reminder of the law already in existence. Its recognition by the General Assembly in 2005 and 2009 was a commitment not to innovate, but to maintain the *status quo*.

A rhetorical concept,[73] it is an innovation only terminology.[74] Already in 1991, before the General Assembly, the USSR observed that reluctance towards humanitarian intervention could be removed simply by renaming it 'humanitarian solidarity'.[75] Evans criticizes the 'rarely invoked and never effectively applied' Genocide Convention for being pure rhetoric.[76] As Hehir rightly observes, one wonders why R2P, which has less legal character than the Genocide Convention, a treaty binding states, and which is less consensual on the international stage, would miraculously escape this problem.[77] A phrase without any meaningful content, chosen for its "commercial" qualities is really more deserving of the term *slogan*.[78] On the world scale, R2P is equivalent to what the *droit d'ingérence* has been on a Francophone scale: a highly marketable, but more or less meaningless concept, defended effectively by its supporters.

This is not to say that this concept has no importance at all. It has been highly effectual in changing the discourse and the perceptions. However, it has not changed state practice, because the link between discourse and practice is not yet sufficiently robust. It depends entirely on the willingness of states, since nothing will force them to intervene nor remain recalcitrant, if that is not their will or intent. It is because R2P depends on political will that it is so difficult to translate into reality.

---

72 R. Jackson, "War Perils in the Responsibility to Protect," *Global Responsibility to Protect*, 2:3, 2010, p. 315.

73 S. Chesterman, "'Leading from Behind'," *op. cit.*, p. 281.

74 L. Boisson de Chazournes and L. Condorelli, *op. cit.*, p. 13.

75 J. Chopra and T. Weiss, "Sovereignty Is No Longer Sacrosanct: Codifying Humanitarian Intervention," *Ethics & International Affairs*, 6:1, 1992, p. 108.

76 G. Evans, "From an Idea to an International Norm," in R. Cooper and J.V. Kohler (eds.), *The Responsibility to Protect: The Global Moral Compact for the XXIst Century* (Basingstoke: Palgrave Macmillan, 2009), p. 17.

77 A. Hehir, The Responsibility to Protect, *op. cit.*, p. 11.

78 F. Mégret, "La responsabilité de protéger: encore un slogan," *Le Devoir*, 27 mars 2006, p.A7; H. Hannum, "The Responsibility to Protect: Paradigm or Pastiche?" *Northern Ireland Legal Quarterly*, 60:2, 2009, p. 145; A. Hehir, *Humanitarian Intervention: An Introduction* (Basingstoke: Palgrave Macmillan, 2010), p. 219.

Because R2P has actually nothing new to offer and the language it uses is itself a problem, we can remain sceptical about it. This is why, despite the efforts of the very efficient R2P supporters, the term "humanitarian intervention" is not going away.[79] Furthermore, as aforementioned, the terms are not equivalent. As far as intervention is concerned, I prefer to call it "military intervention justified on humanitarian grounds." This way, we do not assume that the intervention *is* actually humanitarian, or even that it is "for humanitarian purposes." There is no need to be cognizant of the intentions of intervening states, and their constantly mixed motives. All we know is that it is a military intervention, and that it is justified on humanitarian grounds. This descriptive approach is more cautious.

Humanitarian intervention is ultimately nothing more than a discourse, a way of justification, what Foucault called a "regime of truth." Postmodernism is not the clearest trend in international relations theory, but if there is one point on which we must give it weight it is this: we do not have access to the world *in itself*. What we have access to has always been a *pour-soi*, a discursive construction produced by ourselves: the actors and observers. That R2P has become the main interventionist conceptual framework is the product of a misunderstanding because, as we have seen, this concept is not equivalent to that of humanitarian intervention, it is much broader and intervention is only one of the means envisaged as a last resort. Nevertheless, this assumption gives the impression that critics of R2P are necessarily anti-interventionist, while this is not the case.

The doctrinal landscape appears quite divided, but the apparently stark alternatives are not the only ones available. On one side are the proponents of R2P, which make up what Aidan Hehir rightly called 'the R2P industry [that] reached a point where it has become seemingly impossible for some to admit that the strategy has not worked'.[80] On the other hand, most critics of R2P are anti-interventionist who, either in the name of *realpolitik* or a narrow legalism, oppose the principle of military intervention in foreign territory for humanitarian reasons. Some, however, including Aidan Hehir and myself, advocate an alternative route, which criticizes the R2P without sacrificing the legitimacy of intervention in certain cases and under certain conditions.[81] In Hehir, the realist critique of R2P that I fully share is accompanied by a rather idealistic

---

79 T. Weiss, *Military-Civilian Interactions: Humanitarian Crises and the Responsibility to Protect*, 2nd ed. (Lanham: Rowman & Littlefield, 2005), p. 200.

80 A. Hehir, *The Responsibility to Protect*, p. 11.

81 See J.-B. Jeangène Vilmer, *La Guerre au nom de l'humanité. Tuer ou laisser mourir*, preface by Hubert Védrine (Paris: PUF, 2012).

ambition 'to remove, to a great if not exclusive extent, politics from the determination as to when and where to launch a humanitarian intervention'.[82] He believes that 'International law can regulate humanitarian intervention provided the legal system and its institutions are reformed'.[83] I am much less optimistic than him in this regard, but this discussion would go far beyond the scope of this chapter, which was simply to report a number of misconceptions about R2P.

82 A. Hehir, *The Responsibility to Protect*, p. 179.
83 *Ibid.*, p. 177.

CHAPTER 6

State Responsibility to Protect Deployed Servicemen: The US and Approaches to Operational Risk during the 2000s

Mark Clegg

It has been argued elsewhere that there is a perceived responsibility that liberal states take all possible measures to protect their deployed armed forces. Such responsibility has operational as well as socio-political underpinnings.[1] US doctrine defines force protection as:

> Preventive measures taken to mitigate hostile actions against Department of Defense personnel (to include family members), resources, facilities, and critical information.[2]

The US definition places force protection in the home-base context and seemingly assumes a reactive stance to threats such as anti-terrorism. This is perhaps a reflection of recent events in the US regarding terror attacks on US soil. It may highlight that the protection of deployed forces is gained through proactive measures, which are part of other operational missions.

This paper will argue that the US approach to force protection during the 2000s was distinctly different from the one adopted during the Kosovo intervention in 1999. Shunning the characteristic casualty aversion, the US adopted force protection strategies which appeared to embrace risk in pursuit of mission accomplishment. In so doing, this period highlighted a watershed in US approaches to risk to personnel during military operations. It also demonstrated a re-evaluation of the traditional paradigm of force protection. Importantly, it did not show a US Administration that was disinterested in its responsibility to protect deployed servicemen and women; rather, it illustrated a revision of traditional approaches to that force protection. Of crucial importance in any such analysis of events is the contextual backdrop that

1 M. Clegg, 'Force Protection and Society', *Defense & Security Analysis*, Vol 28, No 2, June 2012, pp. 132–134; see also P Cornish, 'Myth and Reality: US and UK Approaches to Casualty Aversion and Force Protection', *Defence Studies*, Vol 3, No 2, Summer 2003.

2 Joint Publication 3-0, *Joint Operations*, 11 August 2011, http://www.dtic.mil/doctrine/new_pubs/jp3_0.pdf accessed 27 February 2012

 | DOI 10.1163/9789004280380_007

precipitated such a change. Moreover, this chapter will assess shifts in force protection from a holistic viewpoint which acknowledges political as well as military evolutions. The period that this study covers coincides with the early years of the Obama Administration. Consequently, it draws upon his influence as well his relationships with senior military decision makers of that era. It will include Obama's announcements regarding force protection amidst an increasingly interested domestic audience. Additionally, it will discuss the direction and guidance of his most senior generals. All of this speaks to the broader debate over the proper understanding of Responsibility to Protect doctrine since, of course, those who serve in the military are human beings worthy of protection. Additionally, the shift noted above of military members taking on additional risk to themselves in order to better protect civilians in the theatre of operations (and thereby better accomplish their COIN mission objectives), speaks directly to the moral tension at the heart of Responsibility to Protect and the accompanying political difficulties.

Obama and the US Aversion to Failure

President Barrack Obama was inaugurated on 20 January 2009. Within days of taking office, hopes that Obama would be able to drive a successful conclusion in Afghanistan were already looking pessimistic. Indeed, a Newsweek report drawing an analogy with Vietnam argued that, 'while 71% of [US] people believe that Obama can turn around the cratering economy, only 48% think he can make progress in Afghanistan'.[3] The context within which the new Commander-in-Chief faced this 'war of necessity' was profound and looked set to be one of his main challenges and the approach that he took towards the war, including his handling of force protection issues, would likely define his success or otherwise. The shift in strategic culture with regard to force protection, which had occurred in Iraq, had been steered by Bush and so might have been perceived as a characteristic of a Republican president. By contrast, Obama's most recent Democrat predecessor, President Clinton, offered a wholly different way of approaching the issue of protecting deployed US servicemen. Clinton famously held the monopoly on force protection decision making during the build-up and conduct of Operation Allied Force; a situation that dictated NATO strategy in Kosovo. Nevertheless, although decried by

3 J. Barry & E. Thomas, 'Obama's Vietnam', *Newsweek*, 30 January 2009, http://www.newsweek.com/could-afghanistan-be-obamas-vietnam-77749 accessed 27 February 2012

some, it reflected the perceived political context of the era and was embraced by Generals and public alike.

Compounding the issue further, Obama faced a difficult task as, up until the end of 2008, 630 US troops had already lost their lives on operations in Afghanistan.[4] Some observers argued that the 'stigma' of the on-going US commitment in Iraq with its widely-debated fluctuating levels of public support might have been expected to impact on public support for the war in Afghanistan. Furthermore, with the advent of a US president who had opposed the invasion of Iraq, some might have expected comparatively high levels of support for US troops in Afghanistan. However, Miller posited that the US public appeared to be 'judging the Afghanistan war on its own merits'.[5] Regardless, the newly elected president would be expected to approach decisions surrounding force protection as a reflection of his readings of recent US experiences.

As 2009 progressed many continued to question the US commitment in Afghanistan. One poll reported that only 32 per cent of respondents favoured increasing the number of US troops exposed to the dangers of fighting in Afghanistan. Analysts described the current strategy as promising 'more bloodshed in the short run in exchange for a chance of stability in the long term. That is hardly a combination that will appeal to voters, so it will be hard to sustain political support for it for long enough to make it work'.[6] The scene appeared to be evolving into one that was tragically familiar for earlier US presidents; one that saw domestic pressure build in the face of rising casualties.

Force Protection, Politics and Strategy

President Obama had taken over as Commander in Chief following a great deal of revision in the US military. The difficult years of fighting insurgents in Iraq as well as Afghanistan so far had drawn out an impressive ability for the US armed forces to 'learn in contact'. One particularly relevant evolution in this area was US counterinsurgency (COIN) doctrine. Field Manual 3-24 (FM 3-24),

4 'Coalition Deaths by Year – US', http://icasualties.org/OEF/ByYear.aspx accessed 27 February 2012

5 C.A. Miller, 'Endgame for the West in Afghanistan? Explaining the Decline in Support for the War in Afghanistan in the United States, Great Britain, Canada, Australia, France and Germany', *The Letort Papers* (US Army War College, Strategic Studies Institute, Carlisle, June 2010), p. 7.

6 'A War of Necessity?' *The Economist*, 22 August 2009, p. 22.

simply entitled 'Counterinsurgency'[7] and often referred to as the Petraeus doctrine, was widely regarded as a key element of the US progression towards success in Iraq. It dealt with drawing upon and communicating some of history's forgotten lessons regarding how to deal with this difficult dimension of warfare. It recommended a departure from traditional US strategic cultural characteristics of reliance of firepower and technology to overwhelm the enemy. Sometimes labelled as Weinberger and/or Powell doctrine[8] such a heavy-handed approach was increasingly interpreted as an ill fit for the nuances of COIN. Instead, a closer interaction with civilians in pursuit of winning hearts and minds was recommended. The publication contained some 'paradoxical' guidance for commanders seeking force protection during COIN operations. 'Sometimes, the more you protect the force, the less secure you may be' was one strand of guidance that centred upon an acceptance of risk and a focus of close integration with the population. Fundamentally, presence and interaction to win the confidence and support of Afghan civilians, rather than firepower, armour and distance to defeat insurgents, was the prescription for achieving a safer environment for US COIN troops. As such, debate regarding how to succeed in COIN was inextricably linked with force protection considerations.[9]

Obama had launched a review of the way forward in Afghanistan as soon as he took office. However, many became restless with the amount of time that Obama's review appeared to be taking. Some interpreted this as an indecisiveness that exposed deployed US forces to insurgent attacks in order to allow leisurely thinking time in Washington. Domestic cross-party political pressure to protect the welfare of US servicemen was characteristically strong. However,

---

7 FM 3-24 (MCWP 3-33.5) Counterinsurgency (December 2006, Headquarters Department of the Army), http://www.fas.org/irp/doddir/army/fm3-24.pdf

8 J. Record, 'Back to the Weinberger-Powell Doctrine', *Strategic Studies Quarterly*, Fall 2007.

9 FM 3-24 (MCWP 3-33.5) Counterinsurgency, December 2006, Headquarters Department of the Army, http://www.fas.org/irp/doddir/army/fm3-24.pdf; see also D. Kilcullen, *The Accidental Guerrilla* (Hurst and Company, London, 2009). Note: for comprehensive analysis of the US COIN evolution see K.I. Sepp, 'From 'Shock and awe' to 'Hearts and Minds': The Fall and Rise of US Counterinsurgency in Iraq,' *Third World Quarterly*, Vol 28, No 2, 2007 and D.H. Ucko, *The New Counterinsurgency Era* (Georgetown University Press, Washington DC, 2009). Note: for criticisms of the US 'way in war' from a force protection perspective see N. Aylwin-Foster, 'Changing the Army for Counterinsurgency Operations', *Military Review*, November–December 2005; R.A. Lacquement Jr, 'The Casualty Aversion Myth', *Naval War College Review*, Vol 57, No 1, Winter 2004, J. Record, 'Force Protection Fetishism: Sources, Consequences and Solutions', *Aerospace Power Journal*, Summer 2000 and J. Record, 'The American Way of War: Cultural Barriers to Successful Counterinsurgency', US *Air War College*, No 577, 1 September 2006.

the President told US forces that his extensive deliberations were not designed to endanger them in the meantime; rather it was precisely the depth of his analysis which would result in 'the strategy and the clear mission you deserve. We will give you the equipment and support that you need to get the job done. And that includes the public support back home. That is a promise that I make to you'.[10] Such comments indicated that the new president was certainly conscious of the central role of domestic public opinion in successful operations. Indeed, Obama had the 'benefit' of having witnessed, and opposed, his predecessor at work during the build-up and conduct of operations in Iraq. Obama was conditioned by the force protection debates of his journey to the White House.

Observers predicted that, whatever the eventual revised plan for Afghanistan, Congress would be likely to grant its approval. This was due to overall Republican support for the war, complemented by Democrat support for the President.[11] Rather than the cross party friction which had dogged his predecessor, Obama appeared to be benefitting from the political landscape which his early presidency offered. However, it was the shape of his actual plan for reinforcing force levels in Afghanistan that worried some. With a number of reported recommendations from his most senior commanders in theatre to increase troops by anywhere between 10,000 and 60,000 personnel, some predicted that Obama would be tempted, but wrong, to show compromise and aim towards the lower figure.[12] These predictions were confirmed towards the end of 2009. Almost a year after taking office, Obama travelled to West Point to deliver an address which focused upon the challenge facing the US military in Afghanistan. Within his speech Obama emphasised his eagerness to do everything possible to support military personnel deployed to Afghanistan. He explained that as a result of a comprehensive strategy review he had made the decision to increase the US troop commitment to theatre by a further 30,000 personnel.[13] This figure illustrated an inconsistency with his predecessor. While Bush had surprised many by deciding against the majority to reinforce US troops by more than expected, Obama had opted for a more conservative reinforcement which appeared more focused upon hitting the political middle ground than achieving mission success. Hence, despite rising casualty figures

10 'Waiting (and Waiting) for a Plan', *The Economist*, 21 November 2009, p. 54.

11 'Waiting (and Waiting) for a Plan', *The Economist*, 21 November 2009, p. 54.

12 'Obama's War', *The Economist*, 17 October 2009, p. 14.

13 'Remarks by the President in Address to the Nation on the Way Forward in Afghanistan and Pakistan', 1 December 2009, http://www.whitehouse.gov/the-press-office/remarks-president-address-nation-way-forward-afghanistan-and-pakistan accessed 27 February 2012

and increasing criticism it cannot be argued that Obama was predisposed with force protection concerns. Indeed, he claimed no link between increased force levels and increased security for deployed US forces.

However, there was considerable external critique of the plan partly because it included caveats that set timetables for the start of the withdrawal of US forces during 2011. Some described Obama's announcement as an example of how the new President was finding it difficult to adjust 'from campaigning [for office] – which involves promising people lots of good things – to governing… and in trying to please everyone, he has pleased hardly anyone', according to *The Economist*.[14] Observers rushed to criticise Obama for approaching the issue of timeframes in a political rather than purely operational manner. Some argued that his speech should have been less *politician* and more 'commander-in-chief focused single-mindedly on winning a bloody conflict'.[15] While this was a rather simplistic and fundamentally flawed statement coming from otherwise credible analysts, it did indicate the considerable international and domestic focus that existed on the most sensitive of issues. This reaction also highlighted how many had become conditioned by the strategic cultural context that was the legacy of Bush. Although Bush had been replaced for some time and although the theatre in question was a different one, observers criticised Obama from a reference point which appeared more fitting to the Bush era. Nevertheless, some pollsters did conclude that Obama's decision had managed to gain the majority, however slim, of both Republican and Democrat support. Consequently, and of considerable significance, the US polity was more unified at this period than it had been since 9/11.[16] This was particularly poignant when examined against the casualty backdrop of that period. Deaths of US troops in Afghanistan in 2009 had spiked to 310, a significant increase more than doubling the 153 US deaths suffered during the previous year.[17] Although Obama may have made his decision with such figures in mind, his announcement did not contain any overt sign of force protectionism; it appeared wholly focused upon mission success and domestic political unity.

---

14 'Obama the Worried Warrior', *The Economist*, 5 December 2009, p. 54.

15 'The Perils of Keeping Everybody Happy', *The Economist*, 5 December 2009, p. 14.

16 F. Newport, 'Obama's Plan for Afghanistan Finds Bipartisan Support', http://www.gallup.com/poll/124562/Obama-Plan-Afghanistan-Finds-Bipartisan-Support.aspx, 3 December 2009 accessed 27 February 2012

17 'Coalition Deaths by Year – US', http://icasualties.org/OEF/ByYear.aspx accessed 27 February 2012

Communicating an Approach to Risk

Some within the US military during 2009 showed signs of unrest regarding the emphasis that they felt was being placed on force protection at the tactical level in Afghanistan. One junior commander wrote:

> The current Marine Corps policy on the wear of body armor and Personal Protective Equipment (PPE)...is highly restrictive, lacks common sense, and stands in contrast to the Marine Corps warfighting doctrine of Maneuver Warfare...[C]ommanders at the battalion level should be afforded the opportunity to determine what constitutes PPE and provide the authority and autonomy to dictate their own prescribed PPE load based on a solid estimate of the situation, historical precedence, individual experience and expertise.[18]

This provided a useful example of the tension between policy and doctrine as well as between interpretation of the former and application of the latter. Such a strongly-worded condemnation of current policy indicated that some still felt that the US military was over-focused upon force protection issues. This was quite surprising considering the efforts made by the Petraeus team and the majority of comments made by senior commanders in Iraq and therefore could be treated as important but nonetheless the minority view. A more representative view of strategic attitudes to force protection in the US forces was demonstrated by its most senior commander in theatre. General Stanley McChrystal assumed command of ISAF and US forces in June 2009. Importantly, many of the issues which appeared to trouble McChrystal were related to force protection and its relationship with the traditionally accepted levels of war. McChrystal sent a report on progress so far to Secretary of Defense Gates early on following taking command of US and ISAF troops. In the report, which was subsequently leaked to the press, McChrystal described how:

> Preoccupied with protection of our own forces, we have operated in a manner that distances us – physically and psychologically – from the people we seek to protect...the insurgents cannot defeat us militarily, but we can defeat ourselves. [US and ISAF troops should spend] as little time as possible in armoured vehicles or behind the walls of forward operating

---

18 M. Kutilek, 'Maneuver Warfare: Afghanistan and the Combat Load', 20 February 2009, http://www.dtic.mil/cgi-bin/GetTRDoc?Location=U2&doc=GetTRDoc.pdf&AD=ADA510886 accessed 27 February 2012

> bases…[it is] realistic to expect that Afghan and coalition casualties will increase.[19]

McChrystal's report contained echoes of FM 3-24 and the COIN debate since 2001. It was clear that he, with his recent experience fighting insurgents in Iraq, was of the same mind-set as Petraeus and would likely approach his task in a similar manner. However, McChrystal's report did highlight that, as late as 2009, senior US commanders were preaching the accepted wisdom regarding the relationship between COIN and force protection. Having already been driven and implemented by Petraeus in Iraq, formal US doctrine had to be reissued to commanders in Afghanistan. Nevertheless, population-centric approaches to force protection remained a prominent characteristic of the reformed US strategic culture and as such remained foremost in formal orders. McChrystal quickly released his own 'Tactical Directive', which focused upon the challenge facing commanders in theatre and how they were to handle the task of protecting their own personnel.

> I recognise that the carefully controlled and disciplined employment of force entails risks to our troops – and we must work to mitigate that risk wherever possible. But excessive use of force resulting in an alienated population will produce far greater risks. We must understand this reality at every level in our force.
>
> I expect leaders at all levels to scrutinize and limit the use of force like close air support (CAS) against residential compounds and other locations likely to produce civilian casualties in accordance with this guidance. Commanders must weigh the gain of using CAS against the cost of civilian casualties, which in the long run make mission success more difficult and turn the Afghan people against us.
>
> I cannot prescribe the appropriate use of force for every condition that a complex battlefield will produce, so I expect our force to internalize and operate in accordance with my intent. Following this intent requires a cultural shift within our forces – and complete understanding at every level – down to the most junior soldiers. I expect leaders to ensure this is clearly communicated and continually reinforced.
>
> This directive does not prevent commanders from protecting the lives of their men and women as a matter of self-defense where it is

---

19 D. Nasaw & P. Walker, 'White House Says No Decision on More Troops for Afghanistan', 21 September 2009, http://www.theguardian.com/world/2009/sep/21/nato-afghanistan-mission-failure-warning accessed 27 February 2012

> determined no other options are available to effectively counter the threat.[20]

McChrystal's directive, drawing out in some detail his desire for a courageous restraint approach to force protection, was telling on a number of levels. First, and perhaps most importantly, it was entirely grounded in the Afghan context. It reflected only the mission in Afghanistan where the protection of US forces was one element of the dimension to achieve success in theatre. It made no mention, nor did it indicate concern for, the US domestic context. By contrast, while senior British officers were telling UK troops that such wars were to be won or lost in the public perception at *home*, McChrystal exhibited sole focus on Afghans. This was, and is, not the same as concluding that McChrystal was ignorant or had little concern for the impact of casualties on domestic opinion; however, it does indicate that such issues were absent from his orders to his field commanders. McChrystal also focused his directive on tactical decision-making and how commanders at the junior level were to play crucial roles in making force protection decisions whilst minded of his intent. Perhaps surprisingly, he prescribed a 'cultural shift', indicating that, in his opinion, such a shift had not yet occurred despite well-publicised developments in how US forces had operated in Iraq.[21] Again, this highlighted that US strategic cultural attitudes, particularly pertaining to force protection, which had evolved in Iraq but not been reflected by troops and commanders in Afghanistan. When articulating the need for understanding of his intent 'at every level' one must only assume that, again, he is referring to the tactical and operational levels rather than upwards in his own chain of command. Offering no indication of domestic political sensitivity, McChrystal's directive dealt with force protection as a tactical risk management process; a process which was to be managed by low-level commanders empowered with his intent and focused solely on the Afghan context. In his mind, US strategic cultural attitudes to the protection of forces were grounded in accepting risk in pursuit of securing the support of the civilian population.

In a speech to the International Institute of Strategic Studies, McChrystal, continuing this courageous restraint theme, centred on how protecting US and

20 Headquarters, International Assistance Force, Kabul, Afghanistan, 'Tactical Directive', 6 July 2009, http://www.nato.int/isaf/docu/official_texts/Tactical_Directive_090706.pdf accessed 27 February 2012

21 For a comprehensive analysis of US COIN developments during this period see, D.H. Ucko, *The New Counterinsurgency Era* (Washington DC: Georgetown University Press, 2009).

ISAF troops by using excessive kinetic power against insurgents had strong potential to undermine strategic objectives. Moreover, he explained that all such offensive action sent messages to the Afghan population, which simply reinforced insurgent propaganda campaigns. McChrystal saw the Western difficulty with understanding this complexity as grounded in its cultural understanding of war:

> Whether or not we like it, we have a conventional warfare culture – not just our militaries but our societies. Our societies want to see lines on a map moving forwards towards objectives, but you will not see that in a counterinsurgency because you do not see as clearly what is happening in people's minds. We will have to do things dramatically and even uncomfortably differently in order to change how we think and operate.[22]

McChrystal perceived a strong connection between tactical military activity on the ground and its strategic consequences in the attitudes and behaviour of the Afghan people. However, these quotes emphasised that while the General was conscious of the relationship between excessive force protection and the *Afghan* people, he was less concerned with the relationship between the impact of reducing protection and maintaining his own *domestic* public support. Importantly, his comments also illustrated how strategic cultures, like all cultures, tend to evolve gradually, rather than change 'overnight'. Furthermore, members of the same strategic community usually evolve at different paces since they perceive experiences from different perspectives. Interestingly, during October 2009, US political figures appeared to be unsure as to whether or where McChrystal had drawn the line in preventing the use of kinetic power for force protection tasks. Defense Secretary Robert Gates was clear that in his own view 'we will continue to use air power to defend our own troops'. However, he was far less certain about how the senior US general in Afghanistan assessed the same issue as he stated, 'where I think General McChrystal has drawn a line is in using air power in offensive operations'.[23] It was clear that the idea of employing courageous restraint was one of considerable political interest and sensitivity. Nevertheless, while Gates appeared to be more willing to employ force to protect US servicemen than his most senior commander in theatre,

---

22 General S.A. McChrystal, 'Commander, ISAF and Commander US Forces Afghanistan – Special Address', 1 October 2009, http://www.voltairenet.org/article162541.html accessed 27 February 2012

23 'Obama to Increase Troops in Afghanistan by 30,000', *Foreign Policy Bulletin*, March 2010, p. 12.

Gates could not have been accused of being overly focused on force protection above all else. When asked in November 2009 what impact the growing improvised explosive device (IED) threat had made on the decision to send 30,000 extra US forces to Afghanistan, Gates was to the point, stating that 'it was not a significant factor'.[24]

Further inconsistencies in US civil military relations were evident as McChrystal identified that Obama's agreement to uplift force levels in theatre had been accompanied with the news that the US would start to withdraw troops during 2011. The General explained to news reporters that such an announcement had potential to signal a lack of commitment.[25] In contrast, some commentators assessed this apparent contradiction as an attempt to 'strike a balance between assuring Americans that their troops would not remain indefinitely and telling Afghans the US would not cut and run'.[26] Nevertheless, despite such irregularities in official texts from senior US figures, there was no outward sign that force protection was the prominent discussion driving the conduct of the Afghan campaign from a US perspective. Force protection was being mentioned, but in the context of how it was to be achieved as a secondary factor to protecting Afghan civilians. The US domestic dimension received little emphasis.

Managing the Consequences of the US Approach

The threat context facing US forces evolved significantly during this period. During 2009 the ways in which US troops were being killed began to change notably. Although there was a significant overall increase, when broken down into attack method the figures indicated a shift in insurgent tactics. Less than 45 per cent of US deaths were attributable to IED attacks (down from more than 54 per cent) whilst the number of US troops killed by mortar, rockets or rocket propelled grenades increased by nearly a third on the previous year's figures.[27] One of the reasons for this shift may have been insurgent adjustments to a more restrained US troop presence. McChrystal's directives to

24 *Ibid.*, pp. 19–20.

25 G. Whittell, 'Opposing Forces Stand Shoulder to Shoulder Over a Critical 18 Months', *The Times*, 9 December 2009, p. 46.

26 A. Spillius & B. Farmer, 'Obama Gambles on Finding the US a Way Out of Afghanistan', *The Daily Telegraph*, 2 December 2009, p. 16.

27 I.S. Livingstone & M.O. 'Hanlon, 'Afghanistan Index', 31 October 2011, http://www.brookings.edu/~/media/Files/Programs/FP/afghanistan%20index/index.pdf accessed 27 February 2012; IED attacks 2008 84; 2009 142; mortar, rocket & RPG attacks 2008 7; 2009 21.

reduce heavy-handed responses to insurgent attacks appeared to be being obeyed with a 50 per cent decrease in the use of CAS during fire fights.[28] Confident that US forces would not engage in fighting as an early option, in line with McChrystal's directive, for fear of strategic consequence, insurgents may have opted to use direct fire weapons in place of less risky IED attacks. However, the tragic irony was that the adjustment in approach to force protection prescribed to secure the Afghan population above all else actually resulted in a deteriorating security environment. One 2009 report highlighted that 2,412 Afghan civilians had been killed, an increase of almost 300 since the previous year.[29] Although such figures cannot be directly attributed to US or ISAF military actions the overall direction of creating a safer environment for civilians to inhabit appeared some way off. Nevertheless, McChrystal released further guidance on training for COIN operations to commanders, which highlighted a number of issues of particular concern. Most important in countering threats was a need to remain agile to insurgent as well as ISAF tactics, techniques and procedures.[30] McChrystal was wholly engaged in the intellectual debate surrounding COIN and the specific challenges being faced in Afghanistan.

As 2010 progressed, Obama was criticised over his backing for McChrystal's directive to ISAF troops to engage in courageous restraint. This notion, although an extension of the FM 3-24 idea of exposing troops to greater risk in pursuit of longer-term safety, had gained growing public interest. The domestic context appeared to be changing for the worse for the President. Obama told reporters,

> Our troops put themselves at risk oftentimes in order to reduce civilian casualties… They will take a chance, often, in the field of battle where they are trying to deal with uncertain information and they're not sure whether that's an attack coming or not, or which house these shots are being fired from, and because of General McChrystal's direction, oftentimes they're holding fire, they're hesitating, they're being cautious about how they operate even though it would be safer for them to go ahead and take these locations out.[31]

---

28 'Into Taliban Country', *The Economist*, 11 July 2009, pp. 53–54.

29 S.G. Chesser, 'Afghanistan Casualties: Military Forces and Civilians', Congressional Research Service, 6 December 2012, http://www.fas.org/sgp/crs/natsec/R41084.pdf accessed 27 February 2012

30 General S.A. McChrystal, 'COMISAF/USFOR-A Counterinsurgency (COIN) Training Guidance', 10 November 2009, http://usacac.army.mil/cac2/AIWFC/COIN/repository/COMISAF_COIN_Training_Guidance.pdf accessed 27 February 2012

31 B. Montopoli, 'Obama: I Am Accountable for Afghan Civilian Casualties', 12 May 2010, http://www.cbsnews.com/8301-503544_162-20004790-503544.html accessed 27 February 2012

Obama's comments indicated that he fully supported McChrystal and the notion of accepting risk for the sake of longer-term security. The Commander-in-Chief and his most senior military officer appeared to be completely in tune with each other's thoughts regarding the weight of emphasis that was to be placed upon protecting the lives of deployed US servicemen. Set against a difficult backdrop of 'learning in contact' the US strategic cultural position on force protection had evolved significantly and was being defended by US leaders in and out of uniform. Indeed, Obama showed no outward sign of mirroring his Democrat predecessor, Clinton. Nevertheless, the reaction among some US politicians to the 'courageous restraint' mantra was that, whilst it was ostensibly linked to eventual protection of US civilians on home soil, it did so by endangering other US citizens in uniform on operations. Republican Walter Jones told one newspaper journalist, 'You see these kids with their legs blown off and you just hope they were given a chance…[current rules of engagement] are too restricted. …If youre going to send the US military to fight, then let them fight'.[32] Just as the comments above from the US Marine Corps captain were at odds with his senior officer, similar outliers, inconsistencies and frictions remained among the US political divide. They served to complicate the domestic political context but not to such a level whereby force protection assumed the spotlight in discussions regarding progress in Afghanistan.

Additionally, there emerged a growing voice of concern among some in the US military that too much focus was being placed on Afghan safety at the expense of US troop safety; the balanced had tipped too far for some. Many perceived that the appetite to expose US servicemen to hostile action and to restrict the measures that troops had at their disposal when threatened by insurgents had gone too far.[33] Additionally, and tainting his success somewhat, during his tenure as commander, McChrystal had lost 448 US men and women with the month of his departure witnessing 60 US deaths, the worst month for losses yet.[34] US public support for the Afghan commitment was reported by some as showing signs of fragility during this period. Fifty-eight per cent of respondents supported Obama's plan to commence the withdrawal of all US troops from July 2011. However, and equally telling, 38 per cent of those

32 R. Burns & A. Flaherty, 'US War Aim: Protect Civilians First, then Troops', 13 May 2010, http://www.boston.com/news/nation/washington/articles/2010/05/13/us_war_aim_protect_civilians_first_then_troops/ accessed 27 February 2012

33 R.H. Reid, 'Petraeus to Face Soldier Complaints Over War Rules', 25 June 2010, http://www.businessweek.com/ap/financialnews/D9GIEV3G0.htm accessed 27 February 2012

34 'Coalition Deaths by Year – US', http://icasualties.org/OEF/ByYear.aspx accessed 27 February 2012

questioned rejected any setting of timetables for withdrawal at all.[35] This indicated a robust domestic support base behind the US military and also an acceptance of the way US troops were seemingly taking losses whilst employing an approach to force protection which increased their own vulnerability for the sake of the security of Afghan civilians. The poll majority view to withdraw to strict timelines did not signal a public aversion to the steadily mounting US military casualty statistics according to some; neither did it illustrate a civilian groundswell in reaction to the military's approach to force protection at the time. Rather, Miller argued, it drew attention only because US public support for the Afghan war had started off at such a high level.[36]

The relationship between McChrystal and the White House deteriorated during this period. Ultimately, comments made during the widely publicized '*Rolling Stone*' magazine interview[37] brought to an end the tenure of McChrystal. This was seen as too public a strain to exist between McChrystal and the President. Some observers argued that Obama should have ignored the article, as the task in Afghanistan was far more important. They reasoned that a sound commander at the helm of US forces was a more pressing priority than US concerns regarding civil-military relations.[38] Nevertheless, on announcing the replacement of McChrystal, Obama displayed no sign that changes were afoot regarding how US troops were to be protected on operations. 'Let me say to the American people, this is a change in personnel but it is not a change in policy. General Petraeus fully participated in our review last fall, and he both supported and helped design the strategy that we have in place'.[39] This reinforced the character of the evolving US strategic culture; its attitudes towards force protection were not linked to McChrystal, but to its way in the warfare of the new era. Interestingly, the dominant call to review the US approach to force protection came from foreign media. Illustrating a profound exchange of standpoint on the issue of accepting risk to troops for the sake of the mission, while the British media questioned whether the notion of 'courageous restraint' should be subjected to detailed review, Obama and the American public

---

35 J.M. Jones, 'Majority of Americans Favour Obama's Afghanistan Timetable', http://www.gallup.com/poll/141068/majority-americans-favor-obama-afghanistan-timetable.aspx 29 June 2010 accessed 27 February 2012

36 Miller, 2010, p. 11.

37 M. Hastings, 'The Runaway General', 22 June 2010, http://www.rollingstone.com/politics/news/the-runaway-general-20100622 accessed 27 February 2012

38 'General Failure', *The Times*, 24 June 2010, p. 2.

39 'President Obama on Afghanistan, General McChrystal & General Petraeus', 23 June 2010, http://www.whitehouse.gov/blog/2010/06/23/president-obama-afghanistan-general-mcchrystal-general-petraeus accessed 27 February 2012

appeared to show no significant signs of concern on the matter.[40] Such reports possibly said as much about UK strategic culture as it did about the US.[41]

Conclusion

US strategic cultural attitudes towards force protection during this period were robust and unified. While Obama and McChrystal ended their professional relationship over very public and difficult circumstances, their approach to the protection of deployed US servicemen was not the cause of such tensions. This was particularly significant as, during their shared tenure, US casualty figures in Afghanistan climbed sharply. Obama attracted widespread criticism for handling the decision to reinforce US forces in theatre with an attached timetable for withdrawal; critics labelled his approach as playing domestic politics at the expense of Afghan civilians. However, if such accusations were justified, the President would surely not have stood by as his senior military commander issued formal directives which had clear instructions for US troops to strip back force protection measures in pursuit of greater security for Afghan civilians. Equipment, vehicles and overwhelming fire support from the air, previously trademarks of the traditional US military advantage, were all substituted for closer interaction with Afghan civilians; above all, 'courageous restraint' was to be employed in order to avoid any unnecessary Afghan deaths. McChrystal's explicit predictions that his strategy would result in further US military deaths were found to be true and were accompanied by reductions in US public support for the Afghan war. However, and crucially, there was a significant shift from the way the US had dealt with the protection of its service personnel during the wars preceding Iraq. Obama approached force protection in a way that was far closer to that of Bush rather than to Clinton, proving that political background was subservient to the evolution of strategic culture. Although some of the shifts that had occurred under Petraeus in Iraq had to be re-emphasised and doctrine restated, US strategic culture had clearly undergone a considerable evolution by 2010.

40 T. Harding, 'Courageous Restraint Putting Troops' Lives at Risk', 6 July 2010, http://www.telegraph.co.uk/news/worldnews/asia/afghanistan/7874950/Courageous-restraint-putting-troops-lives-at-risk.html accessed 27 February 2012

41 See M. Clegg, 'Protecting British Soldiers in Afghanistan: UK Strategic Culture and the Politicisation of Force Protection', *The RUSI Journal*, Vol 157, No 2, June 2012.

CHAPTER 7

Military Medical Personnel: A Unique Responsibility to Protect

Anthony Dew and Don Carrick

Military Medical Personnel ('MMP') present a unique dilemma – they are deployed to the front line in order to save life and so find themselves alongside other soldiers who are engaged in fighting the enemy and yet they are non-combatants, afforded their status in the very first Geneva Convention, as envisaged by Henry Dunant after the battle of Solferino. This non-combatant status is based on the way they are supposed to be employed, so it is essential that they only be employed in ways that maintain such status. Modern warfare has blurred front lines at the same time as modern military medicine, in order to maximize survival rates, has pushed the provision of medical care as close to the point that wounds are received as possible, and consequently, close to, if not in the actual fighting itself. They are no longer a separate supporting role, but rather an integral part of the combat effectiveness of a military unit in combat. At the same time, some enemy combatants, such as the Taliban appear to be deliberately targeting MMP. Is this merely seeking to undermine the morale of opposing forces by carrying out prohibited attacks, or, in the current operating environment, is this actually a legitimate tactic to degrade the military effectiveness of the units they are seeking to challenge? This chapter will look at the background of the protected status of MMP, the legal and moral basis of it, and the changes in the modern battlefield that threaten it.

The Historical Background

In 1859 Henri Dunant witnessed the results of a battle that left tens of thousands of men dead and wounded. The Battle of Solferino of June 24, 1859 was fought between the Austrians and French and was one of the bloodiest battles of the nineteenth century. The wounded received almost no medical attention. In response to what he witnessed, Dunant established the Red Cross movement. His work led to the First Geneva Convention of 1864 which established the responsibility of the Armed Forces of the signatory countries to provide medical care to both (or all) sides of the conflict, dependent only on their medical need and protected from attack by an emblem that was the reverse of the

 | DOI 10.1163/9789004280380_008

Swiss flag – a red cross on a white background. This sign or emblem was to indicate protection under International Humanitarian Law (IHL) for all medical services of the Armed Forces, volunteer workers and victims of conflict.[1]

This protection has worked well in conventional conflict, but since the Second World War the number of state-on-state conflicts has declined and a phenomenon of intra-state conflicts has emerged, in which non-state actors predominate and the dominant mode of warfare is guerrilla or irregular. This type of conflict has been variously described as 'new war', 'low intensity conflict' and 'war amongst the people': it is the latter description that we will adopt in this chapter because it best captures the typical characteristic of such conflicts, namely that they tend to be fought either literally 'amongst the people' in civilian population centres or figuratively through the media in people's homes.[2] In addition, they are typically accompanied by an increase in the number of non-state actors involved and in the number and variety of asymmetric methods of warfare employed by them. In this new form of war the primary aim is often to control the population by using terror as a tactic: as a result, non-combatants and civilians have become the targets. Behaviour banned under IHL has become an inherent part of the strategy of this type of warfare in which non-state actors or insurgents with a globalised cause use guerrilla tactics against conventional – usually western – forces, aiming for an asymmetric advantage. This shift has also been accompanied by a proliferation in the number and scope of humanitarian organisations that are on the battlefield, with the accompanying challenge of identifying representatives of the parties and in negotiating consent-based access to the war zone.[3] As a result, the spectacle of huge field armies confronting each other in set-piece battles has probably disappeared for the foreseeable future, to be replaced by small unit engagements in localized, increasingly 'dirty' and morally and legally ambiguous conflicts.

Whilst the character of conflict has evolved, so too has the nature of battlefield medicine. Advances in medicine have been translated to the battlefield at the same time as recent experience in conflict has led to improvements in medical care from lessons learnt in treating battlefield casualties. This has led

1 International Committee of the Red Cross, *Study on the Use of the Emblems*, ICRC, http://www.icrc.org/eng/resources/documents/publication/p4057.htm (accessed February 27, 2012), p. 22

2 General Sir Rupert Smith, *The Utility of Force*, p. 17.

3 Benjamin Perrin, *Humanitarian Assistance and the Private Security Debate: An International Humanitarian Law Perspective*, Canadian Red Cross, http://www.redcross.ca/cmslib/general/oteoc_ben_perrin.pdf (accessed March 1, 2012), p. 5

to a dramatic increase in the survival rates of soldiers after injury; in the Vietnam War 76% of American soldiers survived their injuries[4] whilst in a recent study in Afghanistan the survival rate of wounded ISAF personnel was 89%.[5] This increase has several contributory factors: the recognition of catastrophic haemorrhage as the leading cause of death and the ability to treat it with tourniquets and blood clotting agents, the shortened time in which life saving first aid is provided, and the rapidity of medical evacuation by helicopter to well equipped hospitals.[6]

This has led to a change in the way that medical care is provided in the contemporary operating environment. MMP now operate in company with infantry and other units and typically have Regimental Aid Post in Forward Operating Bases (FOBS), co-located with forward units. Larger FOBS may have a primary care doctor whilst smaller FOBS are manned by Combat Medical Technicians or Medical Assistants: they, or doctors, accompany the majority of patrols in Afghanistan and so are quickly able to deliver first aid treatment, although they are correspondingly close to any attacks.[7] Serious casualties are rapidly evacuated to modern medical facilities using Medical Emergency Response and Treatment helicopters, which carry a highly trained team of medical staff that are able to initiate advanced treatment in flight.[8] Recognition that medical personnel, units and transports have been actively targeted has led to the development of doctrine that describes different levels of care, depending on how 'permissive' the environment is, with procedures adapted to be performed whilst under fire.[9] Because of the need to respond quickly to injuries that cause bleeding, the 'Golden Hour', in which medical first aid is imperative, has been shortened to the 'Platinum Ten Minutes', during which

---

4 Richard A. Gabriel and Karen S. Mez, *A History of Military Medicine. Volume II* (New York: Green Wood Press, 1992), p. 273.

5 A. Stalker, J. Ollerton, S. Everington, R. Russell, C. Walker, and S. White, "A Three-Year Review of Emergency Department Admissions – Op Herrick 4 to 9," *Journal of the Royal Army Medical Corps.* 157 no 3 (2011), p. 215.

6 United Kingdom, *Battlefield Advanced Trauma Life Support.* Joint Service Publication 570, 4th edition (NP: 2008), p. 6.

7 Personal experience of author confirmed in interviews with Lt Mark Middleton RN 2 February 2012 and Lt Col Hair RAMC 23 February 2012. See also MCM Bricknell, "Reflections on medical aspects of ISAF IX in Afghanistan," *Journal of the Royal Army Medical Corps.* 153 no 1 (2007), pp. 44–51.

8 Kehoe et al., "Current Controversies in Military Pre-Hospital Critical Care," *Journal of the Royal Army Medical Corps.* 157 Suppl 1 (2011), p. 305.

9 United Kingdom Ministry of Defence, *Battlefield Advanced Trauma Life Support.* Joint Service Publication 570, 4th edition (NP: 2008), p. 3.

control of haemorrhage is the priority, with life saving skills such as the application of tourniquets shared with all soldiers in order to ensure rapid first aid to casualties. One in four soldiers is given advanced training to become a team medic, able to provide a number of life saving techniques close to the point of wounding.[10]

Because of these changes medical care, and therefore MMP, are on the front line with their patients, with a resultant blurring of the boundaries between combatant and non-combatant. Defining 'Medical Personnel' and differentiating them from the soldiers around them whilst limiting their use to the care of the wounded have therefore become major challenges. If medical personnel are close to the front line then it risks them being associated with offensive action and if the protective symbol becomes associated with offensive patrols then its protective effect will be lost.

A further complication arises from the fact that, despite their protected status, medical personnel may provide a perfect target for insurgents: if they wear their protected symbol then they will stand out from the rest of the patrol. When a casualty is inflicted on an enemy there is naturally a flurry of activity surrounding the casualty as his wounds are treated and an evacuation attempted. These contingencies provide an opportunity for a secondary attack whilst the force is distracted and 'bunched up', whilst the arrival of a relatively slow and vulnerable aircraft also presents a tempting target for Insurgents. Attacking these 'Casevac' helicopters may have profound effects: the integrity of the casualty evacuation pathway is fundamental to the 'moral component' of the fighting force and attacking it may well undermine the morale and willingness to fight of a military unit. However, during an insurgency, medical personnel may represent the only medical care on the battlefield, and as insurgents do not usually have the level of sophisticated medical arrangements available to UK or other coalition forces, so those of them that target medical personnel or any component of the evacuation pathway may, paradoxically, be targeting the only medical support available to them if they themselves become casualties. The use of protective symbols in such an environment is therefore extremely challenging, potentially marking medical personnel out to the enemy or giving away the position of a patrol or even providing the enemy with a 'point of aim' and a vulnerable person in the patrol whose removal will adversely affect all of the members.

It is widely acknowledged that MMP and their associated transports have come under attack in Iraq and Afghanistan and interviews with senior British medical personnel confirm this, although it is not always possible to establish

10 *Ibid.*, pp. 1–18.

clear examples of cases since commanders tend to assume that the highly visible protective symbols will be targeted and so allow their removal. However, during the Iraq war in 2003 there were reports of Iraqi soldiers specifically targeting the Red Cross emblem on the sides of thinly armoured ambulances[11] and also of commandeering ambulances to get to the front line and then fighting from them.[12] More recently, there are examples of attacks recorded in television documentaries produced by cameramen who have deployed to the front line. For example, in a 2009 documentary *Doctors and Nurses on the Front Line*, there is footage of the Medical Emergency Response Team helicopter coming under fire from Taliban machine gunners.[13] Similarly a documentary by Al Jazeera shows an American Casevac helicopter that has received damage from small arms fire.[14] In the latter case the Red Cross symbol is clearly displayed although the British crew in the first documentary explain that they do not display the Red Cross because this would make them even more of a target. More recently, ISAF published a report of a helicopter clearly marked with the Red Cross coming under attack in Helmand province, Afghanistan.[15] The threat from the Taliban in Afghanistan has led to the requirement that all medical helicopters be escorted by a helicopter gunship and that all ground ambulances are protected by armour.[16]

To examine the phenomenon of attacks on military medical personnel in Afghanistan, interviews were conducted with two senior officers whose experience collectively included five tours of Afghanistan in charge of the medical support to front line troops.[17] Both described anecdotes of soldiers being targeted for looking 'different' within a patrol and intelligence that suggested that the medical stretcher had been identified by Taliban snipers and the bearer

11 S. Edgar, "The Personal Experiences of the Regimental Aid Post.1st Bn The Royal Regiment Of Fusiliers. OP TELIC, IRAQ," *Journal of the Royal Army Medical Corps*. 150 (2004), p. 27.

12 Human Rights Watch, *Off Target: The Conduct of the War and Civilian Casualties in Iraq* (USA: Human Rights Watch, 2007), p. 70.

13 ITV1, *Doctors and Nurses at War, Part 3 of 3, The Front Line* (ITV1, February 17, 2009).

14 People and Power, *Blood and Dust*. Video clip (Aljazeera, 2011), http://www.aljazeera.com/programmes/peopleandpower/2011/09/2011915105947578551.html (accessed December 15, 2011)

15 ISAF, "Insurgents attack Medical Evacuation Helicopter" ICRC Press release May 14, 2011, http://www.rs.nato.int/article/isaf-releases/insurgents-attack-medical-evacuation-helicopter.html (accessed May 22, 2012)

16 MCM Bricknell, "Reflections on medical aspects of ISAF IX in Afghanistan," *Journal of the Royal Army Medical Corps*. 153 no 1 (2007), p. 46.

17 Interviews with Lt Mark Middleton RN 2 February 2012, and Lt Col Hair RAMC 23 February 2012.

was specifically targeted. Because of these intelligence reports medical personnel were not instructed to wear protective emblems and did their best to 'blend in' to patrols, even painting their own medical Bergens to match those of their colleagues. There was evidence that the Casevac pathway was specifically targeted with secondary attacks on medical evacuation helicopters. As medical personnel were deployed to Forward Operating Bases (FOBs), going on patrol with soldiers, they were often part of very small teams in remote locations and this caused a dilemma for their employment when not on patrol. All personnel within deployed military bases will form part of the defence by manning machine guns or other weapons in defensive positions or 'sangers'. Manning these defences goes beyond the limits of the strict self-protection afforded medical personnel but often became necessary because of the shortage of personnel in FOBs. This problem was resolved either by proposing an argument that, for such small teams, collective defence and self-defence were inseparable, or by finding alternative roles for the personnel. The latter was quite challenging and one interviewee described how even manning a radio may put a medic in the position of co-ordinating offensive action. Even in large bases this was an issue with nurses reportedly manning the Sangers behind the hospital in Camp Bastion for at least one operational tour. The design of some vehicles posed a dilemma with medics deployed on 'Jackal' armoured personnel carriers required to operate at least one weapon system (which were mounted and therefore not portable weapons as allowed by the Geneva Conventions) because only the commander's seat was unarmed; this partly stemmed from the perception that the medic was there as a crew member with additional first aid skills and was addressed by pointing out their employment status. An issue arose on one tour in which a doctor was filmed manning a GPMG on a parked vehicle musing about whether he should use it.[18] This was broadcast on national television,[19] but was not commented on by the ICRC despite a letter alerting them of its imminent broadcast by the then Surgeon General.[20] Lt Col Hair described the difficulty of working with NGOs or humanitarian organisations if no Protective Symbol is displayed, the organisations would often not talk to them until an emblem was displayed and even then would insist on the absence of a weapon.

Medical Personnel who do not display a protective emblem can only expect protection where it is obvious what their role is. The evidence that they are targeted simply for being different and therefore a large red cross would make

18 *Ibid.*

19 ITV1, *Doctors and Nurses at War, Part 3 of 3, The Front Line* (ITV1, February 17, 2009).

20 Interview with Lt Col Hair RAMC, February 23, 2012.

things worse is convincing, but it is not clear that medical personnel forward deployed in foot patrols in the current conflict in Afghanistan have ever worn any of the protective emblems. However, the behaviour of the Taliban and the evidence of attacks on medical helicopters and humanitarian workers demonstrate that the Taliban do not respect the protection that protective emblems afford medical transports or humanitarian workers. More widely, there is evidence of the targeting of humanitarian workers and this has led to the loss of the lives of a large number of these workers. This evidence demonstrates that in 'wars among the people' the protection of the emblems is being lost and that its use on the battlefield is reducing. If on its own an emblem will not provide protection for humanitarian workers then they are likely to withdraw from the battlefield and the essential services that Henri Dunant tried to provide to those suffering in conflict, will no longer be available to either injured civilians or combatants. The challenge is to ensure that medics remain protected, however, in order to do this it is essential to understand the legal, moral and ethical arguments that underpin their non-combatant status.

The Legal Background

The Geneva Conventions provide the legal basis for the non-combatant status of medical personnel and for the protective emblems but also limit the way the way medical personnel may be employed and the weapons they can use. There is a difference between the legal status of international and non-international armed conflicts, although there is no practical difference in the actual employment of medical personnel.

The Geneva Conventions are part of a wider body of International Humanitarian Law. The First Geneva Convention was drafted in 1864 as a result of the work of Henri Dunant and provides protection and care for the sick and wounded (those *hors de combat*, literally out of the fight) and for those medical personnel caring for them. Further conventions were added and in 1949 the Four Geneva Conventions which exist today were written with an updated First Convention, the Second Convention replacing the Hague Convention on Maritime Warfare of 1907, a Third Convention covering Prisoners of War and a new Convention on the protection of Civilian Persons.[21] These remain the most universally ratified International Law[22] and are applicable to all states or actors

21 International Committee of the Red Cross, *The Geneva Conventions of August 12 1949* (np), p. 2..

22 Currently 194 states are signatories.

in an armed conflict: they do not consider the legality of the conflict itself and this does not have any bearing on the treatment of combatants during the war. In response to conflicts in the two decades following the 1949 Conventions, two additional Protocols were added to increase the protection of victims of international and non-international armed conflicts, Additional Protocols I and II respectively. Additional Protocol I strengthens the protection of civilian medical personnel, units and transports in international conflict whilst Additional Protocol II safeguards all those not taking part in non-international conflicts and strengthens the protection of medical personnel, units and transports in them.[23] In 2005 the third Additional Protocol introduced an extra protective symbol, discussed more below. Common Article 3 was incorporated in to all the Geneva Conventions in 1949 and covers situations of non-international armed conflicts including insurgencies, guaranteeing the actors of those conflicts the same protection if made *hors de combat* as actors in a traditional conflict.

Medical Personnel are provided protection specifically because of their exclusive employment in caring for the injured. Injured personnel are afforded protection by Article 12 of the First Geneva Convention, which states that:

> Members of the armed forces and other persons mentioned in the following article, who are wounded or sick, shall be respected and protected in all circumstances. They shall be treated humanely and cared for by the party to the conflict in whose power they may be [...]. Any attempts upon their lives, or violence to their persons, shall be strictly prohibited.[24]

Article 13 expands on who is protected and includes anyone who could be injured by conflict. This principle of the humane treatment of all those who are injured by whichever side finds them is fundamental to the way that medical personnel should be employed on the battlefield and their protected status is derived from this.

Article 24 provides protection for permanent medical personnel i.e. 'those exclusively involved in the care of the wounded and sick as well as chaplains attached to the Armed Forces who are to be protected and respected in all circumstances'.[25] Article 25 provides protection for 'auxiliary personnel' and those carrying out medical duties when they come in to contact with the

23 D.J. Vassallo, "The International Red Cross and Red Crescent Movement and Lessons from its Experience of War Surgery," *Journal of the Royal Army Med Corps*. 140 (1994), p. 146.

24 International Committee of the Red Cross, *The Geneva Conventions of August 12, 1949*, p. 27.

25 *ibid.*, p. 33.

enemy. An important principle, described in Article 7, is the non-renunciation of rights: 'Wounded and sick, as well as members of the medical personnel and chaplains, may in no circumstances renounce in part or in entirety the rights secured to them by the present Convention, [...]'.[26] Thus medical personnel must be exclusively employed on medical duties and may not renounce their duty once they have been assigned to it, although they forfeit their protection if they commit hostile acts. The definition of 'medical personnel' is broad and may include technicians, cooks, drivers and administrators provided they are exclusively assigned to the medical staff.[27] Additional Protocol I reinforces the need for personnel afforded protection to be exclusively employed on medical duties, the period of this duty is not specified although there should be no change to employment during an operation.[28] Medical Units and Transports are similarly defined by their exclusive use for medical purposes.[29]

Article 43 of Additional Protocol I defines military medical personnel as non-combatants by defining other members of the armed forces as combatants: 'Members of the armed forces of a Party to a conflict (other than medical personnel and chaplains covered by Article 33 of the Third Convention) are combatants...'.[30] Additional Protocol II, which applies to non-international armed conflict does not repeat this definition, but sets the principle that participation in hostilities defines a person as a combatant and protection for medical personnel is maintained. In summary, MMP are protected by being an exception to the rule, rather than by being included in it.

Despite their non-combatant status medical personnel are permitted by Article 22 of the First Geneva Convention to carry arms in self defence or defence of those in their charge. The definition of weapons of self defence varies between armed forces, but in general is limited to those which can only be used and carried by one person, and against people not objects such as vehicles or buildings.[31] In the UK the limits are stated in JSP 383 as 'sub-machine

26 *ibid.*, p. 25.

27 UK Ministry of Defence, *The Manual of the Law of Armed Conflict* (Oxford: Oxford University Press, 2005), 38.

28 International Committee of the Red Cross, *Study on the Use of the Emblems*. ICRC, p. 51.

29 Jean-Marie Henckaerts and Louise Doswald-Beck, *Customary International Humanitarian Law. Volume 1: Rules*, pp. 91–103.

30 International Committee of the Red Cross, *Protocol Additional to the Geneva Conventions of 12 August 1949, and relating to the Protection of Victims of International Armed Conflicts (Protocol I), 8 June 1977*. ICRC, http://www.icrc.org/eng/resources/documents/misc/additional-protocols-1977.htm (accessed March 8, 2012), article 44

31 Jean-Marie Henckaerts and Louise Doswald-Beck, *Customary International Humanitarian Law Volume 1: Rules* (Cambridge: Cambridge University Press, 2005), p. 86.

guns, self-loading rifles and handguns'.[32] As medical personnel may only use their weapons in self defence, JDP 4–03 explains that the rules of engagement issued to medical personnel may need to be different in order to reflect the fact that they can only respond in self defence or defence of their patients.[33] This is important because personnel who engage in acts hostile to the enemy forfeit their protection; this protection is only afforded to them as an extension to the respect and protection afforded to their patients.[34]

Additional Protocol I states that no distinction in medical care and treatment should be made except for medical reasons and no medical procedures are to be conducted without consent or without benefit to the patient (except for voluntary blood donation or skin grafting).[35] Additional Protocol II enforces the principles of medical ethics and medical professional obligations such that no punishment may be given for acting in accordance with medical ethics, nobody may be obliged to act contrary to medical ethics and professional obligations are to be respected.[36]

Medical Personnel, Units and Transports may be identified by one of three symbols of which the best known is the Red Cross. The Red Cross was first described in Article 7 of the First Geneva Convention in 1864 as the reverse of the Swiss flag but, despite its intended neutrality, it quickly became seen as a religious symbol, particularly by Turkey who declared in 1877 that they would use a Red Crescent. Later Persia announced its use of the lion and red sun symbol and in 1929 all three of these symbols were recognised.[37] Israel refused to use any of the previously recognised symbols and adopted its own six-point star, but met opposition from Arab states. The consequences were that Israel was excluded from the International Red Cross societies and some other states and societies refused to recognise any symbol because of possible religious

32 United Kingdom DCDC, *The Joint Service Manual of the Law of Armed Conflict* JSP 383, 2004 edition (JCDC: Swindon, 2004), 7.15.1.

33 UK Ministry of Defence, *Joint Medical Doctrine*. JDP 4–03, 3rd edition (DCDC: Swindon, 2011), 1A11.

34 Jean-Marie Henckaerts and Louise Doswald-Beck, *Customary International Humanitarian Law. Volume 1: Rules*, p. 84.

35 International Committee of the Red Cross, *Protocol Additional to the Geneva Conventions of 12 August 1949, and relating to the Protection of Victims of International Armed Conflicts (Protocol I), 8 June 1977*. ICRC, Article 11.

36 International Committee of the Red Cross, *Protocol Additional to the Geneva Conventions of 12 August 1949, and relating to the Protection of Victims of Non-International Armed Conflicts (Protocol II), 8 June 1977*. ICRC, http://www.icrc.org/ihl.nsf/FULL/475?OpenDocument (accessed March 8, 2012), Article 10

37 Gary D. Solis, *The Law of Armed Conflict* (Cambridge: Cambridge University Press, 2010), p. 136.

connotations. In December 2005 the parties to the Geneva Conventions agreed on three symbols: The Red Cross on a White background, The Red Crescent and a red square on its edge on a white background – the Red Crystal.[38] These symbols can be used as protective devices – as the visible sign of protection conferred by the Geneva Conventions, or as indicative devices – indicative of a link to the International Red Cross society or movement.[39] The wearing of the symbols is not mandatory,[40] although in order to obviate hostile action and to ensure protection via the Geneva Conventions they must be worn whenever possible.[41] The symbols do not confer protected status but are indicative of it[42] and as long as the function of the individual is known then their protected status must be protected regardless of their wearing of the emblem.[43] To intentionally attack the distinctive emblems is a war crime in international and non-international conflicts,[44] but respect for the symbols is conditional on their proper use and so care must be taken to not misuse them (Rule 59).[45] Thus the distinctive emblems indicate the protected status of the individuals which is derived from their function as medical or religious personnel and should be displayed whenever possible to indicate this to the enemy. As long as the function of the individual is known then their protected status must be respected. Conforming to medical ethics is a requirement of the Geneva Conventions and affects the employment of medical personnel in the field. Their ethical standards and obligations impose on them restrictions and responsibilities in the way that they practice medicine and this must be respected by the Operational Commander. Employment of medical personnel contrary to ethical standards is a breach of the Geneva Conventions. Humanitarian workers, in particular those of the ICRC, have codes of professional conduct which stress their neutrality and impartiality.

---

38 *Ibid.*

39 ICRC, Protocol additional to the Geneva Conventions of 12 August 1949, and relating to the Adoption of an Additional Distinctive Emblem (Protocol III), December 8, 2005.

40 United Kingdom DCDC, *The Joint Service Manual of the Law of Armed Conflict.* Joint Service Publication 383, 7.25.

41 ICRC, *The Geneva Conventions of August 12 1949*, p. 40.

42 Jean-Marie Henckaerts and Louise Doswald-Beck, *Customary International Humanitarian Law. Volume 1: Rules*, p. 104.

43 United Kingdom DCDC, *The Joint Service Manual of the Law of Armed Conflict.* Joint Service Publication 383. 7.25.2.

44 Jean-Marie Henckaerts and Louise Doswald-Beck, *Customary International Humanitarian Law. Volume 1: Rules*, p. 103.

45 United Kingdom DCDC, *Joint Medical Doctrine.* Joint Doctrine Publication 4–03, 3rd edition, 1A18.

Medical personnel on the modern battlefield come from different professional and non-professional backgrounds including doctors, surgeons, nurses, paramedics and combat medical technicians or medical assistants. Combat medical technicians (CMTs) and medical assistants (MAs) are unique to the armed forces comprising soldiers and sailors trained in advanced medical skills to the level necessary to act autonomously on a battlefield. Despite their lack of a professional qualification they provide the majority of medical care in Forward Operating Bases and on ships at sea. Professionals all have a code of conduct, which prescribes their conduct and requires them to put their medical duties before their military ones. CMTs and MAs are initially trained as soldiers or sailors and so may feel their loyalties are different, but, since they are permanently assigned to medical duties, they are regarded by the Geneva Conventions as medical personnel and so have duties given to them by the Conventions and by the customary practice of the other medical professionals who supervise them.

The Ethical Background

Medical ethics is commonly assumed to have originated in ancient Greece with the formulation of what we now call the Hippocratic Oath. The oath confers a duty on the doctors who swear it to work to the benefit of the patient, to maintain confidentiality and to not harm patients; it also contains promises to not perform surgery or abortions and so has fallen out of favour in modern medicine, but a similar oath is still sworn at medical graduation ceremonies.[46] Modern medical ethics generally regarded as being grounded in 'principlism' as described by Tom Beauchamp and James Childress in their seminal work *Principles of Biomedical Ethics*[47] the principles being: Respect for Autonomy, Beneficence or the duty to help others, Non-Maleficence or the duty not to harm others, and Justice or the duty to treat people fairly. These ethical standards form a set of tests that can be applied to different ethical scenarios and are the foundation of medical codes of practice such as the General Medical Council's guidance 'Good Medical Practice'[48] and the Nursing and Midwifery

46 Daniel Sokol, "A Guide to the Hippocratic Oath," BBC News, http://news.bbc.co.uk/1/hi/7654432.stm (accessed May 16, 2012)

47 T.L. Beauchamp and J.F. Childress, *Principles of Medical Ethics* (Oxford: Oxford University Press, 1994), p. 4.

48 General Medical Council, "Good Medical Practice," http://www.gmc-uk.org/Good_medical_practice__English_0914.pdf_51527435.pdf (accessed May 16, 2012)

Council's 'Code'.[49] Medical professionals remain bound to these codes wherever they practice and may be held accountable to them even if they have not been found guilty of a breach of civil or international law.

There is considerable synergy between the Geneva Conventions and medical ethics. The principle of complying with medical ethics is contained in the Geneva Conventions and an additional principle of military medical ethics is contained in the 'Solferino Principle' that 'all wounded or sick combatants, to whatever nation they may belong, shall be collected and cared for'[50] and in the principle of neutrality of medical care. This contains elements of the principles of beneficence and justice; principles of non-maleficence are supported by the non-combatant status of medical personnel. The principles of consent to treatment and treatment only in the interest of patients were included in the Geneva Conventions as a result of ethical violations conducted by Nazi doctors during World War II.[51]

The Solferino Principle and medical ethics impose restrictions and obligations on an Operational Commander and hence on the MMP under his command. He is obliged to provide some medical care, although the amount is not explicitly stated, and to ensure that after any engagement an adequate search is made for casualties and then to ensure their adequate care.[52] 'Adequate care' implies that a minimum standard of care must be offered, although this is not explicitly explained. He must allow his medical staff to practise in accordance with their professional codes and so must allow them freedom to make clinical decisions without interference. This can lead to conflict where medical and military priorities clash: for example, confidentiality is the cornerstone of the principal of autonomy and the sensitive nature of a patient's medical condition must be respected even when the information is required for military reasons, breaking confidentiality is a grave decision for medical practitioners.[53] However, when faced with a conflict between medical and military duties medical personnel are obliged to follow their professional obligations as Additional Protocol I states that 'persons engaged in medical activities shall

49 Nursing and Midwifery Council, *The code: Standards of Conduct, Performance and Ethics for Nurses and Midwives*, http://www.nmc-uk.org/Documents/Standards/The-code-A4-20100406.pdf (accessed May 16, 2012)

50 M.J. Gunn and H. McCoubrey, "Medical Ethics and the Laws of Armed Conflict," *Journal of Armed Conflict Law*. 3 no 2 (1998), p. 135.

51 *Ibid.*, pp. 147–153.

52 *Ibid.*, p. 144.

53 Neuhaus, Bridgewater and Kilcullen, "Military Medical Ethics: Issues for 21st Century Operations," *Australian Defence Force Journal*. no 151 November/December 2001, p. 52.

not be compelled to perform acts or to carry out work contrary to the rules of medical ethics or other medical rules designed for the benefit of the wounded and sick…'.[54]

Soldiers who have been given additional training to be able to provide advanced medical techniques (team medics) on the battlefield may need to consider their medical responsibilities and priorities. If a casualty is sustained in an engagement and a soldier has medical skills, is the priority winning the firefight or saving the casualty? If the soldier provides first aid is he then afforded the protection of the Geneva Conventions? Neither the medical professional bodies nor the Geneva Conventions consider team medics as medical personnel since they are not employed exclusively for medical duties and are clearly deployed in an offensive role. Their training is insufficient to confer on them ethical or moral responsibilities beyond those of an ordinary citizen equipped with life saving skills who must make a decision if he is to employ them or not. However, the Geneva Conventions, specifically AP1, do provide protection whilst they are carrying out first aid as clarified by the ICRC Emblem Study.[55]

The non-combatant status of military medical personnel is unique on the battlefield, where non-combatant status is normally defined by non-involvement in the conflict; medical personnel and chaplains are the only non-combatant members of the Armed Forces.[56] Whilst IHL defines the difference between combatants and non-combatants, the Principle of Non Combatant Immunity (PNCI) is a *moral* one[57] and it is now appropriate to briefly examine the moral theories that underpin the PNCI in order to better understand the implications for changes that threaten that status.

There are two moral theories that may clash on the principle of non-combatant immunity, namely Utilitarianism and Deontology. Utilitarianism proposes that it is the outcome of a person's action that render it (morally) justifiable, rather than on the decision-making process that achieves the outcome. Utilitarianism gives equal value to all lives, although using utilitarian reasoning, an argument can be made that it is justifiable to kill a person, non-combatant as well as combatant, if by doing so you reduce the overall number of deaths and, by concentrating on the outcome instead of the methods, it may

54 International Committee of the Red Cross, *Protocol Additional to the Geneva Conventions of 12 August 1949, and relating to the Protection of Victims of International Armed Conflicts (Protocol I), 8 June 1977*, Article 16.

55 International Committee of the Red Cross, *Study on the Use of the Emblems*, p. 47.

56 Gary D. Solis, *The Law of Armed Conflict*, p. 136.

57 Helen Frowe, *The Ethics of War and Peace* (Routledge: London, 2011), p. 151.

permit all types of warfare and the deaths of all types of people, including civilians, as long as the best overall outcome is achieved.[58] Critics of this approach object that war could never be justified by utilitarianism because its effects would almost always be worse than not going to war and that once actually at war, the theory permits almost any action.[59]

By contrast, a deontological or absolutist approach 'holds that there are moral rules that should be obeyed in all circumstances without exception'.[60] It is the act not the eventual outcome that is right or wrong in its own terms. This approach is important because it is the basis for the formulation of laws, but an absolutist would also never permit killing 'one innocent in order to save many lives'.[61]

Some compromise between the extremes of the two positions could be achieved. For example, a modified approach to utilitarianism is rule-utilitarianism which accepts that rules are important, but only if by following them you maximise the expected utility. These rules should be argued from principle by people 'behind a veil of ignorance, but believing that their country may well be involved in a war at some time'.[62] Similarly, a deontological absolutist approach could be softened by allowing for exceptions to be made in defined circumstances: the very act of killing in battle – justifiable as acts of individual or collective self-defence – is the classic example of an exception being made to the general rule.

Utilitarian and absolutists therefore both justify the status of non-combatants but from different perspectives. A utilitarian would argue that a person should not be attacked if by not attacking them, or by following a rule that they should not be attacked, that long-term utility is maximised. This might include not attacking non-combatants on the basis that by attacking them you risk inflaming the conflict or drawing more people in making peace less likely and the war last longer. Absolutists argue that there are two types of restrictions in warfare – on the type of person targeted and on the type of attack, although these can be combined.[63] In this theory there must be something about the person that justifies their combatant or non-combatant status. There are a few

---

58 Thomas Nagel, "War and Massacre," in *War and Moral Responsibility*. eds. Marchall Cohen, Thomas Nagel and Thomas Scanlon (Princeton: Princeton University Press, 1974), p. 5.

59 *Ibid.*

60 David Fisher, *Morality and War* (Oxford: Oxford University Press, 2001), p. 94.

61 Fisher, op. cit., p. 95.

62 R.B. Brandt, "Utilitarianism and the Rules of War," in *War and Moral Responsibility*. eds. Marchall Cohen, Thomas Nagel and Thomas Scanlon (Princeton: Princeton University Press, 1974), p. 32.

63 Thomas Nagel, "War and Massacre," in *Ibid.*, p. 13.

different approaches to this justification, none of which are entirely satisfactory.

Moral guilt theory proposes that those that wage war have equal moral guilt and are therefore legitimate targets. This was the principle of St Augustine's writing on war but is limited in application to more modern conflict waged by professional armies whose soldiers may have played no part in the decision to go to war, but whose politicians are morally guilty. It does not explain the immunity of guilty civilians or the non-immunity of just soldiers.[64] An alternative is to define the status of combatants on the basis of their threat and to argue that by posing a direct threat then a person must be a combatant.[65] The trouble with this definition is the narrowness of its definition of combatants which would not include soldiers who are not actively involved in killing or are only present to support other soldiers who do the fighting, such as those gathering intelligence or delivering supplies who provide an indirect threat.[66] However, if the definition is applied more broadly, then it can be permissible to attack anybody who contributes to the threat by supporting the front line soldier, but it is then difficult to draw a line between those who provide active support by supplying ammunition and those civilians in factories who produce ammunition or between military chefs and the farmers who produce the food.[67] In order to make this distinction, differentiation can be made between persons who contribute to the necessities of the soldier's means of fighting and the necessities of the soldier as a human being. Somebody who contributes to the means of fighting by supplying bullets or guns may be targeted, but those providing human necessities such as food should not.[68] Again this definition falls short since it may also include civilians who work in armament factories or those who produce armoured vehicles who would not normally be considered combatants. The UK Manual of the Law of Armed Conflict takes the view that it is the direct nature of the threat rather than its type of contribution that is important; that combatants are permitted to take part in conflict and therefore may be attacked, but that civilians, as long as they do not take part, are protected from attack:

> Taking a direct part in hostilities is more narrowly construed than simply making a contributing to the war effort. Thus working in a munitions

64 Uwe Steinhoff, *Civilians and Soldiers* in Civilian Immunity in War. ed. Igor Primoratz (Oxford: Oxford University Press), p. 56.

65 Helen Frowe, *The Ethics of War and Peace*, p. 160.

66 *Ibid.*

67 *Ibid.*

68 Michael Walzer, *Just and Unjust Wars* (Basic Books: New York, 2000), p. 146.

> factory or otherwise supplying or supporting the war effort does not justify the targeting of civilians so doing.[69]

It distinguishes between the munitions factory, which is a legitimate target, and the people working in it who are not, but may be incidentally killed.[70] This last point is one of military necessity and proportionality which are both principles of *Jus in Bellum* – the military gain in attacking the factory must not be disproportionate to the number of civilian deaths. Ultimately it may help to consider the PNCI as a useful convention: Mavrodes argues that the 'immunity of non-combatants is not an independent moral rule but rather a convention which sets up a morally desirable alternative to [total] war'.[71]

Military medical personnel pose a dilemma when considering PNCI; they are deployed on a battlefield by an armed force which is unlikely to be acting in the best interests of both sides by doing this. Although they may claim that they are acting as civilians[72] they wear a military uniform and are subject to military law. Medical personnel are as morally responsible for the conflict as any other soldier on the battlefield, and are likely to have helped in generating that force and maintaining its health and fitness whilst deployed. If they provide benefit only to one side then deliberately attacking them undermines an important service provided to that side and may weaken its ability to fight. However, it is possible to find several features of medical personnel that make them different from other military professionals. Firstly, the service they provide is to the soldier as a human being rather than specific to his military purpose and, whilst some healthcare is provided to allow him to fight, the majority of benefit is received after the soldier is unable to continue fighting and is no longer a threat to the other side. Secondly, their obligation through professional ethics to put their patients first and to treat anybody who is injured based on medical need means that they benefit both sides; therefore attacking them removes benefit to both sides and so reduces the long term utility to both sides. Thirdly, whilst they are armed they are only entitled to attack in self-defence, something that all non-combatants are entitled to, and so do not contribute a direct threat. The first two of these arguments are unique to medical personnel as non-combatants because they are derived from a duty

---

69 UK Ministry of Defence, *The Manual of the Law of Armed Conflict*, 2.6.3.

70 *Ibid.*

71 George I. Mavrodes, "Conventions and the Morality of War," in *International Ethics*. eds. Charles, Marshall Cohen Thomas Scanlon and John Simmons (Princeton University Press: New Jersey, 1985), p. 88.

72 Helen Frowe, *The Ethics of War and Peace*, p. 103.

to another person – the injured soldier. This principle is reflected in the Geneva Conventions in which the right to protection is derived from the employment on the battlefield in service of their patients. Thus medical personnel morally justify their non-combatant status by their utility to the wounded of both sides, their service to those wounded and their lack of an indirect or direct threat to the other side. That there is an established rule in the Geneva Convention that codifies this status serves as a useful convention that limits the harms of war.

An alternative argument is that medical personnel are non-combatants because of the service they provide (as opposed to a duty) which is identical to that provided in their civilian profession and could equally be provided by any competent medical professional, they are there only because of the armed forces' obligation to search for and care for wounded. If this were true it would provide little moral obligation to the Operational Commander as long as he can be sure that the service is provided. It could be ensured by arming his medics and giving them combat roles until their medical skills are needed as he does in a similar way with his chefs and drivers. However the people that will need the service do not yet exist and so, unlike chefs and drivers, the requirement is as yet unknown and the person that requires that service does not yet know he will need it. Furthermore when he does require it he will be *hors de combat*, no longer a combatant and no longer able to fight and so the service is provided to another non-combatant albeit one that does not yet exist. Thus the commander's responsibility is not to provide a service to his combatant soldiers but to soldiers, from both sides, that will be made non-combatant in the future. At that point he will need to be sure that the medical personnel have remained neutral and that that neutrality is protected for the good of those made *hors de combat*.

A counter argument is that medical personnel provide a service that is a force enabler or force multiplier to their side, the service they provide directly enables troops to fight and encourages their fighting by contributing to the moral component of the force and its will to fight. This argument has merit since all other force enablers who wear a uniform, such as chefs and drivers, are regarded as combatants. Medical personnel certainly enable troops to fight and without medical support it would be morally wrong to ask a soldier to fight but this does not, of itself, make them combatants. The service that is provided once a soldier is wounded does not usually allow them to return quickly to the fight; indeed the Geneva Conventions prohibit those made *hors de combat* from further fighting[73] and so the service provided does not act as a force

73 ICRC, *The Geneva Conventions of August 12, 1949*, p. 25.

enabler. Moral support is not recognised as a force enabler since religious personnel also provide moral support and are not combatants. If we consider the service provided in isolation then it would not be morally acceptable to target a person or organisation providing only medical care to both sides of the conflict. As long as medical personnel treat both sides to the conflict equally then this argument is neutralised. This argument is still focussed at the duties of the medical personnel to the injured of both sides and not to something inherent to them.

This unique argument, that medical personnel are conferred their protected status by their duty to others, confers a responsibility on the force with which they serve to ensure that their employment does not exceed that specified in the Geneva Conventions and that they are therefore not exposed to situations in which their role may be confused. They must be allowed to treat patients from both sides whilst protected by their own side: this does not change in a conflict where medical personnel may become targets because the Geneva Conventions are not a contract which when broken frees the other side from its obligation, on the contrary it is vital that a modern force upholds its principles and maintains the moral high ground. This protection may include enhanced self protection such as body armour but the limits of this are prescribed within the Geneva Conventions as 'those that can be transported by one person'[74] and in JSP 383 i.e. 'sub-machine guns, self-loading rifles and handguns'.[75] Where adequate self-protection cannot be provided, then medical personnel must be protected by others in the deployed force. Force protection by other soldiers such as providing armed escorts to ambulances or medical personnel or manning the defences around field hospitals is essential to allow medical personnel to work, but great care must be taken to ensure there is an obvious distinction between those providing protection and the medical personnel. This does create challenges for the force that must then divert scarce resources to protecting medical personnel.

The operational choices made and the balance struck between the protection of medical personnel and their positioning on the battlefield will affect the medical care afforded to those injured. If the commander makes compromises by not deploying medics to FOBs where they will require greater protection then he may also deny soldiers in those FOBs access to timely medical care and so the right balance must be struck between soldiers with extra first aid

74 International Committee of the Red Cross, "Study on the Use of the Emblems," ICRC, http://www.icrc.org/eng/resources/documents/publication/p4057.htm (accessed February 27, 2012), p. 52

75 United Kingdom Ministry of Defence, *Joint Medical Doctrine*, JDP 4–03, 3rd edition, 1A11.

skills, team medics and medical personnel However, it does not follow that the Force should 'up-arm' medics or increase their self protection to the same level as other soldiers since this undermines the role they have been given.

Examination of the Geneva Conventions and the Emblem Study has shown that displaying a protective emblem is not compulsory although it should be worn whenever possible. Where the protective emblem puts medical personnel at greater risk than other soldiers then it should not be worn. However where its use can be properly protected or if it does not lead to greater risk it should be worn and care must be taken by all medical personnel to wear their protective emblems whenever it is safe to do so and ensure that combatants, on both sides, associate medical personnel with the protective emblems. Great care must be taken not to associate the protective emblems with any offensive actions. Protection of the emblems also includes the Force respecting the emblems displayed and used by the enemy. It they are improperly used by the enemy then the Force must ensure that, before an enemy unit is attacked whilst displaying an emblem, firm proof is available that it is actively being used to attack his side.

However, this requirement of respect for the protected status of MMP only holds good in the context in which it originated, namely state-on-state warfare, and in which there was a quasi-contractual agreement, or compact, between the warring parties to the effect that certain standards of conduct and behaviour would be expected and required during times of conflict (originating in medieval codes of chivalry and latterly seen in honour codes). Thus the modern problem with the Taliban in Afghanistan and in other instances of wars amongst the people, especially those involving jihadists, is that although they might fully understand what is involved in the underlying compact, they do not regard themselves as being bound by its terms and requirements. More importantly, they simply do not *care* if they are in flagrant breach of IHL or the Conventions and Protocols, and therefore have no conscience or guilt feelings as a result. They are beyond persuasion and rational argument. But this does not entail that they have consequently forfeited their own human rights and that they are beyond the demands of common humanity: throughout the conflict in Afghanistan, injured and wounded Taliban fighters have been accorded exactly the same levels of care as ISAF medical treatment resources would allow. Once again, keeping the legal, ethical and moral high ground is of central importance.

Conclusion

Commanders and others higher up the chain of command have a responsibility implied from the legal and moral basis of the non-combatant status of medical personnel to protect their neutrality, ensure their employment is limited only to medical duties and secondary duties that do not compromise this, and to provide adequate physical protection from limited force protection assets to ensure they can operate. They must understand and respect the protection afforded by the protective emblems and work to ensure it is understood and respected by the enemy to ensure it is not lost from the battlefield.

Medical Personnel are unique on the battlefield, they are deployed by a side that is serving its own interest but act to the benefit of all those who are injured and derive their protective status from their duty to help those injured personnel. This confers a responsibility to protect them on all forces on a battlefield and in particular on modern, western forces to protect not only their physical safety but also their employment on the battlefield *and* their neutrality.

CHAPTER 8

The Responsibility to Dissent: Whistleblowing and Military Effectiveness

Colin T. Sullivan

Whistleblowing is an act of dissent and as such, the introduction of a whistleblowing culture into the military may seem at odds with an institution characterized by respect for authority, duty, and loyalty. However, if handled correctly, whistleblowing can bring many advantages, even – and especially – for the military. That said, the act of whistleblowing is seldom risk free and, thus, the aim of this chapter is to ascertain whether the adoption of a whistleblowing culture in the military would be beneficial or detrimental to military effectiveness. We will focus on the British military in order to limit the scope of this chapter to a reasonable range of inquiry.

The chapter first explains what whistleblowing is, as the term whistleblower is contested. The chapter will then differentiate between a whistleblower and other individuals. The term whistleblowing is often used in today's media, but rarely in the right context. Whistleblowers are often confused by journalists for other less ethically motivated individuals who would be more accurately labelled turncoats, snitches, informers and betrayers; and as such, whistleblowing is associated with negative tabloid exposé stories. This explains some of the negativity surrounding the issue of whistleblowing and is just one reason why whistleblowers are seldom regarded positively. Next, the chapter assesses why whistleblowing matters before demonstrating why whistleblowing in a security organisation is a sensitive issue and how the law has failed to protect issues of national security against whistleblowers. Following this, the chapter considers what barriers exist for whistleblowers and discusses how retaliation and loyalty are considerable factors when deciding whether to blow the whistle or not. On conclusion of this section, the paper moves on to account for why whistleblowers choose to dissent. Given that whistleblowing is not always a popular act, the legal protection that whistleblowers are afforded is explained next by using the police and the military as a comparison. The significant benefits to whistleblowing are then demonstrated before the chapter assesses the dangers of a world without whistleblowers. The chapter concludes by arguing that in a globalized world where the military is fiscally constrained and the dynamics of the security environment are extremely fluid, the military should encourage whistleblowing to

 | DOI 10.1163/9789004280380_009

drive down risk, increase efficiency and highlight weaknesses in areas of defence and security. Whilst initially uncomfortable, the chapter argues that disclosure is a vital component of an ethical organisation and ultimately leads to greater effectiveness.

What is Whistleblowing?

The definition of whistleblowing is contested, including its etymology. Most assume the label harkens to either a "policeman blowing his whistle to stop an illegal activity" or else a "referee using a whistle to call a foul" in a sporting event.[1] Public Concern at Work (PCAW), a whistleblowing charity in the UK, include a number of familiar definitions including: 'Bringing an activity to a sharp conclusion as if by the blast of a whistle';[2] 'raising concerns about misconduct within an organisation or within an independent structure associated with it';[3] giving information (usually to the authorities) about illegal or underhand practices';[4] exposing to the press a malpractice or cover-up in a business or government office'[5] and providing a safe alternative to silence'.[6] Glazer and Glazer define a whistleblower as one who, 'acts to prevent harm to others, not him or himself, while possessing evidence that would convince a reasonable person'.[7] The UK Government describes whistleblowing as: 'making a disclosure in the public interest'. This means simply that if you believe there is wrongdoing in your workplace (e.g. your employer is committing a criminal offence) you can, 'report this by following the correct processes, and your employment rights are protected'.[8] Just what constitutes an act of wrongdoing of sufficient weight to warrant whistleblowing is contentious. One of the best examples of a comprehensive definition of wrongdoing can be found in the Freedom of

1 http://www.wordorigins.org/index.php/site/whistleblower/

2 Oxford English Dictionary.

3 Nolan Committee, "Promoting High Standards of Behaviour in the Public Sphere," Public Concern at Work, http://www.pcaw.org.uk/files/best_practice_guide-2006.pdf (accessed 8 February 2015)

4 Chambers, Public Concern at Work, http://www.pcaw.org.uk/files/best_practice_guide-2006 .pdf (accessed 8 February 2015)

5 *Ibid.*

6 *Ibid.*

7 Myron P. Glazer and Penina Glazer, The Whistleblowers, (New York: 1989), p. 4.

8 http://www.direct.gov.uk/en/Employment/ResolvingWorkplaceDisputes/Whistleblowing intheworkplace/DG_10026552 (accessed 13 March 2011)

Information Act of Antigua and Barbuda. The Act defines wrongdoing in this context as:

> A serious threat to health or safety of an individual or a serious threat to the public environment, the commission of a criminal offence, failure to comply with legal obligation, a miscarriage of justice, corruption, dishonesty or serious maladministration, abuse of authority or neglect in the performance of official duty, injustice to an individual, and unauthorized use of public funds.[9]

This definition highlights the positive intentions of whistleblowers. It would be difficult to argue against the reporting of such issues but, without a whistleblowing policy which provides the legal protection of such disclosure in the workplace, there is significant evidence that many of these activities routinely go unreported.[10]

For the purposes of this chapter, whistleblowing is defined as: a means of disclosing information which is in the public interest, by an individual employed within an organisation regarding issues of wrongdoing which have a negative impact that the whistleblower believes is being conducted by another individual or set of individuals within that organisation.

The term whistleblower invokes a surprising contrast of either positive or negative connotations, varying by individual. Some perceive whistleblowers to be freedom fighters, individuals with high moral and ethical values with the courage of their convictions. They believe whistleblowers to be people who are driven to ensure that justice is *seen to be done* when issues of corruption, illegal, or fraudulent activity are evident in the working environment. Others have a less idealized view and see whistleblowers as organisational mavericks or internal terrorists who are seeking to bring down institutions or organisations from within. They are viewed as trouble makers and attention seekers who do

---

9 RTI-rating.org http://www.rti-rating.org/files/pdf/Antigua.pdf (accessed 8 February 2015)

10 See Peter B. Jubb, *Whistleblowing: A restrictive Definition and Interpretation*, (Journal of Business Ethics, Vol 21, 1999), pp. 77–94. Jubb describes whistleblowers through the lens of libertarianism. He defines the act of whistleblowing as: '…a deliberate non-obligatory act of disclosure, which gets onto the public record and is made by a person who has or had privileged access to data or information of an organisation, about non-trivial illegality or wrongdoing whether actual, suspected or anticipated which implicates and is under the control of that organisation, to an external entity having potential to rectify the wrongdoing'.

not deserve the support of the organisation and, as such, are quickly isolated and rendered inoperable when discovered.

One such example of isolation of a whistleblower was the case of Sharmila Chowdhury, a 51-year old 'radiology service manager at Ealing Hospital NHS Trust'.[11] As part of her role she was responsible for ensuring that the accounts within her department were accurate. Soon after taking the position, she noticed discrepancies in the money being paid to senior doctors in the trust. Chowdhury, 'repeatedly warned the hospital's most senior managers that doctors were dishonestly claiming thousands of pounds every month'. Her concerns highlighted that senior doctors seemed to be, 'moonlighting at a private hospital while being paid to diagnose NHS patients'.[12] The doctors concerned raised a counter claim against Chowdhury, accusing her of fraud for being paid for undertaking assessments of x-rays, which she was actually conducting in her own lunch break. As a result, the Trust decided to sack Chowdhury from her post. During the employment tribunal surrounding this case, 'the Trust admitted during the disciplinary hearing that it had failed to find any evidence to support his [the doctor's] claim. Despite this, Ms Chowdhury was sacked for gross misconduct in order to placate the consultants, 'who were fed up with Ms Chowdhury's interference in their business'.[13]

This case helps demonstrate that whistleblowers, in attempting to do what they believe to be the right thing, may not always be viewed as helpful by those within the organisation. In attempting to raise concerns about a potentially corrupt act that was in the public interest, Chowdhury clearly falls into the bracket of whistleblower, however the distinction is not always so clear. The case of Private First Class (PFC) Bradley (Chelsea) Manning (US Army) demonstrates the vagaries in defining what a whistleblower actually is and also draws out the emotions held by those who hold one perspective or another.[14] In the recent high profile case of whistleblowing over the internet, the disclosure of more than 250,000[15] classified US State Department documents to the whistleblowing web site Wikileaks hit the headlines in spectacular fashion.

11 Nina Laikhani, "Sacked NHS Whistleblower Vindicated," http://www.independent.co.uk/life-style/health-and-families/health-news/sacked-nhs-whistleblower-vindicated-2023809.html (accessed 14 April 2011)

12 *Ibid.*

13 *Ibid.*

14 Note that Manning now identifies as female and uses the first name Chelsea.

15 Michael Cook, "Wikileaks: The Case Against, A Clear and Present Danger," Mercatornet, http://www.mercatornet.com/articles/view/a_clear_and_present_danger/ (accessed 5 April 2011)

The disclosure of politically and militarily sensitive information caused an outpouring of contradictory and contentious comment on the matter. The case divided the US nation into those who believe the exposing of classified information was a threat to the nation's security and put the lives of soldiers serving in Afghanistan at risk, and those who believe the exposing of potentially unlawful acts, such as the Apache Helicopter Attack on un-armed civilians in Iraq, was morally and ethically justified. Daniel Ellsberg, a famous US whistleblower who, decades earlier, was held on the same charges as Manning stated: 'much of America is split when it comes to Bradley [Chelsea] Manning and his [her] alleged leaking of hundreds of thousands of State Department records. He [she] is touted as a hero by some, while a traitor by others'.[16]

Manning ultimately plead guilty to 10 of 22 charges and was sentenced to 35 years in prison at Fort Leavenworth, Kansas.[17] But the case remains highly contentious and presses the issue of just where the line should be drawn between legitimate whistleblowing and treasonous behaviour. If a policy of allowing whistleblowing in the UK military were to be adopted, the clear distinction between a whistleblower and a traitor would need to be established. This is a significant challenge as the issue is subjective and has political ramifications. However, the protection of accusations of treason would be essential if a whistleblowing culture were to be productive. By legally clarifying the difference between a whistleblower and a traitor, the military could benefit from the positive aspects of whistleblowing whilst protecting itself against other non-whistleblowing activities such as malicious reporting or leaking of sensitive information which has no public interest and could damage national security.

What Makes a Whistleblower?

In assessing whether permitting whistleblowing would be beneficial or detrimental to military effectiveness, one must first understand what makes a whistleblower. It is important, for instance, to make the distinction between a whistleblower and an informant or snitch, as although many believe they are the same thing they are distinctly different. In David Banisar's whistleblowing paper on behalf of the World Bank, he makes the point that the difference lies in the liability of the person disclosing the information. Banisar suggests that, 'Informants are often themselves involved in some sort of unethical enterprise

16 Daniel Ellsberg, "Daniel Ellsberg Supports Bradley Manning and Wikileaks," http://www.ellsberg.net/articles (accessed 6 April 2011)

17 Julie Tate, "Judge sentences Bradley Manning to 35 years," The Washington Post, 21 August 2013.

and are using the disclosure of information as a means to reduce their liability, either voluntarily, or due to coercion'.[18] This theory is supported in a paper by Wohl, in which the argument is made that the, 'vast majority of informants trade information for money or immunity from prosecution'.[19] Therefore, when deciding whether military personnel who divulge information are whistleblowers or leakers, for instance, the deciding factor will be the motivation of the individual. If the information was divulged in exchange for reward to the individual such a cash payment, or to provide the individual with personal leverage, such as to influence the decision over the procurement of equipment in order to support their favoured outcome, they would not be classed as a whistleblower but as a leaker. However, the widow of Sgt Steve Roberts who was shot dead by Iraqi dissidents, provided information regarding the lack of body armour to protect soldiers in Iraq to the press,[20] out of continued health and safety concerns for her husband's colleagues, and the ethical and moral principles involved in sending soldiers to war without the correct level of protection. She told Five Live: "Steve died because he did not have a flak jacket. If that is not a major issue, I have to ask Mr Hoon how many men have to die before he sees it as a major issue?" Even though Mrs Roberts had little to gain personally from exposing this issue, and the issue was in the public interest, she does not fit into the category of whistleblower as she was not employed by the British military.

There is also a distinguishable difference between a whistleblower and an individual who has a duty to inform wrongdoing. Many cases of reported wrongdoing are categorized as whistleblowing when they are subtly different. The distinction lies in the motivation to inform: 'In the case of required disclosure, the person faces the choice of being subject to criminal or other sanctions for the act of non-disclosure'.[21] A chartered accountant, for instance, has a legal obligation to report fraudulent activity exposed during the conduct of his work. Not to do so would result in legal action being taken against him. The whistleblower often has no other motivation other than their ethical or moral compass and volunteers the information accordingly. The information they disclose does not necessarily have to be of an illegal nature but may be a

18 David Banisar, "Whistleblowing, International Standards and Developments," (Sandoval: Irma, E, 2011).

19 Ethan D. Wohl, "Confidential Informants in Private Litigation: Balancing Interests in Anonymity and Disclosure," in '*Federal Practice and Procedures*' ed. Charles Alan Wright and Kenneth W. Graham (Oxford, 1992), p. 338.

20 http://news.bbc.co.uk/1/hi/uk_politics/3397769.stm (accessed 4 May 2011)

21 David Banisar, *Whistleblowing, International Standards and Developments*, (Sandoval: Irma, E, 2011).

concern about health and safety; inefficiency or poor practice. Given that whistleblowers are not motivated by self interest, but by improving the efficiency or effectiveness of an organisation, reducing organisational risk, or exposing illegal activity etc. the argument for adopting a positive whistleblowing culture in an organisation is strong.

Does Whistleblowing Matter?

The ability to speak freely is a democratic right and is essential for a whistleblower to be effective. Recent events in the Middle East are evidence of how much people are willing to sacrifice in order to gain the right to have the freedom to choose how they live and the freedom to say what they wish. Freedom sits at the very heart of democracy and relies on our core ability to speak the truth. Only by speaking the truth can we impart information and allow others to make their own mind up about the conclusion. Mill summed this up quite succinctly when he wrote: 'The only freedom that deserves the name, is that of pursuing our own good in our own way, so long as we do not attempt to deprive others of theirs, or impede their efforts to attain it'.[22] Mill suggests that central to the issue of freedom is the capability to determine and pursue one's own core values. Kitcher states that: 'knowledge is important for the realisation of freedom and freedom of discussion is important for the role it plays in enabling people to gain relevant forms of knowledge'.[23] The ability to discuss issues and speak freely, Kitcher suggests, is 'the most fundamental value,' because one's ability to converse 'leads to knowledge' and one's ability to gain knowledge without fear of repression or retribution leads to truth.[24] The liberal notion of the freedom of speech suggests 'speech that is unconstrained'.[25] Only by divulging information through speech that is unconstrained can the truth be ascertained. If the speaker has been impeded in any way, then the purity and integrity of the information that is divulged may be questioned and the truthfulness of the speaker brought into doubt.

The act of whistleblowing is very much the manifestation of pursuing one's own core values by disclosing the truth about a subject of which you have

22 John Stuart Mill. "On Liberty and Other Essays," (Boston: Beacon Press, 1957), p. 17.

23 Philip Kitcher. "Varieties of Freedom and Their Distribution," (Social Research, Vol 77: No 3, 2010), p. 857.

24 *Ibid.*

25 L.M. Heldke, "Do You Mind if I Speak Freely? Reconceptualising Freedom of Speech," in *The Ethics of Liberal Democracy: Morality and Democracy in Theory and Practice*, ed., R.P. Churchill, (Oxford, Berg, 1994), p. 112.

knowledge. However, speech is a powerful tool, which can motivate action. The action that results from blowing the whistle is not always welcome within an organisation and this may be the reason that many whistleblowers find themselves isolated once they have spoken out. MacKinnon suggests that, 'words are often tantamount to acts as they are vehicles for removed cerebration'.[26] When one blows the whistle in the workplace, the issue is not just what words are said, it is the acts that the words are designed to motivate. The Racial and Religious Hatred Act, brought into force on 1 October 2007, is a good example of how United Kingdom (UK) laws have been amended to take account of the influence words can have on motivating action. The Act 'makes provision about offences involving stirring up hatred against persons on religious grounds'.[27] Section 29B of the Act specifically mentions, 'A person who uses *threatening words* or behaviour, or displays any written material which is threatening, is guilty of an offence if he intends thereby to stir up religious hatred'.[28] The concern is not necessarily about what is said, but what the repercussions may be of what is said.

The right to voice one's opinion is something that UK citizens take for granted and is not something that would be sacrificed easily. The privilege to speak out against injustice is viewed as a democratic human right and has been supported by the UK legal and judicial system for centuries. Perhaps surprisingly, however, human rights in the UK were not officially legislated for until the introduction of the Human Rights Act 1998. Article 10 of the Act, called 'Freedom of Expression', has placed into UK law, among other human rights, the right to have, 'our own opinions and discuss these opinions freely and without fear of reprisal or interference from the Government'.[29] Yet the Act also allows for a degree of interpretation and may also:

> ...be subject to such formalities, conditions, restrictions or penalties as are prescribed by law and are necessary in a democratic society, in the interests of *national security*, territorial integrity or public safety, for the prevention of disorder or crime, for the protection of health or morals, for the protection of the reputation or rights of others, for preventing the

26 Catherine MacKinnon, *Feminism Unmodified*, (Cambridge: MA, 1987), p. 208.

27 The Racial and Religious Hatred Act, http://www.legislation.gov.uk/uksi/2007/2490/made?view=plain (accessed 5 April 11)

28 Section 29B of the Racial and Religious Hatred Act, http://www.legislation.gov.uk/uksi/2007/2490/made?view=plain (accessed 5 April 11)

29 About Human Rights, "Your Freedom of Speech," http://www.abouthumanrights.co.uk/your-freedom-speech.html (accessed 5 April 2011)

> disclosure of information received in confidence, or for maintaining the authority and impartiality of the judiciary.[30]

This clause is what the UK Government uses, specifically in terms of the restrictions that the Official Secrets Act (OSA) applies in certain circumstances, in order to override the human requirement of free speech. Hence, whilst the ability to speak freely sits at the heart of a democracy, there are significant sections of UK society that do not have this right and are restricted in what they can say.

The Official Secrets Act 2002 restricts what can be discussed on the following subject matters: 'Security and intelligence, defence, international relations, information obtained in confidence from other states or international organisations, information likely to result in the commission of an offense and information likely to impede detection and special investigations under statutory warrant'.[31] The categories are so broad that they cover almost all subject matter that military personnel are likely to become acquainted with and as such, severely restrict what can be freely discussed in public forum. Members of the UK Armed Forces, for instance, are not able to disclose any information that may affect national security, even if it is in the public's interest. The term national security is not a term that has a legal definition, 'but is capable of wide interpretation,'[32] and as such, many issues can be encompassed by it. Who decides what falls under the national security umbrella rests with Ministers and as such, they are not impartial in making this decision. It is only Ministers, for instance, who can issue a national security certificate, which may be used to block a request under the Freedom of Information Act (FOIA). Ministers can only block a request under the FOIA if they are concerned about, 'the effect that disclosure would have, not on the content or source of the information'.[33] This distinction is important as it stresses that it is the repercussions from the information that is cause for concern and not the information in its own right.

The same issue revolves around the freedom of speech. There is a fine balance between protecting the nation's security and restricting the human rights of its citizens. By adopting a whistleblowing policy that respected both issues, this balance could be achieved and could be of significant benefit to both.

30 A Guide to the Human Rights Act 1998, https://www.justice.gov.uk/downloads/human-rights/act-studyguide.pdf (accessed 11 April 2011)

31 House of Commons, "Public Administration Select Committee: Leaks and Whistleblowing in Whitehall," http://www.publications.parliament.uk/pa/cm200809/cmselect/cmpubadm/83/8302.htm (accessed 13 April 2011)

32 Freedom of Information Act, http://www.legislation.gov.uk/ukpga/2000/36/contents (accessed 7 February 2015)

33 *Ibid.*

Stifling the military's ability to raise issues of public interest could actually result in weakening national security. In a survey of federal employees undertaken in the US, on factors that would motivate them to, 'report illegal or wasteful activities. Fully 96% of the 13,000 respondents labelled "very important" activities that might endanger life'.[34] Post September 11, the Government Accountability Project (GAP), one of the largest US whistleblowing websites, received over three times its usual amount of calls for the same period. Calls were made from a number of government sectors highlighting issues of: 'negligence and security breeches at airports around the country; a former Customs special agent expressed concern over inadequate inspection at border security related to railcards; and an expert at the Department for Energy reported concerns about safeguards against attacks at nuclear weapons facilities'.[35] All were taken seriously and investigated. The provision of a whistleblowing framework that provided the facility for military personnel to express their concerns through an independent body may assist in identifying lapses in security, gaps in procedure or negligent acts which, if exposed, could reduce risk and therefore increase military effectiveness.

Whistleblowing and Security

Whilst the present law may deter whistleblowers, it does not stop them. Although the OSA is prohibitive in what can be disclosed, personnel working in areas of national sensitivity have chosen to blow the whistle when they felt the issues were of such importance that they were willing to risk their liberty to expose them. There are two quite recent cases that demonstrate that even with the limitations that the OSA places on individuals involved in handling sensitive information, disclosure can still occur. By stating they were acting out of "necessity of circumstance," whistleblowers have disclosed information that was subject to the OSA and have successfully avoided conviction. The "necessity" law is a "common law" which David Shayler successfully used to defend his actions when he leaked sensitive material as an employee of MI5.

Katherine Gunn also intended on using the same common law in her defence. Gunn was employed as a language analyst at the Government Communications Headquarters (GCHQ). Whilst undertaking her duties in 2003, Gunn had sight of an email from Frank Koza, who was a senior operator in the National Security Agency (NSA) in the US. In the email, Koza ordered

34 Johnson, *Whistleblowing: When It Works and Why*, p. 20.

35 *Ibid.*

deployed NSA staff to 'conduct aggressive, covert surveillance against several United Nations Security Council members,'[36] in order to gain information, which may have helped the US swing the votes of six key nations in support of the war with Iraq. Gunn believed the email contravened the Vienna convention on diplomatic relations which govern the 'privileges and immunities, diplomatic and consular relations,'[37] between states. She copied the memo and, after a period of contemplation, delivered it to a friend who had connections in the press. When the Top-Secret memo eventually hit the front page of the Observer, Gunn was questioned and, 'confessed to her role as the leaker'.[38] Unsurprisingly she was forced to leave GCHQ and was subsequently 'charged with breaking the Official Secrets Act, facing the threat of a trial and a two-year prison sentence'.[39] Gunn intended on using the common law "necessity of circumstance" to defend her actions which would have relied on, 'Gunn proving that she had only acted in contravention of the law (OSA) in order to prevent another crime from being committed'.[40] The UK Government eventually dropped the charges against Gunn as, 'in her view, the government did not want to disclose advice on the legality of the Iraq war to their defence...'[41] Gunn claims that she did not feel guilt over what she did and stated: 'I wanted to get it out. And I would do it again'.[42]

More recently, in 2009, a Senior British Army Officer was arrested, 'on suspicion of passing sensitive information to a researcher working for the campaign group Human Rights Watch (HRW) in Afghanistan'.[43] The lack of transparency over civilian casualty figures seems to have been the motivating factor in this case. Civilian casualty figures continue to be a sensitive issue in Afghanistan and HRW have been tracking the casualty data and reporting their findings

---

36 History Commons, http://www.historycommons.org/entity.jsp?entity=frank_koza (accessed 11 April 2011)

37 UN Treaty Collection, "Vienna Convention on Diplomatic Relations," http://treaties.un.org/Pages/ViewDetails.aspx?src=TREATY&mtdsg_no=III-3&chapter=3&lang=en (accessed 11 April 2011)

38 Oliver Burkeman and Richard Norton-Taylor, "The Spy Who Wouldn't Keep a Secret," http://www.guardian.co.uk/politics/2004/feb/26/interviews.iraq (accessed 11 April 2011)

39 *Ibid.*

40 Wing Commander Nicola Severs, Interview with Author, dated 6 April 2011.

41 House of Commons Public Administration Select Committee, "Leaks and Whistleblowing in Whitehall," http://www.fas.org/irp/world/uk/leaks.pdf (accessed 11 April 2011)

42 Burkeman, "The Spy Who Wouldn't Keep a Secret," http://www.guardian.co.uk/politics/2004/feb/26/interviews.iraq (accessed 11 April 2011)

43 Audrey Gillen, "British Army Officer Accused of Leaking Afghan Deaths Data," http://www.guardian.co.uk/uk/2009/feb/05/afghanistan-british-army-owen-mcnally (accessed 11 April 2011)

throughout the Afghan campaign. The Officer was working in the International Security Assistance Force (ISAF) Headquarters and was accused of providing HRW with sensitive civilian casualty data, which was reportedly used in a HRW brief that showed civilian deaths had tripled between 2006–2007.[44] An MOD statement was released which stated, 'We can confirm that a British army officer has been arrested in Afghanistan on suspicion of breaching the Official Secrets Act. He is being returned to the UK for questioning. The investigation has been referred from the MoD to the Metropolitan police and is now under consideration…'[45] Putting one's liberty and career on the line in the name of truth is not a new phenomena. Historical evidence also suggests that whistleblowers will risk breaking the law if they feel they have no alternative and the benefit of getting this issue into the public domain is of vital importance.

Daniel Ellsberg is one of the most famous whistleblowers in US history. A retired US Marine who, having left the services in 1957, went on to earn a Ph.D. in Economics at Harvard. Ellsberg subsequently went on to work within the Defense Department, 'as Special Assistant to Assistant Secretary of Defense (International Security Affairs) John McNaughton, working on the escalation of the war in Vietnam. He transferred to the State Department in 1965 to serve two years at the US Embassy in Saigon, evaluating pacification in the field'.[46] In 1967, due to his in-depth knowledge of the Vietnam campaign, Ellsberg was commissioned, as part of a large team, to conduct a, 'sweeping study of the Vietnam War',[47] with the intent of creating an, 'encyclopedic history of the Vietnam War'.[48] The study was later to become known as the 'Pentagon Papers'.[49] On its completion, the study was classified, 'Top Secret – Sensitive,' due to the significant number of copied official government documents contained within the paper which could, 'cause embarrassment,' if disclosed.[50]

Ellsberg's research on the Pentagon Papers led him to become increasingly disillusioned with the way the US had conducted its affairs in Vietnam: 'Seven thousand pages of documentary evidence of lying by four Presidents and their

44 *Ibid.*

45 *Ibid.*

46 Daniel Ellsberg, http://www.ellsberg.net/bio (accessed 11 April 2011)

47 John T. Correll, "The Pentagon Papers," *Air Force Magazine*, February 2007, http://www.airforce-magazine.com/MagazineArchive/Pages/2007/February%202007/0207pentagon.aspx (accessed 11 April 2011)

48 *Ibid.*

49 United Press International (UPI), "1971 Year in Review: The Pentagon Papers," http://www.upi.com/Audio/Year_in_Review/Events-of-1971/The-Pentagon-Papers/12295509436546-7/ (accessed 11 April 2011)

50 Correll, "The Pentagon Papers," *Air Force Magazine*, February 2007.

Administrations over 23 years to conceal plans and actions of mass murder,' drove Ellsberg to copy the papers and, 'get it out somehow'.[51] Ellsberg tried in vain to bring these atrocities to the attention of a number of senior US personalities including a number of senators and even Henry Kissinger with whom Ellsberg was on 'first name terms'. In the absence of any takers, Ellsberg, in February of 1967, told Neil Sheehan of the New York Times about the papers and they 'began discussing the possibility of publication'.[52] The publication of such sensitive documents was a fatal blow for the Nixon administration. Kissinger, in his memoirs said, 'The massive hemorrhage of state secrets was bound to raise doubts about our reliability in the minds of other governments, friend or foe, and indeed about the stability of our political system'.[53]

Ellsberg knew the potential ramifications of the information he had at his disposal but felt that the US administration was following an unethical path and felt morally justified in intervening. In an interview with Walter Cronkite, a trusted anchorman with CBS news at that time, Ellsberg was asked: 'what he considers the most important revelations to date from the Pentagon documents'. Ellsberg responded, 'I think the lesson is that the people of this country can't afford to let the President run the country by himself, even foreign affairs, without the help of Congress, without the help of the public…'[54]

Ellsberg was ultimately indicted for 'violating the Espionage Act,' a crime punishable by death, but the case was eventually declared a mistrial due to illegal wire tapping.[55] In a recent interview with Ellsberg he was asked, 'if someone today had the Pentagon Papers, or the modern equivalent, would he still go to the press?' Even though Ellsberg came close to being executed for his whistleblowing act, the ethical judgment that drove him to blow the whistle remains. Ellsberg stated that the current legal system would not deter him: 'I would have gotten a scanner and put them on the Internet'.[56] The military can try to use the law to protect itself against such acts but it will never be in a position to stop the disclosure of information if the whistleblower feels the risk to their liberty is worth taking in order to get the information into the public

51 *Ibid.*

52 *Ibid.*

53 Henry Kissinger, *Years of Upheaval*, (London: Phoenix Press, 1979), p. 245.

54 Correll, "The Pentagon Papers," *Air Force Magazine*, February 2007.

55 *Ibid.*

56 Noam Cohan, "What Would Daniel Ellsberg Do with the Pentagon Papers Today?" *New York Times*, 18 April 2010, http://www.nytimes.com/2010/04/19/business/media/19link.html (accessed on 11 April 2011)

domain. However, by employing a robust whistleblowing framework, 'the risk of disclosure outside of the organisation is significantly reduced'.[57]

Barriers to Whistleblowing

There are significant barriers to whistleblowing. Retaliation is a compelling reason for individuals who are considering whistleblowing to avoid doing so. Out of the seventy case studies reviewed for this chapter, some form of retaliation had occurred in over 80% of cases. Retaliation can come in different forms, 'from minor harassment at the workplace to far more severe consequences'.[58] It is not uncommon to find employees who have suffered mental breakdown and/or negative life changing consequences as a result of blowing the whistle. In 1993, 'the federal Merit Systems Protection Board, the [US] government agency which hears Whistleblower Protection Act (WPA) claims,'[59] conducted a study in which they asked participants, 'why observers chose not to report illegal or wasteful activities? Three of the top four reasons concerned fear of retaliation'.[60] In a more recent study undertaken by the same organisation in 2000, where disclosures included 'health and safety dangers, unlawful behaviour, and/or fraud, waste and abuse, fully 44% of survey respondents who made formal disclosures experienced retaliation, compared to just 4% who had not made a formal disclosure'.[61] Public Concern at Work (PCAW) state: 'It is vital for effective risk management that employees are confident that they can raise their concerns with their employer without suffering any detriment'. They go on to say that: 'Without this confidence, employees may stay silent where there is a threat, even a grave one, to the employer or its stakeholders'.[62]

The US Project on Government Oversight (POGO) includes a list of the most common retaliatory action on their website, for instance:

57 Cathy James, Acting Director of Public Concern at Work dated 9 November 2011.

58 David, Banisar, *Whistleblowing, International Standards and Developments*, (Sandoval: Irma, E, 2011).

59 Project On Government Oversight, "*Homeland and National Security Whistleblower Protections: The Unfinished Agenda*," (Washington: 2005), p. 6.

60 *Ibid.*

61 *Ibid.*

62 Public Concern at Work, http://www.pcaw.co.uk/faq/FAQ_employers.htm (accessed 13 April 2011)

> Taking away job duties so that the employee is marginalised; taking away an employee's national security clearance so that he or she is effectively fired; blacklisting an employee so that he or she is unable to find gainful employment; conducting retaliatory investigations in order to divert attention away from the waste, fraud or abuse the whistleblower is trying to expose; questioning a whistleblower's mental health, professional competence or honesty; setting the whistleblower up by giving impossible assignments or seeking to entrap him or her and reassigning an employee geographically so he or she is unable to do their job.[63]

In July 1997, the US Department of Defence (DoD) issued a Military Whistleblower Protection Directive.[64] The policy document lays out the conditions for the protection of military and military employed civilian personnel in section four. The policy states that:

> Members of the Armed Forces shall be free from reprisal for making or preparing to make a protected communication[65] and no person may take or threaten to take an unfavourable personnel action, or withhold or threaten to withhold a favourable personnel action, in reprisal against any member of the Armed Forces for making or preparing to make a protected communication.[66]

Despite this protection, the figures for retaliation in the US DoD have doubled from, 'three hundred in 1997 to nearly six hundred in 2007'.[67]

One example of such retribution was that of Joe Darby. Darby was the Army reservist who was responsible for alerting the world to the atrocities that were being conducted in Abu Ghraib prison in Iraq. When the then US Defence Secretary, Donald Rumsfeld, publically thanked Darby for blowing the whistle on the issue, Darby and his family were subjected to extreme retaliatory action.

---

63 Project On Government Oversight, http://www.pogo.org/search/search.jsp?query=retaliation (accessed 12 April 2011)

64 Department of Defence Directive "Military Whistleblower Protection," No: 7050.06, http://www.dtic.mil/whs/directives/corres/pdf/705006p.pdf (accessed 6 May 2011)

65 A Protected Communication allows Military Personnel to raise issues of concern to a Member of Congress or The Inspector General.

66 Department of Defence Directive, "Military Whistleblower Protection," No: 7050.06.

67 Project On Government Oversight, http://pogoblog.typepad.com/pogo/2010/12/largely-missing-from-the-wikileaks-debate-the-state-of-military-whistleblower-protections.html (accessed 12 April 2011)

Within the service, Darby was referred to as a traitor and eventually the threats to him and his family became so severe that they were placed in hiding.[68]

A report compiled by POGO concluded that, 'investigations [in the US] fail to provide whistleblowers with a hearing by a truly independent court or administrative body that can hold agencies accountable for the retaliation'.[69] On 6 April 2011, the US introduced the 'Whistleblower Protection Enhancement Act of 2011 (S. 743). This bill will ensure the protection of legitimate disclosures of wrongdoing be protected, increase accountability to the public and save billions of taxpayer dollars by helping expose waste, fraud and abuse'.[70] Importantly, the bill provides those personnel working in the National Security and Intelligence arena with an, 'administrative appeals process to prevent leaks and provide legal, safe channels for disclosures of wrongdoing'.[71]

The evidence suggests that the US Government recognise the value of whistleblowing, even in sensitive areas such as National Security and Intelligence. It also indicates that there is an understanding that retaliatory action against whistleblowers will suppress their actions and lead to higher levels of waste, fraud and abuse. In providing, 'safe channels for disclosing wrongdoing,'[72] this amendment also seeks to protect would be whistleblowers so that they are not driven to expose issues through the media or other external sources. The inclusion of National Security and Intelligence in the Protection Enhancement Act is important as it allows personnel a route by which they can safely expose the most sensitive information. Protection is afforded to the whistleblower even if the disclosure could be potentially embarrassing to the US Government. The Act allows sensitive issues to be exposed early and therefore reduces risk to US citizens before the issue of concern is exposed by its failings. If the UK military adopted a similar approach, individuals could also expose risk in UK defence and security sectors without fear of prosecution or retribution. Whilst potentially embarrassing once disclosed, issues would be dealt with earlier and, as such, would be beneficial to military effectiveness.

68 Project On Government Oversight, "The Perils of Blowing the Whistle," http://pogoblog.typepad.com/pogo/2006/08/darby_the_peril.html (accessed 12 April 2011)

69 Project On Government Oversight, Homeland and National Security Whistleblower Protections: The Unfinished Agenda, (Washington: 2005), 7, http://www.pogo.org/our-work/reports/2005/wi-wp-20060428.html (accessed 6 May 2011)

70 Project on Government Oversight, http://www.pogo.org/pogo-files/alerts/whistleblower-issues/wi-wp-20110406.html (accessed 13 April 2011)

71 *Ibid.*

72 *Ibid.*

Why do Whistleblowers Dissent?

Whistleblowing is an act of empowerment but is seldom rewarded. The disclosure made by a whistleblower is normally aimed at a, 'higher authority,'[73] as they are not normally in a position to formally challenge the authority of those who are committing the wrongful act otherwise they would use their authority to rectify the situation. As such, they are often forced into using whistleblowing as a tool of last resort when all other checks and balances have failed. As whistleblowers are ethically and morally motivated, they find the urge to disclose issues of concern hard to resist. The research conducted on a significant number of case studies suggests that whistleblowers reach a tipping point after which they feel ethically motivated to act. They believe the information they have access to, is in the public interest and feel unable to withhold this information any longer. Whistleblowers believe that, 'being complicit with an immoral activity corrupts the self'.[74] Alford suggests that, 'whistleblowers disclose because they dread living with a corrupt self more than they dread the other outcomes'.[75] For some individuals, this tipping point may be reached after a number of events occur. In this instance, the individual concerned finds the repetitive and accumulative nature of the abuse to be the deciding factor in blowing the whistle.

This was the case for John Wicks, the Parliamentary expenses scandal whistleblower who felt he had no alternative but to blow the whistle after he had been repeatedly exposed to Parliamentary expenses information by a source who was dealing with MPs' accounts on a daily basis. The source revealed information to Wicks, which indicated potential fraud or misconduct on a gross scale. Wicks, having discussed the issues in detail with the source, eventually requested a sample copy of the information on a disk: 'An analysis of the contents of the disc – containing the records of five MPs – quickly confirmed my worst fears. The way in which MPs were abusing the system was an absolute

73 Peter B. Jubb, Whistleblowing: A Restrictive Definition and Interpretation, https://springerlink3.metapress.com/content/h7767141h662t64q/resource-secured/?target=fulltext.pdf&sid=d1j2vm45foyfetz5wkioxzmm&sh=www.springerlink.com (accessed 13 April 2011)

74 Anthony Hayes and Sandeep Kapur, "An Economic Model of Whistleblowing Policy," http://jleo.oxfordjournals.org/content/25/1/157.abstract (accessed 11 March 2011)

75 Fred C. Alford, Whistleblowers, in Anthony Hayes and Sandeep Kapur, "An Economic Model of Whistleblowing Policy," http://jleo.oxfordjournals.org/content/25/1/157.abstract (accessed 11 March 2011)

scandal and everyone had a right to know'.[76] The tipping point for Wicks seems to have been the persistent lack of willingness of Parliament to be transparent over the issue of expenses. Wicks said, 'I, along with members of the public, had been following in the press the ongoing saga of MPs' expenses and was well aware that Parliament and the Speaker had fought hard to suppress this information'.[77] Wicks, was referring to the significant number of Freedom of Information (FOI) requests that had been refused under Parliamentary regulations. A FOI application, 'gives you the right to ask any public body for all the information they have on any subject you choose. Unless there is good reason, the organisation must provide the information within 20 working days'.[78]

MPs' were eventually requested to disclose the total figure of their expenses in an edited version of the accounts. Clearly the information only became relevant if all the detail behind the claims was made public: 'Following a decision of the High Court in 2008, the Commons prepared to release redacted receipts relating to allowances'.[79] But MPs' in the House of Commons again tried to argue that the detail contained in the expenses, such as addresses, represented a security risk and that the requests were, 'unlawfully intrusive'.[80] The intentional watering down of the detail in the expenses scandal caused Wicks to reach his tipping point and, in response, he released the full unedited version to the Telegraph.

Other individuals may be exposed to a single issue that is of such magnitude that they feel ethically motivated to act immediately. Katherine Gunn would fit into this category when she blew the whistle on the Top-Secret Koza memo. Military personnel are equally challenged by the ethical and moral dilemmas they face and may also reach the threshold at which they feel they can no longer stay quiet about the issue. Unfortunately, the lack of a whistleblowing policy in the military means that those individuals are faced with the stark choice between reporting the issue to the media, which is currently against military regulations, remaining silent, which may be a very dangerous option as will be

76 John Wick, "I am Proud to Have Exposed MPs' Expenses Scandal," http://www.telegraph.co.uk/news/newstopics/mps-expenses/5370852/John-Wick-I-am-proud-to-have-exposed-expenses-scandal.html (accessed 11 April 2011)

77 *Ibid.*

78 Directgov, "Government, Citizens and Rights: Freedom of Information," https://www.gov.uk/make-a-freedom-of-information-request/the-freedom-of-information-act (accessed 11 April 2011)

79 Oonagh Gay, "Parlimentary and Constitution Centre: Hansard," http://www.parliament.uk/briefing-papers/SN05784/the-publication-of-mps-expenses-by-ipsa (accessed 11 April 2011)

80 Anil Dawar, "MPs' Fight to Block Expenses Revolations," http://www.theguardian.com/politics/2008/may/07/houseofcommons (accessed 12 April 2011)

shown later in the chapter, or reporting the issue up through the chain of command.

Whistleblowing on acts of wrongdoing by not using the chain of command would present a significant challenge to the core ethos of the UK's Armed Forces. The military rely heavily on discipline and is a hierarchical rank-based structure in order to ensure that discipline is maintained within the organisation. Personnel are encouraged to use the chain of command to raise concerns and stepping outside of the command chain is vociferously discouraged. Often, the would be whistleblower may wish to raise these concerns outside of their immediate chain of command as the immediate supervisor may well be implicated in the act of wrong doing. As the Committee on Standards in Public Life put it:

> The essence of a whistleblowing system is that staff should be able to bypass the direct management line because that may well be the area about which their concerns arise, and that they should be able to go outside the organisation if they feel the overall management is engaged in an improper course.[81]

The ability to step outside of the chain of command in order to raise a concern is likely to be viewed as undermining the chain of command and therefore would be viewed as an act of ill discipline. However, the precedence for allowing reporting of issues outside of the chain of command has already been set in recognition that the chain of command is not always best placed to deal with issues.

In an attempt to address the issue of fair and independent advice and support outside the chain of command, the Armed Forces have established a Service Complaints Commissioner (SCC). The SCC is outside of the command chain and her independence forms an integral part of the Service Complaints system. The Commissioner is not required to report through the complainants' command chain but is responsible to the Secretary of State for Defence instead. The SCC was established in 2007 to deal with the complaints of serving individuals and their families post the Deep Cut investigation. Although independent of the chain of command, as a Commissioner, the Armed Forces Act 2006 only allows the SCC to deal with, 'wrongs done against individuals,'[82] and not issues that may affect the wider service interests such a fraud, corruption or criminal acts that relate to health and safety etc. However, as whistleblowers

81 Public Concern at Work, http://www.pcaw.co.uk/faq/FAQ_employers.htm (accessed 13 April 2011)

82 http://www.legislation.gov.uk/uksi/2007/3352/pdfs/uksiem_20073352_en.pdf (accessed 13 April 2011)

are not individuals who raise concerns regarding themselves, but are individuals who are ethically motivated to challenge wrong doing on behalf of others, the SCC is unable to assist. This gap in provision of support to military personnel is currently exploitable by the media. However, if the SCC were to be made an independent ombudsman, in line with recommendations from the SCC's annual report for 2010, her powers could be broadened to deal with issues such as those raised by whistleblowers could be addressed. An Armed Forces Ombudsman would also provide the link between the whistleblower and Ministers who could decide on whether disclosure was in the public interest and could provide independent investigation in conjunction with other tools of the state such as the National Audit Office. Raising concerns through the chain of command, as has been demonstrated, often results in retaliation and as such deters personnel from blowing the whistle. This is a significant constraint on improving the effectiveness of the military.

Protection of Whistleblowers

The protection of an individual's right to remain in gainful employment without fear of retaliation after blowing the whistle, is an important factor that leads to honest and open reporting. However, retaliation against whistleblowers was of such concern that it led to changes in employment law. The UK Public Interest Disclosure Act (PIDA) was introduced in 1990 and provides the legal basis on which retaliatory action can be legally challenged. Since whistleblowing protection has been introduced under PIDA, there has been, 'a significant increase in the number of whistleblowing cases across the public and private sectors'.[83] PIDA was established to protect those individuals who blow the whistle on: 'breaches of civil, criminal, regulatory or administrative law, miscarriages of justice, dangers to health, safety and the environment, and the cover up of such malpractice'.[84]

The application of whistleblowing protection across government agencies is inconsistent. Whilst PIDA applies to the vast majority of the UK working population, amendments to the OSA in 2002 withdrew the protection that PIDA provides for disclosures 'that violate the OSA'.[85] The result of this ruling is

83 Cathy James, Acting Director of Public Concern at Work, Interview with Author, dated 9 November 2010.

84 PIDA, "Guide to Law & Practice," http://www.pcaw.org.uk/guide-to-pida (accessed 8 February 2015)

85 Banisar, *Whistleblowing, International Standards and Developments*.

that the UK military is not protected from whistleblowing. However, it was not the only public sector to be affected by the ruling. Whilst successive governments recognised that the police service should have the same protection that PIDA provides to civilian employees, '[police] officers were not then brought within PIDA because they were not classed as employees or workers and PIDA was technically an employment law measure'.[86]

Recognising that this would have a detrimental effect on the willingness of officers to report malpractice and the transparency of the organisation, the Association of Chief Police Officers (ACPO) and a number of MPs lobbied the then head of the Department for Trade and Industry (DTI) to amend the Police Reform Bill to allow police the equivalent protection. Their argument was supported by a number of reports, one of which was compiled by Her Majesty's Inspectorate of Constabulary (HMIC), which recognised the reputation of the Force could be ruined by corruption if left unchecked. The Police Complaints Authority (PCA) also recognised that an equivalent protection to that which PIDA provided to their civilian colleagues was essential to allow safe whistleblowing to occur. One PCA report on corruption concluded:

> The provision of information and evidence from fellow officers is often the most effective means of cracking down on serious officer misconduct including corruption. The PCA is aware of cases where internal informants or whistleblowers have come under pressure from their superiors to submit false statements or to withdraw damaging statements about their colleagues' behaviour. To the whistle blower the choice can be to collude with malpractice or to jeopardise their career. At the same time whistle blowers can experience victimisation, intimidation, ostracism and threats by colleagues which inevitably lead to high levels of distress.[87]

This view was supported in the HMI Paper which again stated: 'There is a strong feeling amongst officers and support staff that retribution, subtle or direct, would result from making complaints against colleagues. There is a perception no one commends such officers for demonstrating moral courage'.[88]

---

86 Public Concern at Work, http://web.archive.org/web/20110614045154/http://www.pcaw.co.uk/policy/policereformbill.htm (accessed 8 February 2015)

87 Police Complaints Authority Report, http://www.publications.parliament.uk/pa/cm200102/cmselect/cmhaff/612/612ap10.htm (accessed 14 April 2011)

88 Her Majesty's Inspectorate of Constabulary, Police Integrity: Securing and Maintaining Public Confidence, (June 1999), p. 3.

In response to this considerable evidence, the Police Reform Bill was amended in 2002 to allow police officers the same employment protection rights and privileges that their civilian counterparts were afforded under PIDA. A number of the issues that resulted in the police receiving the protection that PIDA offers are also relevant to the UK Armed Forces. Military personnel are not classed as employees and as such would not be subject to employment law. In the same way that the Police Reform Bill (2002) rectified this situation for the police, giving officers modern terms and conditions such that the objection, 'no longer holds water,'[89] the same amendments could be made for the UK Armed Forces. As with the Police Force, military personnel also work alongside civil servants who are equally exposed to information regarding issues of a sensitive nature and yet civil servants within MOD have a whistleblowing policy that protects them under PIDA.[90] Now that national security is handled in a far more comprehensive, cross-government manner, the lack of coherence in whistleblowing protection between the Police Service, the UK Armed Forces and the Security Services seems questionable and would need to be rectified if the military were to benefit from a whistleblowing policy being introduced.

The Benefits of Whistleblowing

Whistleblowers have had a positive impact on almost every part of our life. If you drive a car, use the train, fly on a plane, eat food, use the National Health Service (NHS) or hold your money in a bank, you can be assured that at some stage a whistleblower has assisted in making the provision of these products and services safer and potentially cheaper. Despite this, whistleblowing still has a stigma attached to it. Whistleblowing should be seen as a positive culture to adopt and not viewed as a subversive act.

A survey conducted by Public Concern at Work showed that the number of whistleblowing cases across Whitehall is increasing. The number of cases of fraud which were reported by Whitehall whistleblowers in 1995/96 was one hundred and fifty three. Subsequently, by the year 2002/03, this number had increased to four hundred and twenty six. The estimated saving to the Treasury

89 Public Concern at Work, http://web.archive.org/web/20110614045154/http://www.pcaw.co.uk/policy/policereformbill.htm (accessed 8 February 2015)

90 MOD Statement of Civilian Personnel Policy, Handling Matters of Conscience, Reporting Concerns at Work and "Whistleblowing" in the MOD – The Public Interest Disclosure Act (PIDA) 1998, Version 1 – Dated 1 December 2008.

over this five-year period alone was, 'an estimated three million pounds'.[91] In 1978, the US adopted the first whistleblowing hotlines aimed at identifying fraudulent acts, wasteful practices and corporate abuse.[92] The response to their usage has been mixed with some seeing them as potential sources of entrapment and others as welcome routes to the anonymous exposing of issues of concern. What cannot be contested is the financial savings that these hotlines have made. The US DoD introduced a whistleblowing hotline in the late 1980s and by 1989, was receiving, 'one thousand calls per month'. The total saving to the DoD in 1997 as a result of information provided by the DoD Whistleblowing Hotline was $391M.[93] The US DoD estimates that the act of fraud alone within the various departments within the DoD in 2009 cost the US taxpayer, $567,495,057.[94] The figure is staggering; even more so when considering that this figure does not include savings made in wasteful procedures and practices in areas such as procurement.

One such practice was discovered by Ken Pedeleose, a senior industrial engineer who was employed by an arm of the DoD. Pedeleose, blew the whistle on the parts provided to the DoD by Lockheed for its C-5 aircraft. The DoD were being charged, '$744.00 for washers, $714.00 for a rivet, $5,217 for a 1-inch metal bracket and $2,522 for a 4-inch metal sleeve'. These findings alone resulted in savings to the US DoD, 'of $34 million'.[95] All together, whistleblowers have assisted the US Government in recovering between, '$5–$25 Million in 1986, to over a billion dollars today'. A very recent whistleblower raised concerns over the price that the MOD was paying for light bulbs. It seems the MOD were paying over £22 for light bulbs that could be purchased for £0.65.[96] Had the UK Armed Forces had a whistleblowing hotline such as that in the US, or a whistleblowing policy that allows personnel to raise issues such as this in a more controlled framework, the individual concerned may well have been less inclined to go to the press causing further embarrassment for the MOD and the government. Furthermore, in straightened times across Defence, the adoption of a positive whistleblowing policy may well provide significant savings.

91 Public Concern at Work, http://www.pcaw.org.uk/policy/treasuryfraudreports.htm (accessed 13 April 2011)

92 Johnson, *Whistleblowing: When It Works and Why*, pp. 106–109.

93 *Ibid.*

94 http://www.dodig.mil/Inspections/APO/fraud/FraudStatistics_pdfs/DCIS_Fraud StatisticsFY09.pdf (accessed 13 April 2011)

95 Douglas Kinan, "The Massachusetts Courts," http://web.archive.org/web/20111117041543/ http://caught.net/cases/suffolk.htm (accessed 8 February 2015)

96 http://www.bbc.co.uk/news/uk-12643966 (accessed 8 February 2015)

Whistleblowing is the best means of detecting fraud. The Associate of Certified Fraud Examiners (ACFE) conducted a survey on behalf of the United Nations (UN) in 2010. The report found that, 'the typical organisation loses 5% of its annual revenue to fraud. Applied to the estimated 2009 Gross World Product, this figure translates to a potential global fraud loss of more than $2.9 trillion'.[97] They assessed that the 'median loss caused by the occupational fraud cases in our study was $160,000. Nearly one-quarter of the frauds involved losses of at least $1 million'.[98] Importantly, the ACFE conducted research into detection of fraud and found that whilst, 'Anti-fraud controls appear to help reduce the cost and duration of occupational fraud schemes,'[99] it was individuals blowing the whistle on fraud that led to detection in the vast majority of cases. Indeed, the figures show that internal and external auditing combined only detected '18.5%' of fraud whilst whistleblowers accounted for '40.2%'.[100] The UK Defence Vote is in excess of £38 billion. A typical organisation loss rate of 5% through fraudulent activity could result in a loss of £1.9 billion per annum. Evidence suggests that the adoption of a whistleblowing policy within the MOD could result in a significant amount of this being recouped. Any money recouped via whistleblowing could be channelled back into the military, thereby incentivising personnel to report wasteful or fraudulent acts.

The UK Government has recognised the positive role that whistleblowers can play in routing out waste, corruption, unethical, immoral and sometimes illegal activity. When establishing the purpose of the PIDA, Lord Nolan, Chair of the Committee on Standards in Public Life summarised the reason for introducing the Act as follows:

> All organisations face the risk of things going wrong or of unknowingly harbouring malpractice. Part of the duty of identifying such a situation and taking remedial action may lie with the regulatory or funding body. But the regulator is usually in the role of detective, determining responsibility after the crime has been discovered. Encouraging a culture of openness within an organisation will help: prevention is better than cure. Yet it is striking that in the few cases where things have gone badly wrong in local public spending bodies, it has frequently been the tip-off to the press or the local Member of Parliament – sometimes anonymous,

---

97 Association of Certified Fraud Examiners, http://www.acfe.com/uploadedFiles/ACFE_Website/Content/documents/rttn-2010.pdf (accessed 8 February 2015)

98 *Ibid.*

99 *Ibid.*

100 *Ibid.*

> sometimes not – which has prompted the regulator into action. Placing staff in a position where they feel driven to approach the media to ventilate concerns is unsatisfactory both for the staff member and for the organisation.[101]

In a recent House of Commons Public Administration Select Committee report on, 'Leaks and Whistleblowing in Whitehall,' the Committee recognized that whistleblowing, 'allows individuals to raise concerns within their line management chain, provides for an alternative source of advice to that chain in nominated officers and provides for direct appeal to an oversight body'.[102] They also recommended that, '...the Cabinet Office take a lead role in ensuring that all government departments' whistleblowing advice and policies follows best practice in the field...'[103] Despite all the positive effects that whistleblowing can provide, the UK Armed Forces are yet to adopt a whistleblowing policy.

A World without Whistleblowers

Without whistleblowers, many of the wrongs that come to the attention of the regulatory bodies, the police or the public would go unnoticed. The MPs caught up in the recent Parliamentary expenses scandal suggested that the whistleblower that divulged the personnel expenses information of a number of politicians to the media did a great deal of damage to the trust and integrity of the political system in this country. The Rt Hon Alan Duncan MP is quoted as saying, 'the outpouring of fury we've witnessed has been like a spring revolution'.[104] This is the usual type of negative rhetoric that is levied against whistleblowers by the victim of the whistleblowers allegations. However, the British public was seized by the issue and a poll conducted by YouGov at the time revealed that eighty seven per cent of the population thought the scandal was important and ninety one per cent stated that it made them very angry.[105] These

---

101 Public Concern at Work, "Public Interest Disclosure Act: Guide to Law and Practice," (January 2007).

102 House of Commons, "Public Administration Select Committee: Leaks and Whistleblowing in Whitehall," https://www.gov.uk/government/uploads/system/uploads/attachment_data/file/228774/7863.pdf (accessed 13 April 2011), Recommendation 15.

103 *Ibid.* Recommendation 18.

104 http://www.telegraph.co.uk/news/newstopics/mps-expenses/5330641/Best-quotes-on-the-Telegraphs-MPs-expenses-investigation.html

105 http://www.libdemvoice.org/british-election-study-mps-expense-15996.html (accessed 22 Mar 2011)

figures indicate that the public were interested in this issue and felt that the revealing of such information, even though it was against the law, was justified.

Certainly, John Wick, the ex-Special Air Service officer who leaked the information believed that the public had a right to know about the expenses of parliamentarians. In an interview with the Daily Telegraph he said, 'We've all had concerns about the expenses and how they've managed it, purely because of how they've handled our requests for information'.[106] This case study demonstrates that there are issues that are in the public's interest that officials in high office will try *not* to disclose. However, it is undisputable that the action taken by Wicks had a profound and positive effect on rules and regulations that govern parliamentarian's expenses: 'The subsequent expenses crisis led to the passage of the *Parliamentary Standards Act 2009* and the creation of IPSA [Independent Parliamentary Standards Association], which took over the administration of MPs' allowances from the beginning of the new 2010 Parliament'.[107]

The dangers of not allowing personnel to blow the whistle can be severely damaging to an organisation. This is readily accepted in industry and as such, an increasing number of employers are, 'beginning to provide a safe whistleblowing route for staff'.[108] The framework generally allows personnel to raise concerns internally within the organisation but outside of their immediate chain of command. This makes sound business and financial sense as not to do so risks employees remaining silent, which could lead to disaster. The Public Interest Disclosure Act (PIDA) was introduced to UK legislation in the early 1990s due to a number of, 'scandals and disasters' in the 1980s which led to the deaths of innocent people and the ruining of reputations. Most of the public enquires conducted over this period found that 'workers had either been aware of the danger but had been too scared to sound the alarm or had raised the matter in the wrong way or with the wrong person'.[109]

Examples include where enquiries demonstrate that accidents could have been averted had the issue been raised in the correct manner:

---

106 http://www.telegraph.co.uk/news/newstopics/mps-expenses/5369066/MPs-expenses-whistleblower-John-Wick-on-why-he-set-the-scandal-running.html (accessed on 22 Mar 2011)

107 Oonagh Gay, "Parliamentary and Constitution Centre: Hansard," http://www.parliament.uk/briefing-papers/SN05784/the-publication-of-mps-expenses-by-ipsa (accessed 11 April 2011)

108 Guy Den and Calland, Richard, "Whistleblowing: The State of the Art," http://www.u4.no/recommended-reading/whistleblowing-the-state-of-the-art-the-role-of-the-individual-organisations-the-state-the-media-the-law-and-civil-society/ (accessed 13 April 2011)

109 Public Concern at Work, "Public Interest Disclosure Act: Guide to Law and Practice," http://plcsab.proceduresonline.com/pdfs/pub_int_act.pdf (January 2007)

> The Clapham rail crash, where the Hidden Inquiry heard that an inspector had seen the loose wire but had said nothing as he did not want to "rock the boat"; the Piper Alpha disaster, where the Cullen Inquiry concluded that "workers did not want to put their continued employment in jeopardy through raising safety issues that might embarrass management"; the Zeebrugge Ferry tragedy, where the Sheen Inquiry found that staff had, on five occasions raised concerns that ferries were sailing with their bow doors open; the collapse of Barings Bank where the regulator found that a senior manager had failed to blow the whistle loudly or clearly; and the Arms to Iraq Inquiry where the Scott Report found that an employee had written to the Foreign Secretary to tell him that munitions equipment was being unlawfully produced for Iraq.[110]

The human implications of reform should be an important factor considered by any organisation that is undergoing reform, including the UK military which is undergoing change on a significant scale. There are a number of historical cases, some very recent, where the evidence suggests that ethical behaviour inside organisations is weakened by reform focused only on improving the system, and one that does not consider the human factor of undertaking the reform. The diluting of ethical principles in a bid to maximise profit or meet a deadline can have catastrophic effect, which as demonstrated in the following case studies, resulted in the needless loss of a significant number of lives.

On 28th January 1986, the Space Shuttle Challenger was launched in the glare of a media spectacle. Millions of people around the world watched in horror as 73 seconds into the flight, the Shuttle irrupted in a plume of smoke, was torn apart, and came crashing back to earth with the loss of all those on board.[111] A Presidential Commission was immediately established to investigate the cause of the disaster. The Commission correctly identified the technical reason for the disaster as the failure of an O-ring in the Solid Booster Rocket.

The Presidential Commission also established, however, that concerns over the integrity of the O-rings had been made on a number of occasions throughout the Shuttle's history: 'the earliest documentation appeared in 1977 – four years before the launch of the first Space Shuttle in 1981'. The Solid Rocket Boosters were not manufactured by NASA but were contracted out to a company called Morton Thiokol. The Commission discovered that, even as late as the evening before the ill-fated launch, 'worried Thiokol engineers argued

110 *Ibid.*

111 James Oberg, "Seven Myths about the Challenger shuttle disaster," http://www.nbcnews.com/id/11031097/ns/technology_and_science-space/ (accessed 2 May 2011)

against launching on the grounds that the O-rings were a threat to flight safety. [Despite this advice], NASA Managers decided to proceed'.[112]

How could a multibillion-pound organisation with some of the greatest scientific minds on the planet make such a catastrophically bad decision? Roger Boisjoly was a senior engineer for Morton Thiokol and, 'was amongst a number of engineers who raised concerns over the effect that the cold weather would have on the O-rings'.[113] Faced with the potential of cancelling the Challenger launch in 1986, a second hastily convened telephone conference between NASA, Thiokol, and a number of other interested parties, was convened. Given the magnitude of the decision facing the gathered audience that night, NASA gave the Thiokol engineers, 'about forty five minutes to prepare for the meeting'. During the telephone conference, NASA put Thiokol under increasing pressure to provide factual evidence to support their no launch advice. Boisjoly was, 'specifically asked what evidence Thiokol had that O-ring damage in former flights was a result of the cold'. During interviews with the President's Commission, 'Boisjoly characterized this meeting as one where the determination was to launch, and it was up to us [the engineers], to prove beyond a shadow of doubt that it was not safe to do so'.[114]

Lacking in conclusive evidence, the initial decision, expressed by Thiokol, not to launch, was overturned. The root and branch investigation into how and why this decision was made unearthed a catalogue of issues relating to the culture within NASA at that time. In her book, "The Challenger Launch Decision," Vaughan dissects the social and anthropological issues within NASA and identifies how 'group culture,' led to incorrect decisions being left unchallenged and how, 'signals of potential danger,' were identified but had become, 'normalized,' within the Agency.[115] After the accident, 'Boisjoly was plagued with guilt'. When asked why he had not gone outside of the organisation and blown the whistle when the decision to launch was overturned, Boisjoly said that, he believed he had no chance of success: 'If I couldn't convince *those who knew*, what good would going outside do?'[116]

In the case of Challenger, NASA was under increasing budgetary constraints and, as such, maintaining the 'launch schedule,' became an economic

112 *Ibid.*

113 Johnson, *Whistleblowing: When It Works and Why*, p. 34.

114 *Ibid.*

115 Dianne Vaughan, "The Challenger Launch Decision," http://books.google.co.uk/books?hl=en&lr=&id=dOugKDAHY50C&oi=fnd&pg=PR9&dq=nasa%27s+organisational+culture&ots=FCpDPE34X3&sig=UrJffJn89jUbn2vlKeku63V96DU#v=onepage&q&f=false, (accessed 2 May 2011)

116 Johnson, *Whistleblowing: When It Works and Why*, p. 34.

imperative.[117] As the manufacturer of the Solid Booster Rockets, the continued success of the Shuttle programme was also important to Thiokol. During the telephone conference, NASA put the Thiokol representatives under significant pressure to prove that Challenger was unsafe to fly. The head of the Thiokol management team, Jerry Mason, elected to isolate the final launch decision discussion to management only. Boisjoly and his engineering team were unable to cast a vote and, as such, the management team elected to advise NASA that a launch could go ahead.

Unfortunately, many of the lessons from the disaster can be directly linked to a more recent tragedy: 'On 2 September 2006, RAF Nimrod XV230 was on a routine mission over Helmand Province in Southern Afghanistan in support of NATO and Afghani ground forces when she suffered a catastrophic mid-air fire, leading to the total loss of the aircraft and the death of all those on board'.[118] Charles Haddon-Cave QC conducted a review into the accident on the request of the then Secretary of State for Defence, the Rt Hon. Des Brown, MP. The Review was scathing about the ethical conduct of BAE Systems in particular. The Report states that, 'The Nimrod Integrated Project Team and QinetiQ were lulled into a false sense of security,' by BAE.[119] The Nimrod Safety Case (NSC) had 99 known safety issues of which 43 were left 'open' and a significant number were unclassified by BAE however, the Report states that BAE did not bring this to the attention of their customer at the 'Customer Acceptance Conference'. Haddon-Cave states that: The motive was simple:

> ...it was embarrassing to reveal the actual figures and it might lead to an unseemly argument with the Nimrod IPT representatives as to whether the task had been properly completed by BAE Systems and whether final payment could be made.[120]

Much like the pressure to launch Challenger in 1986, there also seems to have been a significant pressure to accept the NSC at the Customer Acceptance Conference. Haddon-Cave refers to a QinetiQ employee who attended the Conference on behalf of the usual QinetiQ attendee who was unable to attend at the last moment. The replacement QinetiQ attendee (Witness O) described

---

117 Dianne Vaughan, "The Challenger Launch Decision," http://books.google.co.uk/books?hl=en&lr=&id=dOugKDAHY50C&oi=fnd&pg=PR9&dq=nasa%27s+organisational+culture&ots=FCpDPE34X3&sig=UrJffJn89jUbn2vlKeku63V96DU#v=onepage&q&f=false, (accessed 2 May 2011)

118 Charles Haddon-Cave, QC, 'The Nimrod Review,' (London: 2006), p. 5.

119 *Ibid.* p. 10.

120 *Ibid.* p. 235.

himself as, 'a fish out of water,'[121] as the other attendees were well acquainted with each other. On the conclusion of day two of the Conference, 'all present were asked to state in turn whether they supported the completion of Phase 2 of the NSC by BAE Systems'.[122] As Witness O had not been involved in the project, he stated that, 'he felt that he could not validate BAE Systems' claim that these documents satisfied the contractual requirements. His account in his statement to the Review of what then happened is striking':

> I have a strong memory that upon stating this, various meeting attendees booed me and muttered things along the lines 'bloody safety engineers always have to caveat their statements'. I can remember this clearly because I have never been booed in a meeting before (and have not been at any time since).[123]

Later evidence shown to the Review Team led Haddon-Cave to suggests that: 'Witness O [QinetiQ] did, in fact, succumb to the pressure at the meeting; and in the end, did not wish to be seen to be standing in the way of what was clearly the strong 'mood of the meeting', namely that BAE Systems had completed the task'.[124]

Whilst BAE have an ethics policy, the Report firmly places the blame on, 'leadership of the Company,'[125] for failing to implement it. Haddon-Cave states that: 'BAE Systems formalised its UK ethics policy in 2002, setting out five key principles of ethical business conduct: "*accountability, integrity, honesty, openness and respect.*" In my judgment, all five principles were breached…'[126] In finalising the Report, Haddon-Cave comes to a number of important conclusions including: 'A positive Reporting Culture helps to mitigate errors by encouraging employees to report information about hazards or safety concerns that they encounter. It also enables trends to be picked up and acted upon'. Whilst this comment refers to the adoption of this culture within the Military Aviation Authority, the same lesson could equally be applied across Defence. The Report also highlights a number of, 'impediments to adequate reporting,' including concern over whether reporting an issue will result in a positive outcome, 'apathy,'[127] or scepticism that management will act on reports'.[128]

---

121 Charles Haddon-Cave, QC, 'The Nimrod Review,' (London: 2006), p. 327.

122 *Ibid.* p. 235.

123 *Ibid.*

124 *Ibid.* p. 327.

125 *Ibid.* p. 261.

126 *Ibid.*

127 *Ibid.*, 572.

128 Charles Haddon-Cave, QC, 'The Nimrod Review,' (London: 2006), p. 572.

These are often factors which also impede whistleblowing activity. Also included in the Report are, 'five important factors in ensuring the quality and quantity of incident reports: (1) protection from disciplinary proceedings where appropriate; (2) confidentiality or anonymity where necessary; (3) separation of the agency or department that collects and analyses reports from those with the authority to discipline; (4) rapid, useful, accessible and intelligible feedback to the reporting community; and (5) ease of reporting'.[129] Interestingly, there are a number of similarities between these five factors and those factors that should be incorporated into whistleblowing policy. As discussed, PIDA legislation protects employees from disciplinary action being taken against them for blowing the whistle on issues in the work place. The first of the five factors highlighted above would seem to support the argument that this protection is offered to the military.

Advice on whistleblowing policy offered by PCAW also states that: 'The organisation will, when requested, respect the confidentiality of a member of staff raising a concern'.[130] This meets the exact criteria of factor two listed above. In addition, PCAW also recommend that, 'Staff have the option to raise concerns outside of line management,' and receive advice on, 'when and how concerns may properly be raised outside the organisation (e.g. with a regulator). This would meet the majority of factor three identified in the Nimrod Report above. The advice from PCAW also recommends, 'timely and constructive feedback,' as part of the audit process and, 'ensure that staff are aware of and trust the whistleblowing avenues'.[131] These final recommendations fit neatly with factors four and five of Haddon-Cave's Nimrod Review.

Conclusion

Genuine whistleblowers do not undertake the act of whistleblowing lightly. They are motivated by what they believe is right and what is in the interest of the majority, not what is in the interest of themselves. They choose to blow the whistle because they feel strongly that what they are exposing is in the public interest and, in order to see justice prevail, blowing the whistle is the only remaining avenue left open to them. Whistleblowers are distinctly different from those individuals who sell their stories for personal gain, expose issues to the media for malicious purposes, or use the press to exert pressure in order to

129 *Ibid.*

130 http://www.pcaw.org.uk/files/best_practice_guide-2006.pdf (accessed 2 May 2011)

131 *Ibid.*

advance their own cause. Unfortunately, the media's indiscriminate use of the term is undermining the true value of whistleblowers and as a result, less credence may be paid to their plight. This would be a tragedy, as true whistleblowers often have a story worth telling and ignoring their concerns is seldom to the benefit of the organisation.

The right to speak freely and impart the truth without fear of retribution is a fundamental human right that has now been enshrined in British law. Whilst this right is not currently afforded to the UK Military, the law or military regulations should not be used to suppress information that is in the public's interest, as to do so may increase the risk to national security and the very people you are trying to protect. The establishment of a robust UK Armed Forces whistleblowing policy, which is enshrined in law and is independent from the chain of command, could be one way of ensuring the ethical concerns of UK Military personnel are addressed. Whilst many within the military may view the independence of the process as undermining the chain of command, an independent complaints process already exists within the UK Military and without it, a military whistleblowing policy would be fatally flawed. In addition to independence, a military whistleblowing policy would also require legal protection for those who choose to blow the whistle as without it, acts of retribution would be highly likely, especially in the military where loyalty and duty plays a significant role. This protection could be in the form of an equivalent to the PIDA, similar to that established for the Police Service in 2002.

In almost all walks of life, the evidence clearly demonstrates the benefits of whistleblowing. The positive influence of whistleblowers cuts across the spectrum of the public and private sectors and has influenced banking reform, the food industry, transportation, health and safety and the emergency services, to name but a few. The restrictions that the OSA places on the British Military means they are currently unable to exploit the benefits of whistleblowing however, the evidence of not having a military whistleblowing policy is evident in the news articles that we read and the tragedies that unfold. The British military is operating in a climate of severe fiscal constraints and a fluid globalized security environment. In order to assist in ensuring that the military provide the most efficient and effective capability to cope with these challenges, the evidence overwhelmingly suggests that whistleblowing must be deeply embedded into the military's ethical culture and become a way of life. Whilst this may initially be uncomfortable for some to accept, the British Military must adapt to disclosure, as it is a vital component of an ethical organisation and will ultimately lead to greater effectiveness.

CHAPTER 9

Dehumanizing the Enemy: The Intersection of Neuroethics and Military Ethics

Shannon E. French and Anthony I. Jack

Introduction

How do you teach troops to kill without losing control of exactly whom they kill, how, when, and in what way? It is an ancient question, as old as human conflict. Some may wonder why we continue to ask it. After all, the vast majority of modern, professional combat troops never commit atrocities. For every My Lai, Haditha, Mahmudiyah killings, or Kandahar massacre, there are thousands of military engagements that are conducted fully within the restraints of the Law of Armed Conflict.

Of course, the fact that such crimes are rare is cold comfort to the victims of atrocities, their loved ones, and their communities. And those aberrations from proper military conduct that do occur are costly in other ways. Public support for the military and its missions temporarily wanes in the wake of atrocities, while more lasting harm is done to efforts to win the "hearts and minds" of the enemy. At the same time, dangers to troops increase as new enemies are recruited on the strength of their revulsion at the crimes committed. General David Petraeus observed in 2009 that photos of the mistreatment of prisoners at Abu Ghraib "serve as potent recruiting material to attract new members to join the insurgency."[1]

An additional cost that must not be overlooked is the moral and psychological harm suffered by the perpetrators of war crimes. The idea of perpetration-induced trauma is no longer new or especially controversial.[2] While some atrocities are the isolated acts of disturbed or damaged individuals who would probably commit similar crimes in a non-combat setting, most violations of the laws of war cannot be traced conveniently back to some pre-existing psychological or physical pathology. Certain conditions of war itself create war criminals, and the risk is highest for troops who must fight in the kind of

1 Matthew Alexander, "McCain Backs Torture As Recruiting Tool for Al Qaida; Policy Led to the Deaths of US Soldiers in Iraq," *Huffington Post*, August 31, 2009.

2 See especially Rachel M. MacNair, *Perpetration-Induced Traumatic Stress: The Psychological Consequences of Killing* (Westport, CT and London: Praeger Publishers, 2002).

 | DOI 10.1163/9789004280380_010

conditions present in asymmetric conflicts involving insurgencies and unconventional warfare.[3] That grim reality places the burden firmly with those who order and lead troops into combat to do everything in their power to reduce the chances of those young men and women crossing lines that cannot be uncrossed and committing acts that may scar their minds and mar their souls.[4]

The UN's Responsibility to Protect doctrine explicitly requires individual states and the international community to "protect populations from genocide, war crimes, ethnic cleansing and crimes against humanity."[5] This cannot be achieved without a better grasp of the psychological, biological (especially neurological), and cultural factors that come together to trigger such tragic events. Even with the best will in the world, militaries cannot improve training techniques or adjust deployment strategies appropriately unless they are armed with the right knowledge.

The urgency of this problem is understood, and it has been tackled by several astute scholars who are well informed about the military or have direct personal experience with military service, writing from the perspective of disciplines such as philosophy and psychology. We wish to build on this important work and add new insights from the field of neuroscience. Technology such as neuroimaging allows us to see how the human brain reacts to different stimuli. It is essential that we gain a better understanding of how our troops can respond to combat conditions and relate to their enemies in that context. We can then allow that knowledge to inform how troops ought to be trained and led so that vulnerable populations are protected and troops have the best possible chance of surviving their military experiences psychologically sound, with both their humanity and the public image of the US military intact.

---

3 See Stephen J. Rockel and Rick Halpern, *Inventing Collateral Damage: Civilian Casualties, War, and Empire* (Toronto: Between the Lines, 2009).

4 The reader should not interpret the use of the word 'soul' as a commitment to a dualistic metaphysics. Rather this is intended as a metaphorical use of language. It is our view that certain types of moral sentiment, which can be scientifically studied and which we believe have real and measurable effects on mental health, are difficult to capture using purely secular language, and can be more readily grasped by most people (including the non-religious) when theistic language is used. For a careful discussion of empirical evidence which has encouraged us to this view, the reader might examine: Jack, A.I., Robbins, P.A., Friedman, J.P., and Meyers, C.D., 'More Than a Feeling: Counterintuitive Effects of Compassion on Moral Judgment', in J. Sytsma (ed.), *Advances in Experimental Philosophy of Mind* (London: Bloomsbury, forthcoming).

5 "2005 World Summit Outcome," United Nations General Assembly, Sixtieth session, items 48 and 121 of the provisional agenda. A/60/L.1, 40 pages.

An important issue concerns where the responsibility lies to research, identify, plan and execute policy changes that will reduce the probability both of war crimes and psychological damage to troops. Our view is that the UN's Responsibility to Protect doctrine places a clear mandate on military leadership to ensure that these processes take place. It is not enough merely to point the finger of blame at subordinates for lapses in conduct. Taking responsibility requires making an effort to understand the powerful forces at play and being willing to act to shape them as much as possible to decrease risk. To fail to prioritize these activities in the face of compelling evidence for their significance and potential utility represents an abrogation of the duty imposed on military leadership by the R2P doctrine. Our goal here is to provide that evidence and illuminate a direction for research and training that will help military leadership to meet this vital aspect of its responsibility to protect.

The Psychology of Harm

What factors influence our willingness to harm fellow humans? A naïve psychological view might suggest that our willingness to harm is a simple function of our perception of the need for self-defense. However, a number of observations suggest a quite different picture of the key psychological factors involved. In some situations, which have famously provoked considerable moral consternation, people appear remarkably ready and willing to inflict harm on others. In other situations, people display a truly remarkable reluctance. In neither case is the desire to protect oneself from direct physical harm the motivating factor.

First, we may consider some notable cases in which individuals have demonstrated a surprising willingness to harm others. In the 1960s, Stanley Milgram conducted a series of infamous but enlightening experiments concerning the willingness of individuals to inflict pain on an innocent person out of obedience to a perceived authority. He found that most people (some two-thirds of the population) can be led quite easily to transgress moral limits and perpetrate undeserved harm on others.

Milgram set up an experiment in which subjects were asked to flick switches to deliver increasingly strong jolts of electricity to a person in another room who was supposedly being given a memory quiz. The person taking the quiz was actually an actor (as was the "scientist" telling the subjects when to administer the shocks), and the electrocutions were faked. As the number of imaginary volts went up, the actor in the other room would scream as if in terrible pain, demand to be let go, and even complain about a potentially deadly heart condition. Then he would fall completely silent, as if having collapsed or died.

Still the subjects, ordinary people, would continue to respond to the (fake) authority figure's commands.

> This is, perhaps, the most fundamental lesson of our study: ordinary people, simply doing their jobs, and without any particular hostility on their part, can become agents in a terrible destructive process. Moreover, even when the destructive effects of their work become patently clear, and they are asked to carry out actions incompatible with fundamental standards of morality, relatively few people have the resources needed to resist authority. A variety of inhibitions against disobeying authority come into play and successfully keep the person in his place.[6]

Milgram found that the odds that his subjects would resist authority rose significantly when he introduced variations into the experiment such as having an apparent peer rebel against the authority's commands (which seemed to give the subjects courage to resist the authority, too) or having a second authority challenge the first (which left the subjects unsure which authority to obey and shattered the subjects' illusion that they were not responsible to make their own decisions).[7] A highly significant practical issue concerns what other psychological resources might allow troops to identify and resist misguided authority and/or their own negative emotional impulses. We believe that a number of relatively straightforward measures can, when combined, provide troops with powerful resources sufficient to counterbalance natural psychological pressures to be complicit in war crimes. These steps, which are discussed in further detail in the sections that follow, include: fostering explicit awareness of the powerful psychological processes at play (including the effects of authority and dehumanizing); providing training programs, informed by and consistent with current science, to improve psychological agility; increasing alertness to warning signs that indicate psychological slippage, establishing mechanisms for remediation or removal from combat of individuals at risk for full-blown psychological disintegration, and consistently instilling and reinforcing a powerful and emotionally felt moral code tied to a legacy of honor – the code of the warrior.

Do the factors that Milgram was able to isolate and identify in the laboratory have ecological validity? In other words, can they be seen to be at play in real-world atrocities? Christopher R. Browning's excellent work, *Ordinary Men:*

6 Stanley Milgram, *Obedience to Authority: An Experimental View* (New York: Harper Perennial Modern Thought, 2009 edition), p. 6.

7 Milgram, pp. 107 and 118.

Reserve Police Battalion 101 and the Final Solution in Poland[8] provides compelling evidence for this. Browning describes how members of the Nazi police battalion 101 were led to commit the mass murder of Jewish women, children, and elders:

> The largest group within the battalion did whatever they were asked to do, without ever risking the onus of confronting authority or appearing weak, but they did not volunteer for or celebrate the killing. Increasingly numb and brutalized, they felt more pity for themselves because of the "unpleasant" work they had been assigned than they did for their dehumanized victims. For the most part, they did not think what they were doing was wrong or immoral, because the killing was sanctioned by legitimate authority. Indeed, for the most part they did not try to think, period.
>
> BROWNING, 215–216

Most of the "ordinary men" Browning studied were not eager killers, and they suffered a wide range of negative psychological effects as the result of their actions.

While both Browning and Milgram point to the important role of authority, Browning's study indicates this cannot have been the only factor. The members of police battalion 101, for example, could have resisted, and they chose not to do so. Browning notes that there were "nonshooters" in the battalion who asked to be exempted from the killing and were allowed not to participate.[9] Browning argues that pressure from authority and peers would likely not have been enough to push the members of police battalion 101 past their moral qualms without the broader context of Nazi society that was awash in propaganda calculated to dehumanize the Jewish people: "A combination of situational factors and ideological overlap that concurred on the enemy status and dehumanization of the victims was sufficient to turn 'ordinary men' into 'willing executioners'."[10]

The conclusion that can be drawn from these studies, and other work in social psychology, such as the Stanford prison experiment,[11] is that authority and dehumanization can combine to create an alarming willingness for

8 Christopher R. Browning, *Ordinary Men: Reserve Police Battalion 101 and the Final Solution in Poland* (New York: Aaron Asher Books/HarperCollins Publishers, 1992).

9 Although somewhat less blameworthy than their peers, these men are certainly not laudable. For while they did not participate directly in the killings, they also did nothing to stop or even protest them. As Browning clarifies: "…they did not make principled objections against the regime and its murderous policies, they did not reproach their comrades" (Browning, p. 215).

10 Browning, p. 216.

11 Philip G. Zimbardo, *The Lucifer Effect: Understanding How Good People Turn Evil* (New York: Random House, 2007).

individuals to harm others, even when they face no immediate danger to themselves. In other cases, people may be surprisingly resistant to harming others, even in the face of grave danger. As Lt. Col. Dave Grossman illuminated in his groundbreaking book, *On Killing: The Psychological Costs of Learning to Kill in War and Society,* it is actually not that easy to train troops to kill enemy combatants, let alone to mass-murder civilians.

In the context of a traditional battle with uniformed forces on both sides, one would expect less resistance to killing. After all, it is a case of kill-or-be-killed. Self-preservation is a strong instinct. Nevertheless, Grossman's research concludes that in many such historical engagements, troops were reluctant to take kill shots. He notes that in the Civil War, 90% of the muskets recovered from the battlefield were still loaded, and some 50% of these had been reloaded multiple times without being fired – one was discovered with 23 rounds jammed into its barrel.[12] Even in the face of enemy fire, to which they presumably succumbed, an appreciable number of soldiers would reload and reload, over and over again, unwilling or unable to actually fire upon their enemy.

Grossman cites the well-known post-WWII study by Brigadier General S.L.A. Marshall, *Men Against Fire,* which concluded that only 15–20% of soldiers attempted to shoot to kill.[13] The methodology of the Marshall study has been challenged, but there remains significant support for its general conclusions.[14] The US military found it so persuasive that, following the Marshall study, training methods were altered to endeavor to improve so-called "kill ratios" – that is, to increase the lethality of our troops.

Dehumanizing and Trauma

David Livingstone Smith discusses some of the implications and effects of the Marshall study in his insightful book, *Less Than Human: Why We Demean, Enslave, and Exterminate Others*:

> Although it sounds very nasty, and Marshall never put it quite this way, his observations imply that military training should concentrate on

12 Lt. Col. Dave Grossman, *On Killing: The Psychological Cost of Learning to Kill in War and Society* (Boston: Little, Brown and Company, 1996), p. 23.

13 Lt. Col. Dave Grossman, *On Killing: The Psychological Cost of Learning to Kill in War and Society* (Boston: Little, Brown and Company, 1996), p. 3.

14 See K.C. Jordan, "Right for the Wrong Reasons: S.L.A. Marshall and the Ratio of Fire in Korea," *Journal of Military History* (2002) 66 (1), pp. 135–162.

> overriding the recruit's moral integrity, so that he or she will have no scruples about killing on command. Moral reservations are – in Marshall's words – a "handicap" that prevents the soldier from doing his job. [...] The US armed forces overhauled their system of military training to try to solve the problems that Marshall identified. [...] Apparently as a result, US soldiers' ratio of fire increased during the Korean conflict, and by the time the Vietnam War rolled around, American troops had become much more efficient killers. But this solution created a whole new problem. The troops did better in battle, and the ratio of fire skyrocketed, but so did the incidence of combat-related psychological disorders.

As will become apparent, we believe the research suggests that dehumanization can play a more nuanced role in military training. Hence, we do not join with Livingstone Smith's view that effective military training involves a wholesale overriding of the recruit's moral integrity. Instead, we think that their moral sentiments need to be preserved and carefully directed. Recruits need to learn how to put aside temporarily some very natural and very powerful human moral responses, if they are to be effective in combat. This puts our troops in some moral peril, yet we do not think this has to be done at the cost of throwing away their moral compasses. Our aim is to shed light on how we can help recruits achieve a stable balance when we ask them to walk a moral tightrope. To do this, we base our account not just on cutting edge research in psychology and neuroscience, but also on an appreciation of and respect for modern military practice.

Grossman illuminates some of the methods that have been adopted over the years to help troops achieve emotional distance from their enemies. Troops have been drilled to fire on human-shaped targets but not to think about the act of killing itself. The focus has been placed on the mechanics of aiming and firing and responding quickly to changing scenarios. Troops have been taught to "neutralize targets" as efficiently as possible and the word "kill" has been carefully avoided.

Livingstone Smith points out that modern civilian society seems to support this approach and itself fails to confront the reality that waging war involves authorizing the intentional killing of other human beings:

> [W]e (contemporary Americans) go to great lengths to avoid acknowledging the simple and obvious truth that war is all about killing people. Read the newspapers and listen to the speeches of our politicians. Young men and women are called to "serve their country" by going to war. When they're killed, we're told that they "gave their life for their country" (a foolish idea:

> soldiers' lives are taken, not given). But how often do you hear young people asked to go to war to *kill people* for their country?[15]

In other words, we persuade people to kill on our behalf by describing the actions of war, where possible, in terms that sound wholesome, moral, and inspiring; and where this is not possible we use neutral objectifying terms that cloak the emotional impact of these actions. A positive impact of this is to emphasize the warrior virtues, such as loyalty, discipline, honor, courage, and sacrifice (which are all very real and necessary), yet a more unfortunate consequence is that this language downplays the negative effects of war on those who kill. It is a cruel bait-and-switch, made worse by the lack of sustained support for veterans who are living with those effects. As novelist C.S. Harris laments: "We don't take good care of the men we ask to risk their lives and health for us, do we? We use them, and then when they're no longer of value, we toss them away."[16]

Propaganda is not only employed to recruit troops, however. It is also applied to maintain the aggressive stance of troops against an enemy with whom they are already engaged. Propaganda that tries to deny the humanity of enemies and associate them with subhuman animals is a common and effective tool for increasing aggression and breaking down the resistance to killing. This dehumanization can be achieved through the use of animal imagery and abusive language. As Grossman explains:

> It is so much easier to kill someone if they look distinctly different than you. If your propaganda machine can convince your soldiers that their opponents are not really human but are "inferior forms of life," then their natural resistance to killing their own species will be reduced. Often the enemy's humanity is denied by referring to him as a "gook," "Kraut," or "Nip."[17]

This enemy-as-subhuman approach plays off of what psychologists call "in-group bias." In other words, humans are basically tribal or clannish. We tend to fear and devalue those who are not members of our "tribe" and view them as potential threats:

> We are innately biased against outsiders. This bias is seized upon and manipulated by indoctrination and propaganda to motivate men and

15 Livingstone Smith, p. 225.

16 C.S. Harris, *What Darkness Brings* (New York: Penguin Publishing, 2013).

17 Lt. Col. Dave Grossman, *On Killing: The Psychological Cost of Learning to Kill in War and Society* (Boston: Little, Brown and Company, 1996), p. 161.

> women to slaughter one another. This is done by inducing men to regard their enemies as subhuman creatures, which overrides their natural, biological inhibitions against killing. So dehumanization has the specific function of unleashing aggression in war.[18]

This type of dehumanization is one of the key factors that Browning highlights in the transformation of the members of police battalion 101 into efficient mass-murderers. Milgram also notes, "Systematic devaluation of the victim provides a measure of psychological justification for brutal treatment of the victim and has been the constant accompaniment of massacres, pogroms, and wars."[19]

Given that dehumanization plays such an important role in enabling murder and other atrocities, one response would be to suggest that all forms of dehumanization should be resisted, rather than being incorporated into military training. However, this view is also problematic for anyone who is not a pacifist. If we accept some version of Just War Theory, and therefore endorse the view that violent military force is sometimes required in defense of a just cause, then we are cornered by the reality that troops do need to be trained to kill. Indeed, for justified military actions, there is a strong moral argument that military training should, first and foremost, be directed at enabling our troops to kill in the most effective and efficient manner possible. We doubt this can be accomplished without allowing some form of dehumanization of the enemy (although, as we will later note, this should be coupled with equally intentionally re-humanization). Hence, the central question here is, are some forms of dehumanization less morally perilous than others? First, are there ways of dehumanizing the enemy that might promote military effectiveness in combat, yet achieve this end without lowering troops' resistance to *all* types (and targets) of killing, i.e. those not sanctioned by the laws of war? Second, how can we mitigate the psychological costs of war, for both moral and practical reasons?

The act of dehumanizing, both in the context of war and psychological experiments, is strongly associated with psychological trauma. The Milgram and Stanford prison experiments provoked changes in the ethical oversight of psychological experiments because of the trauma experienced by participants who were horrified by their own willingness to harm others. More recent research indicates that the mere act of ostracizing others, such as excluding someone from a simple game of catch when instructed to so by the

18 Livingstone Smith, p. 71.

19 Milgram, p. 9.

experimenter, induces a variety of negative psychological effects in the ostracizer, including increased negative affect and decreased senses of personal autonomy and social connectedness.[20] It is little wonder, then, that the much more extreme and visceral actions that follow from dehumanizing an enemy have often been anecdotally cited as an important factor in the psychological adjustment of troops returning from conflict.

While more work is needed to establish direct links between dehumanizing and diagnoses such as post-traumatic stress disorder in veterans, recent findings in psychological science, combined with accounts from military scholars, already make a compelling case that the horror, shame, and guilt associated with having participated in actions that they cannot reconcile with their 'civilian' sense of self represent major factors that determine veterans' subsequent health, well-being, and psychological adjustment. For instance, recent research indicates that negative affect[21] and a perceived sense of social disconnection[22] have powerful effects on both physical and psychological health. Amazingly, these factors are more predictive than physical or external conditions, which have traditionally been thought to be more important, such as economic circumstances, safety, hunger, and homelessness.[23] When we consider why troops have often been unwilling or unable to shoot at the enemy, it is worth considering that they are indeed engaged in a form of self-defense: their unconscious motivation is not so much to protect the integrity of their bodies but rather the integrity of their sense of self.[24] The challenge, then, is to construct training

---

20 Legate N., Dehaan C.R., Weinstein N., and Ryan R.M., Hurting You Hurts Me Too: The Psychological Costs of Complying with Ostracism. *Psychological Science*, February 27, 2013.

21 Pressman S.D., Gallagher M.W., and Lopez S.J., 'Is the Emotion-Health Connection a "First-World Problem?"' *Psychological Science* (2013).

22 Hawkley L.C., and Cacioppo J.T., 'Loneliness Matters: A Theoretical and Empirical Review of Consequences and Mechanisms', *Annals of Behavioral Medicine* (2010) 40, pp. 218–227.

23 Pressman S.D., Gallagher M.W., and Lopez S.J., 'Is the Emotion-Health Connection a "First-World Problem?"' *Psychological Science* (2013).

24 While this claim may seem surprising to readers who are not familiar with research in social psychology, the authors intend this to be a quite uncontroversial statement. A great deal of research in social psychology, including but not limited to the citations already made, can be summarized as showing that we are very powerfully motivated to preserve our self-image. Indeed, this can be seen as the primary function of offering rationalizations (reasons/justifications for our actions). Rationalizations are a ubiquitous feature of human behavior, and scientific research has shown they frequently fail to hold up to close scrutiny. See for example: Nisbett, Richard, and Wilson, Timothy, 'Telling More Than We Can Know: Verbal Reports on Mental Processes', *Psychological Review* (1977) 84, pp. 231–259; Haidt, Jonathan, *The Righteous Mind: Why Good People Are Divided by Politics and Religion* (Pantheon, 2012).

and conditions that help our troops return from war whole, both in body and in soul.[25]

Optimal Cognitive Function

Ideal troops should not just be reconciled to their military actions in a manner that allows them to return to a well-adjusted civilian life, they should also have a high degree of mental flexibility in the field. They should be trained in a way that optimizes their ability to fluidly switch among roles such as active combatant, peacekeeper, and military escort/trainer. However, the psychological demands associated with switching between such dissimilar roles should not be underestimated. Our research demonstrates that there is a fundamental tension between the brain areas that we use to understand the experiential viewpoint of others and the brain areas we use for emotionally disengaged analytic thinking, focused visual attention, and motor planning.[26] In general, when we turn on one of these networks of brain regions, then we suppress activity in the other. The mutually antagonistic relationship between these networks is a fundamental feature of the human brain – it is a very marked neurophysiological effect involving much of the human cortex, and it was observed long before we understood its cognitive significance.[27] It can be detected in the brain even when participants are not engaged in any task.[28] It is also a marker of healthy brain function. Disruptions in the mutually

25 The substitution of the word 'soul' for 'sense of self' used in the previous sentence is intentional. Psychological research indicates that we have a complex folk-psychology of the self, and that the concept of the 'soul' is particularly tied to our sense of spiritual and moral identity. It is the ability of our troops to maintain this aspect of their self-image that we believe is put in critical danger by war and atrocity. For work on the concept of the soul, see for example: Richert, Rebekah A., and Harris, Paul L., 'The Ghost in My Body: Children's Developing Concept of the Soul', *Journal of Cognition and Culture* (2006) 6 (3–4), pp. 409–427.

26 Jack A.I., Dawson A.J., Begany K.L., Leckie R.L., Barry K.P., Ciccia A.H., and Snyder A.Z., 'fMRI Reveals Reciprocal Inhibition between Social and Physical Cognitive Domains', *Neuroimage* (2012) 66C, pp. 385–401.

27 Raichle M.E., MacLeod A.M., Snyder A.Z., Powers W.J., Gusnard D.A., and Shulman G.L., 'A Default Mode of Brain Function', *Proceedings of the National Academies of Science*, USA (2001) 98, pp. 676–682.

28 Fox M.D., 'From the Cover: The Human Brain is Intrinsically Organized into Dynamic, Anticorrelated Functional Networks', *Proceedings of the National Academy of Sciences* (2005) 102, pp. 9673–9678.

suppressive relationship between these brain networks has been clearly linked to a variety of major mental disorders and to poor performance on tasks.[29]

What this extensive research tells us is that the tension between analytic and empathetic thinking is an inescapable feature of our evolutionary heritage. Our arms were designed by evolution to be wonderfully adaptive and efficient structures, capable of many uses. Yet they will never be effective tools for scratching our own backs. No one in his right mind would break his elbow in the hopes that doing so might allow him to maintain the arm's existing functions and also enable him to reach effectively behind himself. Similarly, current research indicates that the tension between analytic and empathetic thought represents a fundament constraint of the highly effective neural structure that evolution has designed. Unless and until we acquire a much more sophisticated understanding of neural engineering that contradicts this view, we are well advised to accept that disruptions of this tension will only result in mental disintegration.

On the modern battlefield, our troops are asked on the one hand to be ready to fight an enemy with clear-sighted and dispassionate efficiency, and, on the other hand, we expect them to be sensitive to the mores of a foreign culture, enabling them to win the hearts and minds of its citizenry while forming strong and mutually trusting working relationships with members of its military. In other words, we ask them to be both highly analytic and highly empathetic. Hence, at first sight, it might appear that the demands of the modern battlefield are simply impossible to manage: they are bound to drive our troops insane. Fortunately, there is reason to believe the situation is not quite so bad. The psychological demands of modern warfare are extreme; however, we believe they can be accommodated within the bounds of healthy human function. This is suggested both by a more careful consideration of what the research shows, and by a parallel example of a working context that requires both analysis and empathy.

First, while the research indicates that we cannot be both analytic and empathetic at the same time, a key feature of our neural function is that we are constantly cycling between these two networks. This natural cycling between analytic and empathetic mental modes is part of what is disrupted in individuals with mental disorders. Tasks temporarily and partially disrupt this natural

---

29 Broyd S.J., Demanuele C., Debener S., Helps S.K., James C.J., and Sonuga-Barke E.J., Default-mode Brain Dysfunction in Mental Disorders: A Systematic Review. *Neuroscience and Biobehavioral Review* (2009) 33, pp. 279–296; Buckner R.L., Andrews-Hanna J.R., and Schacter D.L., 'The Brain's Default Network: Anatomy, Function, and Relevance to Disease', *Annals of the New York Academy of Sciences* (2008) 1124, pp. 1–38.

cycling, pushing us more into one mode or the other for more sustained periods. However, we know that when a task is used to push healthy participants into one mode, and they are then given a task-free break, they tend to compensate by cycling deeper into the opposing mode the harder they were pushed away from it.[30] Therefore, no absolute obstacle is presented by the mere fact that individuals are required to make use of both modes in a particular working context. In fact, provided the switching between modes is well managed, this is likely to be more healthy and sustainable, and less fatiguing, than a work environment that only calls on one of these cognitive modes. The trick is just managing the switching between modes – ensuring that one is in the appropriate cognitive mode to effectively tackle the task at hand. This requires attending to appropriate cues and the possession of a broader cognitive model that allows us to make good use of those cues.[31]

Surgeons face a tension between analytic and empathetic thinking that is similar in some respects to that faced by the modern combatant.[32] The surgeon learns to see his or her patient as a biological machine in need of fixing, a task that is clearly analytic in nature. When surgeons come to wield their scalpels, empathetic thinking is not only of little use to them, but is, in fact, a positive hindrance. There is no use in surgeons contemplating the emotional significance of their immediately harmful actions as they cut into their patients. A number of steps are taken to help avoid the distracting effects of inappropriately engaging empathetic thinking at these moments: the patient's face is usually occluded from view (usually only the anesthetist views the face, in order to be sensitive to facial cues that might indicate waking), and there is generally a prohibition against performing surgery on close friends and

---

30 Pyka M., Beckmann C.F., Schoning S., Hauke S., Heider D., Kugel H., Arolt V., and Konrad C., 'Impact of Working Memory Load on FMRI Resting State Pattern in Subsequent Resting Phases', *Public Library of Science One* (2009) 4: e7198.

31 The research shows that these two modes, corresponding to different 'hardwired' neural systems, can be flexibly deployed and that there are individual differences in our propensity to adopt one cognitive mode or the other. For instance, males who evidence more hostile sexism towards women show less activity in empathetic brain regions when they are shown sexualized images of attractive women. Similarly, humanizing and dehumanizing narratives influence which mode one adopts when viewing depictions of others (see ref 36). Adopting one mode or the other would not usually be a conscious choice, but it is influenced by culture, personality and training. Reference: Mina Cikara, Jennifer L. Eberhardt, and Susan T. Fiske, 'From Agents to Objects: Sexist Attitudes and Neural Responses to Sexualized Targets', *Journal of Cognitive Neuroscience* (2011) 23 (3), pp. 540–551.

32 http://medicaleconomics.modernmedicine.com/medical-economics/content/tags/analysis/why-its-so-difficult-physicians-be-empathetic-and-analytic-s

relatives. Yet the surgeon's job is rarely accomplished in the operating theatre alone. Surgeons usually meet the patient and family members both before and after the surgery: moments when a more empathetic approach is not only useful, but often essential both to ensuring fully informed consent for the procedure has been obtained, and for the patient's recovery.

Clearly, it can be hard to reconcile the adoption of these two very different cognitive modes towards the very same person. Hence, there is considerable concern about the bedside manner of many physicians, and concerns have been raised about the prevalence of dehumanization in medical practice. Nonetheless, these two modes are effectively reconciled by able physicians every day, and work in social psychology suggests a number of concrete steps that are likely to facilitate their reconciliation in general medical practice.[33]

The broad cognitive context in which people work plays a highly significant role in their ability to reconcile these opposing cognitive modes. Accountants who stand up from working on spreadsheets at their computers to attend client meetings or chat with colleagues at the water cooler are not likely to have difficulties. In this case, the cues and cognitive context make adoption of the appropriate cognitive mode a simple matter. This is harder to achieve in a medical context, where the predominant mental model is to view patients as biological machines, and where many types of interaction require swift transitions between modes in response to subtle cues. When should a physician respond to the medical history a patient is describing by integrating it with a medical understanding of the condition, and when should she pause from this task to connect interpersonally with the patient's often distressed experience of that condition? Both modes are important to patient outcomes, but juggling them effectively is not always easy.

The tension faced by modern troops is even harder to reconcile. Physicians may at least reflect that their immediately harmful actions, whether they be surgical or the prescription of drugs with powerful side-effects such as chemotherapeutic agents, are actually aimed at healing patients. One step back and two steps forward is still progress in the right direction. However, no such luxury is afforded to combatants, who cannot miss the obvious fact that the harm they inflict can never be reconciled for the person at whom it is directed. Instead, they can only offset these acts of harm by justifying it in terms of the harm they prevented to their fellow troops, as well as appealing to more abstract notions of their honor, service, and duty, and the larger purpose of the conflict in which they are engaged.

33 Haque O.S., and Waytz A., Dehumanization in Medicine Causes, Solutions, and Functions. *Perspectives on Psychological Science* (2012) 7, pp. 176–186.

The profound psychological dissonance provoked by an act as ultimately harmful as killing can only be offset by the possession of a very strongly embedded cognitive model that allows it to be reconciled. If this positive cognitive model is not reinforced, some troops are bound to resolve the intolerable dissonance by adopting a cognitive model that is destructive, both to their military performance and to their own long-term emotional well-being.

As we will shortly discuss, the destructive effects of dehumanizing, even when contained, are always bound to lurk beneath the surface in armed conflict. The simple reason for this is that dehumanizing represents a natural, and often psychologically necessary, coping mechanism. However, before fully entering into that discussion, it is important to establish some key points. First, some readers may be skeptical that something as abstract as cognitive context is likely to have a major influence on brain function. Second, it is crucial to distinguish between different types of dehumanizing. Third, it is necessary to establish a neural basis for our claim that dehumanizing has negative effects not just on the individual who is dehumanized, but also on the dehumanizer.

Dehumanizing and the Brain

The human brain has a mixed architecture. A great many of the computations it achieves, which allow us to perceive and act, occur largely automatically and in parallel. These processes have some capacity limits, yet it has long been observed that the greatest limits on human performance reflect the limited capacity of our higher cognitive functions. Until recently, it was thought that these effortful and cognitively demanding processes reflected the operation of a single, unified general reasoning system. However, we now know this is not true. There are two largely distinct systems that are involved in cognitively effortful processing. In the brain, these correspond to the two networks of brain areas that we previously described as being involved in analytic and empathetic thought. The distinction between these systems has only become apparent as a result of brain imaging technology. In behavioral tests the two systems appeared to be a single system because of their tendency to mutually suppress, and hence trade off with, one another. It is striking that this division, which was only hinted at in decades of behavioral research on human performance, is so stark and obvious when we look into the brain.

Brain imaging gives us a new way of looking at cognitive effort. Instead of looking at indirect behavioral measures of effort, we can more directly see how different types of cognition engage these two networks. Of particular concern here is how this relates to the phenomenon of dehumanization. Recent work in psychology suggests there is an important distinction between two types of dehumanizing.[34] On the one hand, we can equate people with inanimate objects or machines (in a military context, this is reflected by the use of expressions such as "neutralizing targets"). On the other hand, we can equate people with animate but "lesser" beings, i.e. non-human, dangerous animals, or imaginary monsters (virtually all military propaganda about the enemy involves examples of this, but perhaps the most notorious example is the Nazi propaganda film "The Eternal Jew" that directly equates Jews with vermin[35]). The distinction between these two forms of dehumanizing is supported by behavioral work. This shows, for instance, that these different forms of dehumanizing are associated with different emotions: objectifying people is associated with indifference on the part of the dehumanizer, and feelings of sadness and anger in the dehumanized; whereas animalistic dehumanization is associated with disgust on the part of the dehumanizer, and feelings of shame and guilt in the dehumanized.[36]

We recently conducted a study that examines what happens in the brain when ordinary participants of a wide range of ages view social narratives similar to dehumanizing propaganda.[37] To those who are not attuned to social perception, these narratives might appear broadly similar in content. All involved depictions of people engaged in different activities. For instance, one stimulus depicted a thirsty runner kneeling down to drink from a puddle (acting like an animal), while another stimulus depicted a girl stressed by an exam who nonetheless refuses an opportunity to cheat (the opposite of acting like an animal). It is obvious that these prompts suggest differences about the people depicted. It is perhaps more surprising how clear the differences are in the brains of observers who perceive these different kinds of minds. Specifically, the two limited capacity networks, involved in analytic and empathetic reasoning, showed quite different patterns of recruitment depending on relatively subtle aspects of how people are depicted. The major networks of our brains are

---

34 Haslam N., 'Dehumanization: An Integrative Review', *Personality and Social Psychology Review* (2006) 10, pp. 252–264.

35 Eberhard Taubert, writer, and Fritz Hippler, director, "The Eternal Jew," Deutsche Film Gesellschaft (1940).

36 Bastian, B., and Haslam, N. 'Experiencing Dehumanization: Cognitive and Emotional Effects of Everyday Dehumanization', *Basic and Applied Social Psychology* (2011) 33 (4), pp. 295–303.

37 Jack, A.I., Dawson, A.J., and Norr, M., *Seeing Human: Distinct and Overlapping Neural Signatures Associated with Two Forms of Dehumanization*. Revised manuscript currently under review.

extremely sensitive to these social cues, even though we often fail to realize these profound differences in our how we are thinking.

On the basis of this work, we can identify four broad cognitive modes that humans use to think about other people, which are distinct in terms of the extent and type of cognitive effort involved: (1) When we think of people as objects, we barely engage any effortful cognitive processing. We remain indifferent, including to their suffering, and have cognitive resources to spare. (2) When we think about people as biological machines, as a doctor or neuroscientist does, we engage analytic but not empathetic reasoning areas. (3) When we humanize people (i.e. when we think about their experiential point of view), we engage empathetic but not analytic reasoning areas. (4) When we animalistically dehumanize people, or engage in Machiavellian thinking, we engage both networks. In this mode we think about the person as an agent driven by beliefs and desires, but we refuse to recognize the other as a truly feeling being similar to ourselves. We recognize it if the other person is suffering, but we do not feel concern about it – we may even take sadistic pleasure in it. Not only is this last mode the most cognitively demanding, as it requires both our analytic and our empathetic cognitive resources, but it also breaks with our usual tendency to suppress one network when we activate the other. This cognitive mode has greater similarity to the typical pattern seen in individuals with mental disorders than it does to the typical pattern seen in healthy individuals.

We call this fourth mode a blended cognitive mode because it involves aspects of both analytic and empathetic thinking. It is often useful. It undoubtedly represents an important aspect of healthy human thinking, but it is also limited and unstable. It is engaged when we think creatively, which sometimes yields important insights, but also often yields bizarre, illogical, and unhelpful ideas. It is important when we need to think politically or respond to someone who has malevolent intentions, yet it involves a failure to fully appreciate the other's experiential world. It also occurs more frequently when people are chronically fatigued or sleep deprived. While it is no doubt perfectly healthy to cycle between this and other cognitive modes, it is plausible that individuals who chronically adopt this cognitive mode are putting their psychological integrity at risk.

We believe that we must train our troops to dehumanize the enemy. To ask them to consider the humanity of an individual at the very moment they are killing that person is simply to ask too much. Such a stance would hinder their ability to think in a clear, logical, and efficient manner, putting themselves and their fellow combatants at risk. Yet, we do no better if we allow our troops to animalistically dehumanize the enemy. This stance may provide them with a motivation to kill, but it is neither a desirable motivation nor a cognitively efficient state. Instead, we should encourage our troops to objectify the enemy, at least while they are engaged in the business of combat. This is the only mode that frees their cognitive resources to deal with the strategic and performance demands of combat.

Dehumanizing in a Military Context

Animalistic dehumanization is generally what we associate with atrocities that spring from rage and hatred. They are often acts of revenge, and may trigger vicious cycles of reprisals. Unlike objectifying, this is not an emotionally disengaged cognitive mode. It is an emotionally dysfunctional cognitive mode. WWII combat veteran J. Glenn Gray brings home the agony of the warrior who has become trapped in such a cycle in his modern classic on the experience of war, *The Warriors: Reflections on Men in Battle*:

> The ugliness of a war against an enemy conceived to be subhuman can hardly be exaggerated. There is an unredeemed quality to battle experienced under these conditions, which blunts all senses and perceptions. Traditional appeals of war are corroded by the demands of a war of extermination, where conventional rules no longer apply. For all its inhumanity, war is a profoundly human institution.... This image of the enemy as beast lessens even the satisfaction in destruction, for there is no proper regard for the worth of the object destroyed.... The joys of comradeship, keenness of perception, and sensual delights [are] lessened.... No aesthetic reconciliation with one's fate as a warrior [is] likely because no moral purgation [is] possible.[38]

Objectifying the enemy is a lesser evil. It is better to view our enemies as mere things, like cogs in a wheel or blips on a computer screen, than to hold on to the "image of the enemy as beast," to borrow Gray's language. Yet objectification is certainly not without its moral perils. We know that Nazi propaganda made liberal use of both forms of dehumanization against the Jews and others, and it seems probable that the grotesquely efficient massacres committed in the concentration camps during the Holocaust were primarily conducted through cold, mechanistic objectification. It was meticulously organized mass

38 J. Glenn Gray, *The Warriors: Reflections on Men in Battle* (New York: Harper and Row, 1970), pp. 152–153.

murder. As Hannah Arendt so vividly describes in *Eichmann in Jerusalem: A Report on the Banality of Evil*, "The extermination machinery had been planned and perfected in all its details long before the horror of war struck Germany herself, and its intricate bureaucracy functioned with...unwavering precision."[39]

Objectification certainly has the potential to lead to moral negligence, and thence to horror at one's disregard for the humanity of others. All forms of dehumanization are toxic to some degree, and both animalistic and mechanistic dehumanization can be pressed into service by those constructing conditions for the commission of atrocities. Our troops need to dehumanize their enemies at least to some extent in order to achieve the moral distance needed to do their jobs. Yet, in moments when they reflect upon their actions, they cannot escape the reality that they have killed another human. Even drone pilots, who operate at a safe distance using an interface that is nearly as removed as playing a video game, have been reported to suffer from post-traumatic stress disorder.[40] Similar belated realizations of horror have been reported by the crews of World War II bombers. Only psychopaths can permanently block a re-examination of their actions from an empathetic perspective. Objectifying is a necessary, but temporary, fix. Indeed, if we want our troops to maintain the capacity to question clearly immoral or illegal orders, then we would not want it any other way. And so, in the end, there is no avoiding the need for a larger frame that allows troops to reconcile their actions with the perspectives that are afforded by both analytic and empathetic modes of thought.

If we fail to reinforce this broader positive cognitive frame, then animalistic dehumanizing is bound to rear its head. It appears that a careful and limited disregard for others can be reconciled within such a frame. Surgeons do not feel guilt for cutting into their patients, because they know it was for a good end. Yet if they carelessly cut too much, some guilt is appropriate. The oncologist does not feel bad that the chemotherapy treatment brought a patient to her knees, provided the course was justified. But if a doctor encourages a treatment that would never work, rather than listening to the patient's wish to die more comfortably in the company of loved ones, then, again, re-examination of that action is appropriate.

The larger moral context is essential here, even more so for the combatant who cannot, and for his own well-being should not, escape a degree of sadness at the lives he has ended. Disregard for others, when limited and justified, can

---

39 Hannah Arendt, *Eichmann in Jerusalem: A Report on the Banality of Evil* (New York: Penguin Books, 1977), p. 116.

40 James Dao, "Drone Pilots Are Found to Get Stress Disorders Much as Those in Combat Do," *New York Times*, February 22, 2013.

be reconciled. However, it is a much greater challenge to reconcile hatred, contempt, and acts of killing that are motivated by them. The psychological dissonance of honestly facing such actions can be almost unbearable for the individual. So powerful is our sense of allegiance to our tribe that these actions are often unbearable even if we had no hand in an atrocity, but it was done by the social group with which we identify. Often, the only route to relieving this pressure is the damaging fix of animalistically dehumanizing the enemy.

If our actions cannot be reconciled with recognition of the humanity of our enemies, then our only psychological escape route is to deny their humanity. The inevitable nature of this process can even be observed at a very distant remove from actual combat. When both undergraduates and typical American citizens are told that their in-group has perpetrated violence against an out-group, their sense of collective responsibility causes them to animalistically dehumanize the out-group.[41] We can only imagine how much more powerful this effect is when combatants learn of atrocities committed in the same theatre of war by their fellow troops. Psychological research indicates that witnessing such examples leads to a lowering of the ethical bar for the witnesses, unless the perpetrators are shunned for them.[42] It is exceedingly dangerous for such behavior to become normalized.

We believe that the only way to counter these tendencies is to emphasize a sense of social identification that is explicitly predicated on honorable conduct – that is, to inculcate the right kind of warrior's code.[43] Such a code will insist on bright lines demarking honorable and dishonorable behavior, and will motivate troops to maintain these lines as a sacred obligation they owe to those who have come before them, to their fellow troops, and to themselves. They should be charged to act with honor because they have chosen to bind themselves to a particular set of values and norms; and their discipline should be such that that commitment will not waver, regardless of what perceptions they may have of those they fight. In this way, the process of social identification that is so essential to the psychological integrity of the combatant will

41 Castano E., and Giner-Sorolla R., 'Not Quite Human: Infrahumanization in Response to Collective Responsibility for Intergroup Killing' *Journal of Personality and Social Psychology* (2006) 90, pp. 804–818.

42 Gino F., Ayal S., and Ariely D., 'Contagion and Differentiation in Unethical Behavior: The Effect of One Bad Apple on the Barrel', *Psychological Science* (2009) 20 (3), pp. 393–398.

43 See Shannon E. French, *The Code of the Warrior: Exploring Warrior Values, Past and Present*, Chapter One: "Why Warriors Need a Code," (New York: Rowman and Littlefield, 2003), and also Mark Osiel, *Obeying Orders: Atrocity, Military Discipline, and the Law of War* (New Brunswick and London: Transaction Publishers, 1999).

serve to actively guard against what is otherwise a very natural and powerful human tendency to animalistically dehumanize the enemy.

There is an understandable temptation to employ animalistic dehumanization to motivate troops to kill, because it appeals to the natural passions that arise in combat settings. However, animalistic dehumanization is pernicious because it is at odds with maintaining discipline and control over one's actions and emotions. General Benoit Royal supports this point extremely well in his analysis of *The Ethical Challenges of the Soldier*:

> The soldier at war will always be liable to be overwhelmed by passion, a feeling of revenge, and the appeal of cruelty. In armies worthy of the name, it is right to require those who exercise command, at every level, to contain possible excesses of passion by their subordinates; for similar but more important reasons, it is essential that they prevent themselves using such excesses as a way of dramatically increasing their fervor in combat. ...[T]he essence of the profession of arms [is]...the responsibility that the leader accepts for the use of force and the management of lethal risk.[44]

It therefore makes the most sense to continue the modern trend toward mechanistic, but not animalistic, dehumanization in military training. It is better to train troops to "neutralize targets" than to "exterminate the evil-doers." The latter may produce short-term gains, but it will undermine long-term goals and increase the odds of war crimes.

There is also the issue of reinforcing a cognitive model that clearly determines the appropriate context and targets for dehumanizing. It is one thing for troops to use a sanctioned form of mechanistic dehumanization to enable them to execute their legal orders and kill enemy combatants: legitimate targets. It is quite another for entire populations, including combatants and noncombatants, to be dehumanized en masse. In other words, dehumanization should be linked to a particular task and in response to specific actions or threats, not to a people. In legal terms, the issue is enforcing the rules of engagement. In cognitive terms, if the law is to be followed reliably in practice, troops need to be trained to recognize concrete cues and move rapidly into the appropriate cognitive mode in response. Ultimately, it may be possible to test for this ability and use these tests to determine fitness for combat. The mental readiness of troops to achieve such fluid and appropriate transitions is very

44 General Benoit Royal, *The Ethical Challenges of the Soldier: The French Experience* (Paris: Economica, 2012), pp. 63–64.

important, because of the potential for one inappropriate action, even one that is within the rules of engagement but stems from the wrong psychological motivation, to trigger a vicious psychological circle that encourages more frequent and heinous inappropriate actions. One way to protect against this cycle of dehumanization is to actively humanize the civilian population put at greatest risk by the military engagement.

The US Army is attempting to implement something like this approach through the development of the Human Terrain System (HTS) program. This is the official HTS mission statement:

> The Human Terrain System develops, trains, and integrates a social science based research and analysis capability to support operationally relevant decision-making, to develop a knowledge base, and to enable sociocultural understanding across the operational environment.[45]

The program brings in subject matter experts, such as anthropologists, sociologists, historians, and linguists, to instruct soldiers about the people and cultures they are likely to encounter. Some of these subject matter experts are even embedded with the troops to provide real-time insights and guidance. The US Army has also joined forces with the Cultural Knowledge Consortium (CKC), a research consortium formed "to facilitate access among multi-disciplinary, worldwide, social science knowledge holders [to] foster collaborative engagement in support of socio-cultural analysis requirements…[to support] US government and military decision-makers, while supporting collaboration and knowledge sharing throughout the socio-cultural community."[46]

There is a lot to be gained by improving our troops' knowledge of and respect for the culture of those they fight. This process can assist in collaborative engagement. It is also likely to be protective of mental health. When troops lose that respect, they experience even greater combat trauma. In his deeply perceptive work, *Achilles in Vietnam: Combat Trauma and the Undoing of Character,* psychiatrist Jonathan Shay stresses how important it is to the warrior to have the conviction that he participated in an *honorable* endeavor:

> Restoring honor to the enemy is an essential step in recovery from combat PTSD. While other things are obviously needed as well, the

45 http://humanterrainsystem.army.mil/

46 https://ckc.army.mil/Pages/default.aspx

> veteran's self-respect never fully recovers so long as he is unable to see the enemy as worthy. In the words of one of our patients, a war against subhuman vermin "has no honor."[47]

In other words, training to support the process of "re-humanization" of the enemy must be given the same attention as the training that allows troops to achieve the necessary psychological distance (mechanistic dehumanization or objectification) to be able to kill. This will support and strengthen troops' ability to appropriately shift between empathetic and analytic stances, so that they "learn to take only certain lives in certain ways, at certain times, and for certain reasons."[48]

Ted Van Baarda also makes a persuasive case that this kind of training can increase the likelihood that troops will recognize dangerous dehumanizing stances adopted by others and thus be able to raise red flags and intervene to prevent atrocities before they occur. He cites the example of Sergeant Hugh Thompson's intensely empathetic response to the vicious attack on the villagers of My Lai by American soldiers in the Vietnam War (a horrible crime that could have been even worse if Sergeant Thompson and his men had not intervened to rescue the few surviving villagers). Van Baard notes, "Where dehumanization of the enemy facilitates the commission of atrocities, the power of (re-)humanization serves as an antidote and a source for moral courage."[49] Military training must continually reinforce the principle that honor demands warriors must show as much courage in preventing war *crimes* as they do in prosecuting legal warfare.

As we have argued elsewhere, by upholding standards, maintaining discipline, accepting certain restraints, and respecting their enemies, warriors can create a lifeline that they can use to pull themselves out of the hell of war and reintegrate into their society, should they survive to see peace restored. That is the purpose of the warrior's code of honor. It is a shield that guards the warrior's humanity.[50]

---

47 Jonathan Shay, M.D., Ph.D., *Achilles in Vietnam: Combat Trauma and the Undoing of Character* (New York: Simon and Schuster, 1994), p. 115.

48 Shannon E. French, *The Code of the Warrior: Exploring Warrior Values, Past and Present* (New York: Rowman and Littlefield, 2003), p. 3.

49 Ted Van Baarda, "The Ethical Challenges of a Complex Security Environment," in David Whetham (ed.), *Ethics, Law and Military Operations* (Basingstoke: Palgrave MacMillan, 2010), p. 166.

50 Shannon E. French, *The Code of the Warrior: Exploring Warrior Values, Past and Present* (New York: Rowman and Littlefield, 2003).

Conclusion

All forms of dehumanizing are potentially morally perilous. Hence, it is tempting to hope that we might be able to train our troops to fight without ever dehumanizing the enemy.[51] We acknowledge the pull towards this view; however we have come to the conclusion that it is naïve, and even dangerous, to suppose that our troops can and should consistently adopt a stance that requires them to empathize and identify with their opponents. Two observations we have mentioned strongly suggest this conclusion: the historical observation of low kill ratios in conflicts prior to military training aimed at helping troops to objectify the enemy; and the neurological observation that consideration of the humanity of others interferes with our ability to think and act with a clear-headed analytic mindset. Yet perhaps the most telling objection to this view is a matter of moral and psychological intuition. It strikes us that any attempt to square empathy or humanitarian concern for an individual with committing acts of extreme, intentional violence against that person represents a mindset that is too tortured and dysfunctional to condone. Troops should not be asked to love their enemies while inflicting suffering and death upon them. This is the mindset of an abuser, not a mindset we wish to encourage in troops who will return to civilian life.

Violence should be seen as a last resort, but when it is necessary, those who must engage in it have no better option than to place consideration of the humanity of their targets, temporarily, to one side, using the psychological technique of objectification. Given the inevitability that our troops will be required to commit acts of violence towards others, objectification is a necessary psychological strategy that can both allow them to perform their duties well and also safeguard them from the perils of psychological disintegration. In our view, it is entirely consistent with military honor that troops should be enabled to practice a degree of psychological distance towards the enemy when the situation demands it. Such a carefully controlled and limited degree of interpersonal coldness need not be viewed as wrong. Indeed, when properly exercised, it may be viewed as a virtue. It is similar to the notion, which translates well from our analogy with healthcare, of clinical efficiency.

In other words, while we agree that the strategy of objectifying others is morally perilous, we do not regard it as pernicious. That term we reserve for

51 Nancy Sherman suggests in *Stoic Warriors: The Ancient Philosophy Behind the Military Mind* (Oxford: Oxford University Press, 2005) and elsewhere that troops could practice building empathy with their enemies by "trading places in imagination" (p. 172) and fully embracing their shared humanity.

animalistic dehumanizing. We suggest that objectification is a psychological tool that has a similar moral status to the weapons our troops are charged with operating. It is essential but dangerous and must be deployed with care and precision. Military leadership recognizes the duty to ensure troops are appropriately trained and monitored in their use of weapons. Similarly, it is the duty of leadership to ensure that troops are properly trained and monitored in their use of psychological distancing strategies. Indeed, the considered use of such psychological strategies is no less essential to the honorable and efficient conduct of war than the physical weapons our modern military so visibly relies upon.

The best military leaders acknowledge and understand the full range of emotions combat troops may experience, but make it clear that intentional deviations from the warrior's code will not be tolerated. Experience has taught these leaders that preserving the humanity of their troops ultimately enhances the safety of those same troops. They will insist on holding the line at necessary objectification of the enemy without permitting animalistic dehumanization of the enemy. Such leaders recognize that excessive and vicious dehumanization of the enemy only clouds the troops' judgment, making them greater targets of hatred themselves, and causing them to underestimate their enemies through lack of respect.[52] Despite the difficulties, especially in urban and asymmetric conflict, great leaders demand that their troops do their utmost to differentiate combatants from civilian populations and re-humanize former combatants when they cease to be legitimate targets (i.e. when they become casualties or POWs).

The following is an excerpt from a celebrated speech given by Col. Tim Collins of the British Army, before taking his troops into Iraq in 2003:

> Iraq is steeped in history. It is the site of the Garden of Eden, of the Great Flood and the birthplace of Abraham. Tread lightly there. You will see things that no man could pay to see and you will have to go a long way to find a more decent, generous and upright people than the Iraqis. You will be embarrassed by their hospitality even though they have nothing. Don't treat them as refugees for they are in their own country. […] If there are casualties of war then remember that when they woke up and got dressed in the morning they did not plan to die this day. Allow them dignity in death. Bury them properly and mark their graves. […] It is a big step to take another human life. It is not to be done lightly. I know of men who

52 Shannon E. French, "Sergeant Davis's Stern Charge: The Obligation of Officers to Preserve the Humanity of Their Troops," *Journal of Military Ethics*, David Whetham, guest editor (2009) 8 (2), pp. 116–126.

> have taken life needlessly in other conflicts. I can assure you they live with the Mark of Cain upon them. If someone surrenders to you then remember they have that right in international law and ensure that one day they go home to their family. The ones who wish to fight, well, we aim to please. If you harm the regiment or its history by over-enthusiasm in killing or in cowardice, know it is your family who will suffer. You will be shunned unless your conduct is of the highest for your deeds will follow you down through history. We will bring shame on neither our uniform nor our nation. [...] Let's bring everyone home and leave Iraq a better place for us having been there. Our business now is north![53]

Our troops cannot and should not avoid dehumanizing their enemies to some degree. Just as it is their responsibility to only kill certain people in certain ways at certain times, it is the responsibility of leadership to help them accomplish this by training them to only dehumanize certain people in certain ways at certain times. It takes mental and emotional agility to switch rapidly between different cognitive modes; to go from seeing someone as a "target to be neutralized" to seeing him as a disarmed and wounded prisoner to whom one must render aid. Yet that agility is what morality, martial honor, and military effectiveness demand. Warriors have a duty to act with honor, regardless of whether their enemies do the same. This is a duty they owe to themselves, to each other, and to their mission. Most fulfill it faithfully, sacrificing without complaint, and, to paraphrase Col. Tim Collins, bringing shame on neither their uniforms nor their nation.

The conduct of most troops in the face of extraordinary psychological demands is nothing short of exemplary. Nonetheless, we should not use this as an excuse to avoid the responsibility to provide better protection for their psychological well-being and for the populations with which they interact. Leadership and command climate represent key elements in this equation. A bad leader can create a corrupt command climate and signal attitudes that cause conditions in a unit to run very rapidly out of control.[54] In contrast, the tone that is set by a positive and conscientious authority figure, who maintains discipline and embodies the warrior's code cannot be overstated. It signals the

---

53 "UK Troops Told: Be Just and Strong," BBC News, March 20, 2003. Archived from the original on June 15, 2009.

54 For a military perspective see e.g. Lt. Col. Joseph Doty and Maj. Joe Gelineau, "Command Climate," *Army Magazine*, July 2008. For a social psychological perspective see e.g. Philip G. Zimbardo, *The Lucifer Effect: Understanding How Good People Turn Evil* (New York: Random House, 2007).

right type of cognitive model to the troops, for them to emulate. And there are further steps that the military should take to reinforce the example that great leaders offer and to embed this kind of model firmly in the minds of all our troops.

Our goal here has been to increase awareness of vital factors affecting the behavior of troops in combat and provide a glimpse of how insights that arise at the intersection of neuroscience, psychology, philosophy, and military ethics can help guide improvements in training, command climate, and ground conditions. Our hope is that this will provide meaningful support for the one critical mission upon which everyone can agree: that of bringing our troops safely home – their bodies and, no less important, their moral souls.

CHAPTER 10

Our Responsibility to the Irresponsible

Sophie Paul

Introduction

On the 5th of September 2009 a British reporter working for the New York Times visited Kunduz province in Afghanistan in order to investigate civilian casualties surrounding a NATO air strike on fuel tankers stolen by the Taliban. Coalition and British government sources reported that he had pursued this line of inquiry in an area known to be extremely insecure, and in defiance of counsel from Afghan police and intelligence officers. Indeed Foreign Secretary David Miliband said Mr Farrell had ignored 'very strong advice' not to travel to the area.[1] Farrell was subsequently abducted by the Taliban and held hostage along with an Afghan colleague. His rescue by the British military was undertaken at the cost of four lives; that of a soldier, Farrell's Afghan colleague and reportedly a civilian woman and her child. A military source was quoted as saying, 'this reporter went to this area against the advice of the Afghan police. So thanks very much Stephen Farrell, your irresponsible act has led to the death of one of our boys'.[2] The moral questions raised by this incident produced febrile discussions within the media in the aftermath, 'it seems misguided of the British Government to have approved or perhaps initiated…an operation which cost men's lives, to free a journalist stuck in a hole of his own digging'.[3] This case highlights an important issue regarding the degree to which states have a responsibility to protect their citizens, even when those citizens deliberately choose to place themselves in harm's way and how this is to be balanced against the value of what that individual does versus the responsibility towards the well-being of those who are sent to protect them.

War is of perennial interest to the media, reflected in burgeoning numbers of reporters descending upon operational theatres. By late 2004, for example,

1 David Milliband quoted in Qwerty 2009, "Farrell Case Raises Moral Issues over Forcorrs," (2009), p. 2, http://qwerty2009.wordpress.com/category/journalism-and-conflict/ (accessed 31 October 2014)

2 Andrew Pierce, "Army anger as soldier killed saving journalist who ignored Taliban warning," (2009), p. 1, http://www.telegraph.co.uk/news/worldnews/asia/afghanistan/6163453/Army-anger-as-soldier-killed-saving-journalist-who-ignored-Taliban-warning.html (accessed 22 February 2010)

3 Max Hastings, "Journalist's lust for glory and a risk too far," (2009): 1, http://www.dailymail.co.uk/debate/article-1212700/Lust-glory-risk-far.html (accessed 12 May 2010)

 | DOI 10.1163/9789004280380_011

over 6,000 journalists had registered with the US military's press office in Baghdad alone.[4] The increase in media operators together with the increasingly insecure environment accounted for 57 abductions of journalists in Iraq between 2004 and 2009.[5] The nature of the modern battle space and the media's interest in it, therefore, situates this moral dilemma as an enduring issue for the State and the military as the lever of power often closest to it. Despite a temptation borne of proximity to view such cases as a military issue, the heart of the matter actually lies in the nature, extent and conditionality of the State's obligations to its citizens and whether this can be affected by the moral behaviour of any one individual. Given Stephen Farrell potentially took an irresponsible level of risk, did the State, in this case acting through the military, 'owe' him a response? Or was his arguably reckless conduct so morally flawed as to effectively disqualify him from state assistance?

The 'irresponsibility dilemma' represents the tension between the individual's moral responsibility for their action, the consequences thereof, and the State's customary or moral obligations to its citizens. The analysis will largely be framed by the experiences of the British media and state in Afghanistan and Iraq since 2003 as it is widely accepted by monitoring agencies and commentators alike that it is these interventions which have seen the clash between the new face of media and the new nature of war at its most acute; a clash which to a great extent generates the context of the 'irresponsibility dilemma'.[6] Whilst this study is restricted to the particular circumstances surrounding the media working in these operational theatres, they are certainly not the only group to suffer abduction or murder as a result. Similar moral dilemmas have been presented by contractors and Non-Governmental Organisation (NGO) workers.[7] Such cases have clear parallels to the 'irresponsibility dilemma' and indeed some of the findings can be legitimately extrapolated to apply to them, however, it must be noted that alongside some commonality they also present specific moral equations born of additional factors that would inform the moral calculus, such as whether the motivation for defying Foreign and Commonwealth Office (FCO) advice was remuneration or altruism.

To disassemble and analyse the 'irresponsibility dilemma' the role of state, the responsibilities of the individual and the context must be examined. Tools

4 Herbert Foerstel, *Killing the Messenger* (Westport: Praeger, 2006), p. 25.

5 Committee to Protect Journalists, "Special Reports Iraq: Journalists Abducted 2003–2009," (2008), p. 1, http://cpj.org/reports/2008/04/abducted.php (accessed 8 May 2010)

6 See Howard Tumber and Frank Webster, *Journalists Under Fire* (London: Sage Publications, 2006).

7 Such as the abductions and rescue or rescue attempts of Ken Bigly and Norman Kember.

provided by political thought and theories on moral responsibility will be applied to the context, in turn derived from analysis of both the contemporary nature of war and the latter-day media. There is an enormous body of literature on each separate element of the subject, however, none directly tackle the interplay between state responsibility and how far that extends to an individual who may have behaved in such a way as to arguably strip them of their normal 'rights' or expectations as a citizen. The literature on political thought generally reflects on the origins and governing tenets of state development: 'The history of political thought is the history of the attempts over the centuries to answer the question: "Why should I obey the State?"'[8] Such treatises generally, however, study the way in which society is constructed within a nation state, as freedoms are 'traded' for governance, and tackle the denial or constraint of further individual rights or freedoms only within the context of domestic legal transgressions. The literature does not examine rights and responsibilities in terms of moral behaviour (unless this breaks laws) and does not analyse how, what is effectively a reciprocal relationship operates outside of the nation state. The latter is not only fundamental to this study, but is a factor that will continue to grow in importance in a globalised context. However, whilst not addressed explicitly, some of the extant literature does at least provide some "handrails" about how this might be interpreted in this context and the factors that would need to be taken into account in tackling the consequences of 'irresponsibility dilemma'.[9]

State Responsibility to the Citizen

Classical treatises reflect upon values that can be described as 'modern or even pre-modern, but certainly international'.[10] That they remain pertinent to the post-modern and globalised era can be established by two criteria: credibility and precedent. Credibility can be demonstrated by currency within contemporary academic debate such as the study of the international system where indeed classical authors are validated by their consistent use to, 'define and structure contemporary and theoretical and political debates'.[11] Precedent can

8 Brian Redhead, *Plato to Nato, Studies in Political Thought* (London: BBC Books, 1984), p. 9.

9 E.g. James Pattison, "Whose Responsibility to Protect?" *Journal of Military Ethics* 7 No 4 (2008), pp. 262–283.

10 Jahn Beate, *Classical Theory in International Relations* (2006), http://assets.cambridge.org/97805218/66859/excerpt (accessed 20 April 2010)

11 *Ibid.*

be established through resonance in current state responses to hostage crises where tenets central to Kant and Hobbes's treatises are manifest in the responses of contemporary governmental departments such as the FCO.

The responsibility of a state to its citizens and their reciprocal undertakings can be understood through Social Contract theory, which explains the way people form states and thereby create social order. The term is attributed to Rousseau, however, the principles that inform it can be traced back through the treatises of Hobbes or even Plato. They comprehend not only what an individual gives up in terms of sovereignty to a government, but what that sacrifice is rewarded with in terms of social order, rule of law and the sense or set of stated responsibilities a state has to its citizens. Importantly the civil rights the social contract affords the citizens of a state cannot be seen as natural or permanently fixed, as the contract is based upon the understanding that the end-state is above everything, the benefit of all. The purpose of the State is, therefore, to act in the interests of the majority. In classical thought, Plato's dialogue, Crito[12] can be interpreted as a type of social contract theory. Facing the death penalty, Socrates argues that despite being afforded other options he chose to live in Athens, thereby accepting the reciprocal nature of the social contract and the attendant burden of the prevailing and accepted laws. He further reasoned that given this acceptance he could not then elect to violate these laws even when they were clearly against his self-interest. By prioritising the values of the state, in this case the codified laws, above his own interests, Socrates emphasises the importance of the State or collective interests above the individual.

Hobbes was in turn the first modern philosopher to articulate a detailed contract theory. Hobbes argued that the state of 'nature', or lives governed by self-interest alone would be, 'solitary, poore, nasty, brutish, and short'.[13] The absence of any sense of the collective good, rights or a contract to structure this would prevent the evolution of the 'social' or society. Hobbes argued that this state of nature or anarchy was transcended by the social contract in which the individual ceded a measure of their individual freedoms or rights to engender the same behaviour in others, which in turn led to the development of society. Society by extension requires an entity to lead or manage; a sovereign entity or state thereby came in to being. The State's role in return for the individual surrendering of sovereignty is to provide protection for these rights and provide a framework to regulate society. Importantly, however, Hobbes also

12 Plato, "Crito" in *Classics of Moral and Political Theory*, ed. Michael Morgan, (Indianapolis: Cambridge, 1992), p. 22.

13 Redhead, *Plato to NATO*, p. 105.

recognised that the state system, whilst a natural product of the Social Contract was not regulated or guided by the same principles. The system was anarchic in the sense of lacking leadership and was essentially guided by self-interest and competition. With the lack of a sovereign entity above states able to impose social-contract laws, Hobbes reasoned that states would act in the context of nature and were, therefore, bound to be in conflict. This reasoning provides basis for the realist-based interpretations of international relations proposed by theorists such as Carr and Morgenthau. It also invites the question of state behaviour engendering risk to the citizen. This may inform any judgement on the apportionment of individual responsibility for risk which has in the first instance been engendered by conflict between states or sovereign entities.

Writing in the 18th Century Rousseau's treatise 'The Social Contract' is consistent with the central tenets of previous thinking insofar as the symbiotic relationship between individual and state was acknowledged with the surrender of individual rights supporting the community, thereby subordinating the interests of the individual to the collective good. Rousseau differed from Hobbes, however, in the nature of state authority, disputing the idea of near absolute sovereignty in favour of a more republican approach which would make the sovereign more representative of, and responsive to, the will of the people. The thinking of Plato, Hobbes, Locke and Rousseau form the heart of the philosophy of contractarianism. Whilst their varying strains provide the theoretical basis of constitutional monarchy, liberal democracy and republicanism, there are some common tenets which can be drawn out to inform the debate central to this paper. Violations of contractual obligations such as committing a crime are logically responded to across the philosophies with a corresponding withdrawal of rights, a response reflected in most modern liberal democracies in imprisonment and often disenfranchisement. Beyond the clear cases such as breaching the law, however, violations of the contract are not closely defined. This leaves state responsibility to those who have potentially irresponsibly endangered themselves and, therefore, jeopardised others as a matter of judgement. Such judgement, however, can be illuminated by key principles drawn from political thought. From Plato to Rousseau all emphasise the subordination of the interests of the individual to those of the greater good or 'all'.

Whilst application of historical political thought has been demonstrated to be broadly relevant to the contemporary global environment; in order to prove relevance to the 'irresponsibility dilemma', British state behaviour must be shown to resonate along the theoretical lines presented by the Social Contract discourses, particularly the two central principles previously identified. The

British State has no stated obligation to citizens, beyond the undertaking to provide consular support to British people in trouble abroad. Any assistance beyond this largely administrative role is discretionary and governed essentially by custom and political direction. Indeed consistent with the treatises of Rousseau and Locke, the FCO confirmed that the will of the people was one of the main motivations behind any governmental response to intervene in a hostage situation; the public was generally supportive of rescues of citizens in peril where practicable.[14] The State's will to intervene, however, is governed by an evaluation of broader state interests, comprehending the level of risk engendered by a rescue attempt and the risk generated by non-intervention. There is, therefore, no automatic entitlement to a state response, either political, diplomatic or military in the event of a hostage-taking and all dynamics are considered when the State judges how the greater good or the 'all' is best served.

Individual Responsibility

If individual moral responsibility will potentially inform the State's reciprocal duty to a citizen, it is important first to understand the concept before exploring how an individual can be found morally responsible and the conditions which may dictate the level of moral culpability conferred. Ascribing moral responsibility is a way of judging praiseworthy or blameworthy actions. As such it can be seen as a conservative social mechanism that governs behaviours through criticism or reward, according to prevailing social norms. A commonly held, though not uncontested view is that morality is not scientific or objective, and that judgement on specific issues will be subjective and, therefore, variable.[15] To approach the 'irresponsibility dilemma' methodically, a framework for analysis must, therefore, be established and situated within acknowledged philosophical debate in order to militate against subjectivity. The analysis adopted in this chapter harvests and applies commonly accepted principles across the theories. These common principles establish the interrelationship between causality and responsibility, as well as set out the two

14 FCO, interview with author, 1 March 2010, pp. 5–6.

15 Socrates as related by Plato represented the argument that good and bad, right and wrong, are part of the objective nature of things. The philosophy developed that just as there are scientific laws, there are moral laws that lay down right and wrong, independently of the subjective feelings of individuals: Graham Gordon, *Eight Theories of Ethics* (Abingdon: Routledge 2004), p. 2.

circumstances under which actions or consequences could be excused. A third excusing condition potentially pertinent to journalism is also considered through the application of rule-utilitarianism theory.

Firstly, as its association with governing behaviour in society would suggest, moral judgement can only legitimately be conferred upon humans. Only humans, for example, can be morally responsible agents, as distinct from being causally responsible. An animal can break a vase, for example, whilst a person can deliberately smash it. Both are causally responsible for the breakage, however, only the latter can be morally responsible. The conference of moral accountability however, is more complex than establishing a causal link; it is also dependent upon certain conditions. Whilst there is sharp philosophical debate[16] surrounding the conditionality of moral responsibility, there are some common criteria across the theories that can inform the 'irresponsibility dilemma' as they are widely acknowledged to excuse responsibility, despite causality. These excusing conditions are often traced back to Aristotle and were characterised by him as ignorance and force. In terms of ignorance Aristotle reasons that an agent must have a knowledge and understanding of what they are doing to be responsible. Thus to be morally responsible, 'a person must know (or reasonably be expected to know) what he is doing, and he must not be deceived or ignorant about the circumstances and manner in which he is doing it'.[17] The second excusing condition, force, comprehends that forced actions cannot be morally ascribed to a responsible agent. Aristotle uses a kidnapping scenario to exemplify this condition, the reasoning follows that an agent is responsible only if his action is unforced.

Whilst it is commonly accepted across most theories that there are two sets of 'excusing conditions', a third can be considered regarding journalists; a condition perhaps best expressed as the aphorism, 'the ends justify the means'. This considers that additional risk taken by journalists, which in turn engenders consequences for which they are morally responsible, can be mitigated by the moral purpose or intent of their mission: pursuit of truth in the public interest. This is not a commonly accepted excusing condition and must, therefore, be challenged. The emphasis on the 'ends' leads to the intuitive application of the ethical doctrine of consequentialism, which holds that actions are

16 Consequentialist doctrines judge actions by their effects or intended effects; conversely deontological moral arguments, for example, contend that duty dictates actions and duty should be adhered to regardless of consequence. Further theoretical perspectives are provided by virtue ethics theory and the Ultimate End concept. *Ibid.*, 61, pp. 115–126.

17 John Fischer and Mark Ravizza, *Perspectives on Moral Responsibility* (Ithaca: Cornell University Press, 1993), p. 5.

judged by their effects, or intended effects, rather than by a deontological adherence to obligation or rules. Reaching moral judgement purely as a function of consequence as act-utilitarianism suggests, however, would be a potentially chaotic approach. Judging only on the basis of outcomes would confuse any kind of systematic assessment, a requirement if a state were to consider moral culpability before acting in support of a citizen. Arguably, for example, different citizens could do the same thing, with different consequences and thereby be judged and potentially treated differently by the State. Competing ideas such as deontology or Kantism could also indict such an approach on the grounds that the actions themselves and their morality or lack of it would be ignored.[18] Rule-utilitarianism can be regarded as a compromise between the duty-based approach of Kantism and the outcome-biased consequentialism. It offers a more balanced and systematic approach; balanced because it comprehends the morality of actions themselves as well as the outcome, and systematic because it judges the individual's moral responsibility by adherence to a set of rules rather than by the more random criteria of consequence. Moreover, these rules are accepted on the basis that they are a structure that will most likely deliver positive consequences. In order to be applied to the 'irresponsibility dilemma' these positive consequences must be accepted to be the bringing of truth and balance in reporting to the people.

Such values can be established through analysis of customary practice, legal practice and contemporary state behaviours. Firstly, England is acknowledged to be where the struggle for press freedom began, with John Milton establishing in his *Areopagitica* of 1644 the value of such freedoms and further arguing to Parliament that the licensing restrictions which represented prior restraint should be forsaken for publishing responsibility, thereby setting the cornerstone of press freedom in the UK. The level of freedom achieved and the upholding of these freedoms is proved by the legal liberty enjoyed by the press in the UK today, the level of which is attested to by the 'free' status conferred upon the UK by the annual report from the NGO Freedom House.[19] Contemporary state behaviour also clearly values the principle of a free press, evidenced by statements such as those by ex-Prime Minister Blair, who in 2009 stated, "We fought for freedom in Iraq including freedom of the press. Often what the press says is harsh or unfair. But that freedom is essential and must be upheld."[20] The morality of the 'ends' is

---

18 Gordon, *Eight Theories of Ethics*, p. 137.

19 http://freedomhouse.org/country/united-kingdom#.VFaooUvVvwI (accessed 2 November 2014)

20 Julian Borger, "Blair backs Iraq appeal calls for press freedom" 26 November 2009, http://www.theguardian.com/world/2009/nov/25/tony-blair-iraq-press-freedom (accessed 10 May 2010)

further attested to by practitioners themselves, who argue that they contribute heavily to the moderation or cessation of abuses by exposing and standing witness, 'unquestionably, anything that is away from the light of day in the field of conflict and foreign affairs festers and produces abuses and it still remains the job of the journalist to try and dig things out and to publicise them'.[21] This is seen by many as a duty, 'the prioritisation of the moral and ethical duties of the journalist towards the public and the world in general is part of the professional values framework within which contemporary journalism operates'.[22]

These motives and duties are also formalised into professional codes of ethics, analysis of which show that the codes were designed more for the purpose of serving the public interest than protecting the journalist, a theme specifically identifiable in the UK's two codes, tailored for journalists and editors respectively.[23] Whilst 'rules' are clearly evident and have been independently judged to be ethical,[24] the integrity of this theory and its application to journalism is weakened by the fact that the 'rules' or ethical codes are elective. Indeed that the codes are not necessarily widely known or adhered to is an issue specifically identified by Nordenstreng's study, 'to what extent are they put into practice in real life and to what extent are they even known among the rank and file journalists? On both counts the evidence is rather distressing, supporting a cynical view of the codes as window dressing'.[25]

Applying this theory to the operational environment is further compromised on the grounds of relevance. The Code of Conduct[26] adopted by the British National Union of Journalists does not consider the issue of risk or endangerment of third parties at all. This means that locally employed media workers such as translators are not considered in terms of duty of care nor indeed those charged with providing security, which in this environment is the military. Indeed, it appears to be a code forged entirely within a domestic context. Of note, this is a criticism common to the 50 codes from 46 European countries reviewed.[27] None address risk or danger engendered to others in the

---

21 Julian Manyon quoted in Tumber and Webster, *Journalists Under Fire*, p. 72.

22 *Ibid.*, p. 67.

23 Journalists Code of Conduct, Editors' Code of Practice, http://ethicnet.uta.fi/country/united_kingdom (accessed 4 May 2010)

24 Kaarle Nordenstreng, *Media Ethics in Europe: In Search of Core Values* (2004), p. 6, http://portal.unesco.org/ci/en/ev.phpURL_ID=14199&URL_DO=DO_TOPIC&URL_SECTION=201.html (accessed 10 May 2010)

25 Nordenstreng, *Media Ethics in Europe*, p. 9.

26 National Union of Journalists Code of Conduct, http://ethicnet.uta.fi/united_kingdom/code_of_conduct (accessed 4 May 2010)

27 Press Complaints Commission, Editors' Code of Practice, http://ethicnet.uta.fi/ethicnet_collection_of_codes_of_journalism_ethics_in_europe (accessed 4 May 2010)

course of collection and they do not comprehend the considerations attendant with work in dangerous environments. Importantly the value the people (and therefore the State insofar as it is a reflection of the people), place on press freedom is altered when specifically polled on operational environments. Here the public seemingly favour tighter government control over such information, with a Pew Research Centre report in 2001 showing over half respondents (54% versus 39%) finding, 'the military should have more control over war news than news media have'.[28] With weak evidence of knowledge of, or adherence to, the rules; the lack of relevance to the environment and the value of the 'ends' potentially modified by context, it must be concluded that this theory cannot be legitimately applied to the 'irresponsibility dilemma'.

The New Face of Journalism Meets the New Face of War

Having examined the origins and nature of individual moral responsibility and state responsibility to its citizens, the operational context of the 'irresponsibility dilemma' must be analysed in terms of causality, and to establish where individual and state interests lie, where they coincide and where they clash. First, however, the scale and nature of the 'irresponsibility dilemma' will be established. Journalists working in theatres where the British state has intervened militarily are by definition operating in highly insecure environments where the indigenous security architecture is nascent, fragile and certainly not comprehensive. This backdrop of general insecurity is familiar to many journalists experienced in operating in war zones, however, there has been an escalation in the specific threat to journalists and media workers working in such places in the last 10–15 years, a threat that has increased exponentially with the advent of operations in Iraq and Afghanistan. This can be evidenced by a comparison of lethality between the 1990s and the 2000s in Iraq, which reflects an increase in deaths from one to 140 respectively.[29] This increase in lethality has been attended by a corresponding increase in hostage-taking, with 57 journalists abducted between 2003 and 2009 – a tactic previously so rare that data cannot be sourced.[30] Similarly, in Afghanistan the Committee to Protect Journalists (CPJ)

28 William Hatchen and James Scotton, *The World News Prism* (Oxford: Blackwell, 2002), pp. 23 and 142.

29 1992–2003 1 killed. 2003–2010 140 killed. Committee to Protect Journalists, "Special Reports Iraq" (2008), http://cpj.org/killed/mideast/iraq (accessed 8 May 2010)

30 Committee to Protect Journalists, "Special Reports Iraq: Journalists Abducted 2003–2009," (2008), http://cpj.org/reports/2008/04/abducted.php (accessed 8 May 2010)

has documented at least 16 abductions since 2007, 'it's become a very dangerous world… I don't think there's ever been a period when doing the job…has seemed so full of risk'.[31]

The character of war and adversaries' approaches to journalists are dynamics which have changed greatly in the last 20 years, moreover, they are variables that are mostly outside of the control of any individual reporter. The potential elements of the threat to journalists that will be considered in terms of how they inform the balance between state and individual responsibility are: legal ambiguity; the new nature of war and belligerent; the influence of state actions; the contemporary face of the media in terms of journalists' capabilities, training and experience; demands for real time access to action together with the increased numbers of media actors and finally perceived and actual journalistic partiality. The threat, therefore, is very real; the reasons behind it are, however, multifarious.

Traditional protections for journalists in war are seemingly breaking down. Building on the 1907 Hague Convention, the 1949 Geneva Conventions began codifying journalists' position as civilians on the battlefield. The Conventions can, however, be accused of being less relevant to the contemporary media landscape after, 'exponential technological changes are redefining, broadening and fragmenting the media landscape in dramatic ways'.[32] Indeed the protocols remain steeped very much in the context of conventional war with formal belligerents and clearly definable 'war correspondents'.[33] Today they do not accurately reflect either the, 'practice of modern journalism, or the practice of modern war'.[34] The definition of journalist is the first point of ambiguity, as the business of news production encompasses personnel beyond writers, broadcasters, editors and photographers, particularly in the new media context.[35] Notwithstanding the lack of direct relevance to the new media landscape, the intent behind the Conventions is abundantly clear to any who choose to heed them: journalists should be treated as non-combatants and should not be attacked. The spirit of the law is clear, even if the detail appears often to be

31 Tumber and Webster, *Journalists Under Fire*, p. 116.

32 Nik Gowing, *Skyful of Lies and Black Swans* (Oxford: Oxuniprint, 2009), p. 1.

33 Geneva Conventions and Additional Protocols, http://www.icrc.org/ihl.nsf/CONVPRES?OpenView (accessed 22 March 2010)

34 Kenneth Payne, 'The Media at War. Ideology, Insurgency and Journalists in the Firing Line' *RUSI Journal* 153 No 1 (2008): p. 17.

35 Such production relies on many other specialisations such as fixers, engineers and drivers. The proliferation of electronic media such as the internet and mobile phone technology also means that there are now a range of non-professional media actors on the battlefield, such as the citizen-journalist or blogger.

anachronistic. Bar the almost inevitable catching of some media operators in the crossfire on a confused and ambiguous battlefield, attacks on journalists are not, therefore, founded in legal ambiguity. They are founded in a complex combination of factors, which include changes in the very nature of warfare and media themselves. If the relevance of journalistic ethical codes can be discounted at least in part because they appear to be unknown to most journalists, then the Geneva Convention argument used here needs to be qualified, because the Taliban have probably even less knowledge of, or interest in, any such ethical rules or conventions.

Latter-day conflicts such as Iraq and Afghanistan are marked by their lack of fixed lines and seemingly chaotic situations, which increase the vulnerability of correspondents. The change from more formalised warfare where a front line was easy to establish has been attended by an commensurate increase in the role of the less 'formal' belligerent, characterised as, '...basically huge gang fights between ethnic or religious insurgent groups or terrorist groups. These are untrained gunmen, people who have no knowledge of the laws of war'.[36] Modern conflict is, therefore, characterised by complexity, with multiple non-state actors shaping an ever-more ambiguous battlefield. Moreover, conflicts particularly those involving Islamist insurgency and terrorism, are distinguished by irregular combatants with no *interest* in the customary conventions of war as well as those determinedly opposed to them. Fundamental to the imperative to adhere to international protocols is investment in their development and effects. As non-state actors, insurgent or terrorist groups have no investment or obligation to adhere to such standards they, 'do not feel obliged to fight according to the terms of international laws and norms laid down by sovereign states to govern conventional warfare'.[37] Indeed many see themselves as specifically opposed to such values, or at least the framework and system that begat them. They are ideologically opposed to the western values, the very origins of the Westphalian state system within which such laws evolved. Furthermore, with the US' highly-publicised use of rendition and Guantanamo Bay they can also claim to have been excluded from receiving the protections that are afforded to 'lawful combatants'. Finally, and perhaps most importantly it makes no strategic sense for the non-state actors operating in Iraq and Afghanistan to limit their freedom of manoeuvre and observe international law, as they would be fighting at such a huge disadvantage.

The risk to journalists has not just increased, however, due to greater ambiguity on the battlefield and less-formal belligerents. The very role the

36 Foerstel, *Killing the Messenger*, p. 82.

37 Payne, *The Media at War*, p. 20.

journalist now plays in these conflicts has increased their vulnerability, 'in a war about ideas, they have become the targets'.[38] The war in Iraq, for example, demonstrated to the belligerents the power of the press in the battle for the strategic narrative. It is important to note that whilst this battle has been played out in Iraq it is part of a much broader information war: the struggle between the Western secularist governments and militant political Islamists. This struggle to dominate the narrative has been expressed at the strategic level by the respective leaders. Ex-Prime Minister (PM) Brown acknowledged the critical value of the narrative, 'the cultural war that had to be fought against communism from the 1940s and 50s onwards, is in a sense the model for what we've got to do here',[39] resonating with statements from Blair in 2005 who characterised the effort as, 'a global struggle…a battle of ideas…a battle that must be won, a battle not just about the terrorist methods but their views. Not just their barbaric acts but their barbaric ideas. Not only what they do, but what they think and the thinking they would impose on others'.[40] Similarly, Ayman al Zawahiri, one of the principal leaders of Al Qaeda articulates the central importance of dominating the strategic narrative, whilst also specifically identifying the pivotal role the media have in this, 'I also remind our brothers who work in Islamic media of their crucial, critical role in the Muslim Umma's battle against the Zionist Crusade'.[41] With both sides of the conflict characterising the ideological battle as so important the natural corollary is that the protagonists have a vested interest in what is being communicated, how it is being transmitted and, therefore, the conduit.

The information war is not particular to, or indeed a new aspect of, counterinsurgency. It has been a feature of the Cold War and of previous counterinsurgency battles such as Malaya where, 'an understanding and sympathetic press, particularly in adversity is one of a commander's greatest assets and is worth a great deal more than many other weapons in his armoury'.[42] Where previous conflicts have demonstrated the importance of information, it has now become critical in a context where, 'countering a modern, ideologically motivated insurgency' with, 'global aspiration' has become the battle.[43] Whilst the information war is by no means new, therefore, the importance of it has

---

38 *Ibid.*

39 Payne, *The Media at War*, p. 17.

40 Blair "Full Text: Blair Speech on Terror" 16 July 2005, http://news.bbc.co.uk/1/hi/uk/4689363.stm (accessed 7 April 2010)

41 Zawahiri quoted in Payne, *The Media at War*, p. 17.

42 *Ibid.*, p. 18.

43 *Ibid.*

grown and the centrality of journalists to this battle has meant that they have been affected in new ways. No matter how unwillingly, and despite the intentions of journalists to maintain their position as independent observers, the assimilation of the media *into* the war has meant that the once-established norm of treating journalists as civilians has been eroded, 'When war becomes a spectator sport, the media becomes the decisive theatre of operations...it also transforms journalists from observers into protagonists...'[44] This does not, however, necessarily translate to all sides having an interest in killing or intimidating journalists; indeed notwithstanding the values and professional standards of the counter-insurgent, it would make no sense for that side of the conflict to do such a thing. The insurgents or terrorists, however, have a more paradoxical relationship with the media where there is an interest in using them as a narrative tool, but where there is also an interest in targeting them.

On one hand the media's interest in pursuing stories of violence serves the insurgent or terrorist well, as their violence would have a very limited purpose only without the large audience reporting generates. Similarly where the counter-insurgent has engendered civilian casualties, the propaganda campaign of Al-Qaeda or the Taliban can exploit it effectively only where it is broadly publicised. Conversely however, journalists serve as an effective target for insurgents wishing to demonstrate the weakness of the counter-insurgent, shock their audience or punish a particular editorial line. In the first instance where the counter-insurgent is undertaking to provide security in an operational theatre, killing or kidnapping journalists is an act of terror that seeks to send a powerful message about the efficacy of those efforts. The targeting of media workers by those arrayed against the security forces can, therefore, undermine the coalition's ability to construct an effective information operation by weakening not only the substance of the message, but also the method by which it can be spread, particularly indigenously. In terms of undermining the counter-insurgent, the domestic audience and political will, is also targeted, and journalists, '...become tools. There are the clearly politically motivated kidnappings meant to change a country's policies, and journalists are not viewed as exempt from this...'.[45]

In addition to journalists becoming increasingly and unwillingly caught in the information-war cross-fire, they are also at greater risk by virtue of their nationality, their consequent associations and how such associations are seen by the irregular adversary. George Habash, Leader of the Popular Front for the Liberation of Palestine, was the first to develop the doctrine of international

44 Mark Connelly and David Welsh, *War and the Media* (London: IB Taurus, 2005), p. 276.

45 Adi Ignatius quoted in Foerstel, *Killing the Messenger*, p. 83.

terrorism, thereby internationalizing the guerrilla theories of Guevara and Marighella. He clearly stated, 'In today's world, no one is innocent, no one a neutral. A man is either with the oppressed or he is with the oppressors',[46] thus presaging the threat in the contemporary environment where, 'recognition of journalists as neutral observers has largely gone'. Increasingly journalists covering international conflicts are identified with their countries or are seen as "'either with us or against us."[47] This denuding of journalists' neutrality and closer identification with the policies and actions of their respective states has had a major impact on the threat, catalyzed further by levels of hostility engendered by Western interventions in the Middle East, 'the whole picture has changed with the doctrine of what Tony Blair has described as "liberal intervention" on a global level. We Western reporters are seen as being affiliated with this policy in many parts of the world'.[48]

Most of the threats hitherto presented are engendered by actors or dynamics outside of journalists' control. Elements of the threat can, however, be related to the behaviours and choices of the media in recent years. Insurgents perceive a lack of objectivity in western reporting on Middle Eastern conflicts, which has led some to regard journalists simply as mouthpieces for their governments.[49] Indeed, some journalists do recognise a measure of bias in reporting since the first Gulf War (GW1). David Schlesinger, chief correspondent for Reuters, for example, highlights the 'we' factor in Western reporting:

> The use of 'we' [in Iraq] to mean not 'we' the organisation or 'we' the profession, but 'we' representing the United States or the Coalition means that in many people's minds journalists are not objective observers of the situation. They are actually in play, and I think that is one of the things that makes it more dangerous today...[50]

This partisanship, no matter how mild, is bolstered by the effect of media consumers and the embed system. Jerry Levin, a former CNN correspondent and kidnap victim in Lebanon recognises the need to retain the audience, 'mainstream journalism has never been neutral... Do you really suppose that when the New York Times...or the Associated Press covers a war in which the United

46 Antokol, N., and Mayer, N., *No One a Neutral* (Ohio: Alpha Publications, 1990), p. 11.

47 International News Safety Institute, *Killing the Messenger* (INSI: Belgium, 2006), p. 8.

48 UNESCO, *Press Freedom, Safety of Journalists and Impunity*, p. 22, http://unesdoc.unesco.org/images/0015/001567/156773e.pdf (accessed 16 April 2010)

49 Foerstel, *Killing the Messenger*, p. 86.

50 *Ibid.*

States is involved that they are going to be pulling for the other side to win? They may be critical of the conduct of the war, but they acknowledge that there is an enemy'.[51]

Embedding, whereby journalists are integrated in to a military unit or base engenders bias via a combination of factors: the unconscious identification of the journalist with those alongside whom they live and endure, and the conscious need to safeguard future opportunities to embed. Firstly, by immersion in the lives and battle-rhythm of a unit, 'the embedded reporter is seeing the war from the fighting man's point of view, the foxhole point of view...when you're embedded...you're most likely to strongly identify with the soldiers you are with. They're your protectors'.[52] Bias is further encouraged by the competition for embed slots. The current security environment in operational theatres drives media organisations to seek embedded slots to attain the greatest measure of protection available to their staff, an imperative driven both by moral duty and adherence to insurance preconditions. This in turn results in the British Ministry of Defence (MOD) receiving multiple demands for limited slots on the operational front line with requests from bloggers, documentary makers and book writers competing with mainstream media.[53] With this highly competitive avenue often the only access to operational theatres available, journalists perceive that a severely critical report would result not only in the alienation of those they are working alongside, but more importantly would jeopardise their access to theatre in the future. Terri Judd relayed this understanding as an 'unspoken contract', whereby the opportunity to embed came with the expectation that the attendant output would be generally positive of the military.[54] This is consistent with the view of the Director of Media Communications in the MOD, who acknowledged that the media was motivated to preserve their relationship with the MOD and, therefore, exercised a degree of self-censorship.[55] The accusation of bias in Western reporting is, therefore, founded in fact, and remains a dynamic within control of the media.

Acknowledging the upturn in threat, the ability of journalists to manage the risk this presents to them has also diminished in many cases with the changes in the nature of correspondents. The last 15–20 years has seen the change from the foreign correspondent steeped in a country or region, to the latter-day journalist who often visits operational theatres or areas of conflict on a

51 *Ibid.*

52 Philip Caputo quoted in Foerstel, *Killing the Messenger*, p. 132.

53 Nick Gerr, interview with author, 19 February 2010.

54 Judd, interview with author, 19 February 2010.

55 Gerr interview with author, 19 February 2010.

shorter-term basis, as well as media practitioners such as citizen-journalists and bloggers. The effect of such changes has made media far more pervasive, but many if not the majority of practitioners also far less experienced, 'a lot of our experienced people don't want to go...because the most experienced people understand the risk'. Meanwhile of those less capable, 'a lot of them want to go but...don't really have the experience to gauge the danger'.[56] This diminished experience is arguably mitigated to an extent by better training. The compensating effect of training must, however, be heavily qualified in both quantitative and qualitative terms. Hostile environment training is available to a minority of media workers only, generally those belonging to large, western media organisations where requirement for such training is generally related to the organisation's insurance risk.

Freelancers, local media workers and those contracted to less financially secure media bodies generally do not benefit. The level of compensation it offers must also be qualified – 'Its pretty hard in the classroom or training situation to impart the kind of wisdom and street-smart knowledge that people develop over years just from experience... I'm not saying you can't learn from training, you can. But the most important thing is experience'.[57] The pressures and, therefore, risk engendered by the 24-hour media revolution is also a factor, driven by the requirement for immediate, intimate and exhaustive coverage. This in turn pushes the numerous, often less experienced media closer to ongoing conflict, 'we have a media system in the West which wants to portray this in actuality and live'.[58] The ability and now the expectation to transmit live from the respective front lines, therefore, drives up the risk journalists may take.

The State Calculus Versus the Moral Calculus

The analysis of where moral responsibility lies and which calculations inform a state response in the case of British journalists working in operational environments is extremely complex. As set out above, individual and state rights must be considered in the context of the prevailing environment. However, a state's responsibilities are less clear outside of its immediate jurisdiction. For example, in Basrah in Iraq and Helmand in Afghanistan, the British state accepted responsibility for the area with a stated mission to support and strengthen the nascent, but nonetheless legitimate indigenous state apparatus

56 Foerstel, *Killing the Messenger*, p. 117.

57 Jeremy Thompson quoted in Tumber and Webster, *Journalists Under Fire*, p. 133.

58 Tumber and Webster, *Journalists Under Fire*, p. 127.

to the point where it is robust enough to act independently. It is postulated that in the case of a British citizen in peril in an area where the British state is one of the principal providers of security, 'it is a basic responsibility of government to ensure the safety of people and property within its jurisdiction. Over time Western governments have come to be expected to do this internationally as well'.[59] Indeed the UK state demonstrably represents its citizens in legal cases abroad where they run contrary UK-values. The FCO, for example, consistently makes representations to foreign governments where UK citizens are sentenced to the death penalty, demonstrating the British state's commitment to certain values even in a foreign context. Accepting that the identified Social Contract and moral responsibility principles can legitimately be applied, this study can now synthesise both sets of principles with the operational context.

The Moral Calculus

Firstly, to examine where the burden of moral responsibility ultimately lies in cases where journalists have been taken hostage in the course of collecting information in high-risk areas, a number of factors must be considered: the threat environment and which parties have contributed to this risk factor; how and whether the risk had been reasonably mitigated; the subject's knowledge and understanding of the threat they were facing; and finally, whether the 'ends justify the means' which in this case would amount to moral responsibility being commuted by the justification of the value of free press and the truth. It has been demonstrated that the risk environment facing journalists in operational theatres has become significantly more serious over the last two decades, a process of change that has accelerated since GW1. Importantly, it has been shown that the threat to journalists has its origins in a multitude of factors, most of which are outside of their control. This raises the key question of whether the journalist can be found morally culpable for falling victim to a threat environment they were not causally responsible for generating.

Some of origins of the increased threat can be traced back to the UK state itself and the nature of the interventions it has committed to. The UK's interventions alongside the US in the Middle East and its equity in the broader strategic narrative have contributed to the changes in the threat environment. It might, therefore, be considered that if the state contributes to the threat

59 Antokol, *No One a Neutral*, p. 178. This view is consistent with the European Convention on Human Rights and the way that it had to be applied to extraterritorial areas considered under the control of the UK.

environment, it has a responsibility to those who fall victim to it. Similarly it can be postulated that journalists are not causally responsible for the changing character of the adversary, which can also lead to an escalation in the risk. The threat faced cannot, however, be wholly attributed to factors outside of journalists' control. There are elements of the environment that both their modus operandi and the very demands of the modern media environment have generated. This is rooted in the previously identified, and almost inevitable bias of western journalists and the impetus which drives them further forward to witness actual events.

The origins of the threat environment are, therefore, multifarious with the state itself is responsible for some aspects of it. Certainly if it were a matter of balancing causality in order to attribute moral responsibility, it could certainly be argued that the majority of causal factors are state or adversary-based, with fewer directly attributable to journalists themselves. This simplistic equation is, however, fundamentally flawed. Analysis of the factors governing moral responsibility concludes that awareness of consequences is critical, rather than pure causality. A person deliberately dropping a vase, for example, cannot blame gravity (a dynamic outside of their control) for its demise given the consequences of their actions were known. Accordingly, the understanding of the contemporary threat environment for journalists is widespread with supporting data and advice easily accessible through journalistic bodies. The CPJ is one of several bodies that document and publicise dangers to journalists together with numbers taken hostage, killed or imprisoned around the world.[60] The environment within which they work is, therefore, one in which the risks are known and acknowledged by front-line journalists and editors and indeed is one where these dangers are empirically measured and publicised. Moreover, the very nature of the business they are in circulates this news. Journalists do, therefore, conform to the originally Aristotelian intuition that, 'in order to be… blameworthy a person must know (or be reasonably expected to know) what he is doing'.[61] Ignorance, as one of the two acknowledged 'excusing' conditions that could absolve an individual of responsibility, does not therefore apply.

Force, the second 'excusing' condition is a presupposition common to most theories surrounding moral responsibility, and can ultimately be traced back to Aristotle, who specifies kidnapping as an example.[62] The logic is that if,

60 Other bodies include: International News Safety Institute and the Society to Protect Journalists.

61 John Fischer and Mark Ravizza, *Perspectives on Moral Responsibility*, p. 7.

62 Artistotle, "Nicomachean Ethics" in *Classics of Moral and Political Theory*, p. 260, 1110a–1111b10.

'human beings who control him were to carry him off', the subject could not be responsible for his whereabouts.[63] Whilst this is indeed irrefutable, absolving journalists from responsibility on this basis would fail to acknowledge that they do not fulfil the criteria either logically or according to Aristotle's specific qualifications. Aristotle demands that actions borne of force can only be deemed involuntary if, 'what is forced has an external origin, the sort of origin in which the agent or victim contributes nothing'.[64] He further contends that in some way inviting or being a willing participant in what ultimately becomes an arguably forced action disqualifies a subject from excuse, 'It is ridiculous, then...to ascribe responsibility to external [causes] and not to himself, when he is easily snared by such things'.[65] Journalists have an interest in placing themselves at the heart of an issue or an event and where they do so willingly in a known high-threat environment it is postulated that they have contributed to the situation, deliberately placing themselves in a context where they are easily captured or certainly more likely to be so. This disqualifies them from this excusing condition, meaning they are potentially morally responsible for becoming a hostage and, therefore, the subsequent consequences attending a rescue. Notwithstanding attribution of responsibility for generating the hostage situation, the contention that the hostage can also be found morally responsible for the consequences can be challenged by the argument that action taken by the state or security forces is something subsequent to the kidnap and is entirely outside of the hostage's control. If they have not 'contributed' and have no knowledge of a rescue it could be argued that they fulfil the excuse conditions and are, therefore, morally absolved. This paper contends, however, that the possibility of attempted rescue and the attendant risks are consequences well known to those working in such operational environments. Not only is there precedent, but the UK government's stated position on negotiation with terrorists and the legal prohibition on payment of ransoms leaves rescue as one of the only responses available where it is possible.[66] Whilst certainly not inevitable it is predictable and is a response or consequence a journalist can reasonably be expected to know and understand.

With the theory of rule-utilitarianism judged to be invalid on the grounds of a lack of relevant criteria, none of the three excusing conditions provide journalists with succour from moral attribution. Journalists are cognisant of the

63 *Ibid.*, p. 260, 1110a.

64 *Ibid.*

65 *Ibid.*, p. 261, 1110b15.

66 Rescue of Norman Kember, http://news.bbc.co.uk/1/hi/uk/4844800.stm (accessed 18 April 2010)

threat even if they are not wholly causally responsible for it, and by deliberately putting themselves in harms way they have also contributed to the admittedly independent actions of the aggressors. Journalists are not, therefore, excused by either 'ignorance' or 'force', and must be judged to be morally responsible for their actions and the consequences.

This responsibility can, however, be shared and mitigating factors must also be considered before the State's response can be analysed. Firstly, with regard to the burden of responsibility it is clear that other dynamics and interests are at work with corresponding moral responsibilities. The hostage takers as the aggressors are clearly culpable; whilst the security forces and their chain of command must also bear their share of the moral responsibility for the outcome given they too have acted independently and in the full knowledge of likely consequences. The moral responsibility of the journalist for their predicament is, therefore, shared with their captors and the moral responsibility for the rescue and consequences with both captors and rescuers. That this is a shared moral responsibility, however, does not alter its attribution to the individual. Does this represent a contravention of the social contract, absolving the State of responsibility to the individual? Or does it seriously qualify the nature and extent of any aid offered? Indeed does the moral calculus enter in to the state calculus at all? In an unwritten constitution the answers to these questions must again be sought from the philosophical principles that have been shown to inform state actions and through examination of current state conduct towards citizens who have also been morally compromised.

The State Calculus

The basis of the Social Contract is that individuals give up certain freedoms to a sovereign in return for 'protection' or governance. The State's responsibility to its citizens is in turn balanced against the central tenet of the collective good or the 'all'. To understand the State's responsibilities regarding the 'irresponsibility dilemma', we must first, therefore, understand the interests of the people or 'all' in a hostage crisis as well as what an individual is logically 'due' in return for their sacrifice of individual freedom. This analysis can be characterised as balancing the good of the 'all' against the implied rights of the citizen. In terms of state interest or representation of the 'all', a superficial look at the conundrum would suggest that the balance between one hostage and the many that would be risked in a rescue seems clear. This, however, assumes that the 'all' is restricted to those prosecuting the rescue, when in fact the state and the 'all' are engaged in many other ways. This is highlighted by the very distinction between hostage-taking and a kidnapping, the, 'political form of kidnapping is hostage taking – the act of illegally holding one or more persons captive in order to make political demands'.[67]

Hostage taking is therefore an innately political act, which rapidly transcends the abductee who becomes a vehicle to engage or pressure a state. This can be by issuing overtly political demands, or by demanding ransoms that could strengthen opposition to the State.[68] The former is exemplified by Phillip Sands, a British freelancer reporter, abducted on December 26, 2005 in Iraq as well as by the case of Peter Moore and his four security guards in 2007.[69] Both cases were connected to demands that the UK state withdraw British troops. The latter case is demonstrated by the abduction of Stephen Farrell in Afghanistan where a ransom was demanded, payment of which ran contrary to UK policy[70] as well as to international law.[71] By virtue of the demands, therefore, the State is engaged on a political level and must respond as a state rather than an actor interested only in the personal security of an individual, 'demands are coming in to the government and the government has to respond'.[72] The act of hostage taking and the political demands that attend it, therefore, engages broader state interests such as defending troop deployment policy or preventing payments to insurgent or terrorist groups which will ultimately bolster them. The strengthening of the Taliban through ransom payment, for example, would ultimately result in a greater risk to British servicepersonnel. The collective good as outlined in social contract theory now becomes invested

67 Antokol, Nudell and Mayer, *No One a Neutral. Political Hostage-Taking in the Modern World* (Ohio: Alpha Publications, 1990), pp. 22–23.

68 The two types of abduction often conflate with those motivated by ransom often resulting in the selling of the hostage to an insurgent or terrorist group such as Al Qaeda or the Taliban who will then seek to make political demands or capital from the situation. Foerstel, *Killing the Messenger*, p. 28.

69 Philip Sands was filmed pleading for his life and asking Britain to pull all troops out of Iraq and release all Iraqi prisoners. He was rescued by chance by the US military, http://cpj.org/reports/2008/04/abducted.php Jason Swindlehurst, Jason Creswell, Alec Maclachlan and Alan McMenemy, four security contractors kidnapped with Peter Moore, a computer consultant, on 29 May 2007. Their captors demanded the withdrawal of British troops from Iraq and release of Iraqi prisoners in exchange for the hostages's release, http://www.guardian.co.uk/world/2009/mar/22/iraq-british-hostages-video

70 Thatcher was the first to articulate an official no substantive concessions approach in 1980s. Prime Minister Brown's statement regarding Edwin Dyer 3 June 2009 reiterated this approach. Substantive concessions equate to ransom or prisoner exchanges. FCO, interview with author, 1 March 2010.

71 UNSCR 1267, http://www.un.org/sc/committees/1267

72 FCO, interview with author, 1 March 2010, pp. 5–6.

in and aligned with the interests of the individual. Of note, this alignment is particularly likely within the context of operational theatres, where the State is invested in development. Not only does this broaden the number of issues through which insurgents may wish to try and politically engage, it also increases state sensitivity to dynamics such as the strategic narrative.

State equity in the role of unilaterals centers on the legitimizing of the State's strategic narrative and representing the values of freedom upon which liberal democracies pride themselves. The value of communicating the State's message has always been a high priority, particularly in a counter-insurgency environment where building productive media relationships founded upon timely and above all honest information, has been a cornerstone of a media strategy which again reaches back as far as the Malaya campaign, where it was written that the government's credit 'in the eyes of the people...can only be preserved by strict adherence to the truth'.[73] The in-theatre population is critical to progressing governance over the agenda of insurgents, whilst the support of the population in the coalition countries of origin is also vital to justify expenditure and accept loss of life in a country which often seems remote and irrelevant, 'it is not whose army wins but whose story wins'.[74] The State imparts its message through official releases in the UK or in theatre, information which is often relayed and augmented by reports from embedded reporters. The state relies upon the integrity of this message to convince, and upon the media channels to transmit this. Both these aspects to communicating the strategic message are potentially jeopardised by a lack of independence in the media corps. First, relying mainly on embedded reporters narrows the channels; the MOD Director of Communications, for example, commented that the embed's focus on the tactical level often meant the strategic messaging was difficult to impart. Second and more importantly, however, the integrity of the message and, therefore, its potency would be undermined by a lack of challenge or corroboration. The governing tenet of strategic messaging is truth, 'the most powerful and convincing messages are factually true and are mutually reinforced through our actions. Influence Activities seek to change behaviour through messaging; UK messaging should be founded on absolute truth, as the default'.[75] Independent reporting often makes the difference between a message communicated, and a message believed.

73 Payne, *The Media at War*, p. 18.

74 Nye quoted in Milena Michalski and James Gow, *War, Image and Legitimacy: Viewing Contemporary Conflict* (London, 2007), p. 199.

75 United Kingdom. MOD, *Policy Guidance for the Employment of Military Influence at the Operational Level.* (D/DCDS(Ops)/Policy Papers/Military Influence, 2009), p. 9.

Without independent comment the State's narrative would be perceived as one-sided, isolated and without context. The presence of independent reporting thereby validates a medium that would otherwise be perceived as utterly one-sided, potentially propagandist and probably unconvincing. The 'challenge' function and independent context offered by independent reporting, therefore, legitimizes the state narrative.

In addition to the greater good in terms of broader state interests informing a state response, it has been shown that current state behaviors are also governed by the principle of government reflecting the will of the people. The electorate's interest in a fellow citizen's safety and the desire to see such sentiment reflected in state action resonates with Rousseau's version of the Social Contract which demands a state responsive to, and representative of, the people. Importantly, this is not dependent upon specific circumstances and is therefore detached from any moral judgments regarding the conduct of the individual. Indeed the FCO stated that, 'people...empathize with their plight', a situation which has, 'institutionalized over time' and which shared by politicians, also drives engagement, '[what]...motivates politicians to act or motivates parliamentarians...is...sympathy for these people'.[76]

Given there are compelling factors drawing broader state interest into the resolution of hostage crises, thereby aligning state and individual interest, does the moral responsibility owned by the abductees nevertheless militate against intervention? This question demands that a causal relationship between moral behavior and state responsibility to the subject be established. There is little in political philosophy to assist the tackling of this question, however, current and historical state behaviors towards those found morally wanting are instructive; specifically the UK state's treatment of citizens tried and convicted as criminals both domestically and abroad. Within the UK, for example, the State deems censure appropriate in terms of denial of freedom and disenfranchisement, with the concept of 'civic death' traceable back as far as the reign of Edward III.[77] Degree, however, is all important. The denial of these rights is temporary and not terminal as abandonment of a citizen in a hostage situation is likely to be. That state censure does not extend to this severity or level of abandonment is demonstrated by governmental interest in British citizens sentenced to death abroad. This governmental concern extends beyond perceived miscarriages of justice or relating to systems deemed partial, with active government to government appeals launched even regarding those convicted of heinous crimes by respected judicial systems within the context

76 *Ibid.*

77 The European Convention of Human Rights now disallows disenfranchisement. *Ibid.*

of liberal democracies. The UK government interventions relating to citizens guilty of major moral and legal transgressions such as murder proves that individual moral conduct and state responsibility to citizens are manifestly divorced, 'it would be totally irresponsible and unjust for a liberal democracy to treat some of its citizens as more deserving of strenuous efforts at release. All...citizens kidnapped abroad must be given equal attention, energy and support by government to secure their earliest possible release'.[78]

It can be demonstrated, therefore, that the State does indeed respond to its citizens outside of its own borders for a combination of principle-based and interest-based reasons, and that this is not allied to moral behaviour. The nature of this intervention can, however, be heavily qualified by the overarching principle of the collective good or 'all'. This means that state intervention may be diplomatic only and indeed may be surmounted by other state interests, which will actually cause greater peril to a hostage. In GW1, for example, a number of British and US nationals were held by the Iraqi government as human shields. This did not, however, alter state behaviour as articulated by President Bush, 'Our hearts go out to the hostages and their families. But our policy cannot change. And it will not change'. Whilst their timely release meant state resolve was never tested, both UK and US governments remained committed to maintaining diplomatic and military momentum and safeguarding a fragile coalition over the security of the hostages. This has been further demonstrated by the case of Yvonne Ridley, a British journalist who crossed the border from Pakistan to Afghanistan illegally and illicitly only to fall into the hands of the Taliban. Held hostage between September and October 2001, appeals were made to the British government to defer military action as part of Operation Allied Force, lest it physically endanger Ridley or jeopardise chances for her release. The UK state whilst engaging on Ridley's behalf diplomatically, nevertheless prosecuted the military operation, clearly underlining that the State's broader interests in pursuing its foreign policy aims and maintaining its obligations as a coalition partner, transcended the needs of a single citizen.

The level of risk or irresponsibility displayed by an individual in becoming a hostage is not, therefore, a factor considered in forming a governmental response. In addition to the institutionalised customary behaviours of state and, indeed, the broader interests of the nation, there are also some critical practical and related moral factors. Morally and practically, it would be impossible to accurately calibrate the level of risk taken and form a judgement on what level was worthy of redemption and what level disqualified an individual from assistance. How much risk would be deemed too much, and where each

78 Paul Wilkinson, *Terrorism and the Liberal State* (Basingstoke: Macmillan, 1977), p. 230.

case fell relative to this equation would be impossible to realistically determine. Further practical considerations such as an ability to establish the facts are also relevant. Opportunities to intervene, particularly militarily, often present themselves early in the process. At such a stage, for example, the hostage may not have been 'traded up' to the more politicised and professional levels of an insurgent organisation or sold to a more radical organisation. At such early stages detail on circumstances and methods of abduction are often scarce, again rendering a meaningful judgement on the conduct of the hostage impossible to establish. Moreover, the testimony of the individual at the heart of the crisis would necessarily be missing, meaning that any judgement should it be formed, would be without vital data.

Conclusion

This chapter has sought to unpack the 'irresponsibility dilemma' in terms of the State's responsibility to its citizens, specifically, journalists who choose to place themselves in situations where they may come to harm in the form of kidnap. Clearly, as part of the social contract, states have a responsibility to protect their citizens. This chapter has argued that this is so even where those citizens deliberately and knowingly choose to place themselves in harm's way. In such cases, even taking into account the changes in the character of contemporary conflict, the way that western and non western militaries conduct themselves and the tensions this brings out for those seeking to report the facts on the ground, the individual at the centre of the 'irresponsibility dilemma' is still morally responsible for their predicament and the predictable consequences thereof. Despite the lack of codification in this area, UK policy appears consistent with this view. The State responds to an individual's predicament on the basis of the situation itself, including pragmatic considerations, rather than their moral conduct. This is due to a combination of principle-based and practical reasons in which calibrating state reaction according to a sliding scale of individual moral behaviour would simply be impossible. The moral conduct of the individual is, therefore, irrelevant to state reactions.

The nature of the State response is calculated on the balance between the collective good against that of the individual. In operational theatres, the interests of the state or the 'all' often align with those of the individual, even where that individual might be considered to be at fault. Quickly transcending the individual, hostage situations engage the State through consideration of direct political demands; the potential strengthening of the enemy if demands are acceded to and state interest in the function of 'unilaterals' given their utility in the battle to win the strategic narrative. It is important to note that whilst operational theatres lend themselves to the coincidence of individual and state interests, state responses are very different where this is not the case. UK state conduct with regard to Yvonne Ridley exemplifies that whilst the state will always engage, the nature of this engagement may be strictly limited as the collective good dictates the prioritisation of other interests, which may even jeopardise the safety of the specific individual further.

Therefore, the journalist Stephen Farrell was morally responsible for the consequences he engendered by his risk taking. He knew or could reasonably be expected to have known what would unfold should he be caught exposed and unprotected. He knew it was an insecure area, he knew abductions of journalists and westerners in general was common currency in the theatre of Afghanistan, just as it had been in Iraq, indeed he had personal experience of this. In terms of consequences thereof, he also knew that it is against British state policy to pay ransoms meaning that the predictable consequences were restricted to two likely courses of action: an illegal ransom payment followed by release, or; a military rescue, both of which have precedent. However, his moral culpability does not influence the customary responsibilities of the State, which remains responsible to the individual, with direct intervention likely if the there is opportunity and the balance of interests falls in favour of the 'all'. 'Our', the State's, responsibility to the irresponsible is, therefore, to intervene on a citizen's behalf. How this is achieved is a policy-balancing act that is not based upon the irresponsibility or the culpability of the actor involved.

Index